THINKING RIGHTLY
OF CHRIST

THINKING RIGHTLY OF CHRIST

Bryan Holstrom

AMBASSADOR INTERNATIONAL
GREENVILLE, SOUTH CAROLINA & BELFAST, NORTHERN IRELAND

www.ambassador-international.com

Thinking Rightly of Christ

Printed in the United States of America

ISBN 978-1-935507-25-3

Cover Design & Page Layout by David Siglin of A&E Media

AMBASSADOR INTERNATIONAL
Emerald House
427 Wade Hampton Blvd.
Greenville, SC 29609, USA
www.ambassador-international.com

AMBASSADOR BOOKS
The Mount
2 Woodstock Link
Belfast, BT6 8DD, Northern Ireland, UK
www.ambassador-international.com

The colophon is a trademark of Ambassador

To Lauren, Brooke, Ethan, and Thomas

Contents

Prologue

"Who Do Men Say That I Am?"

(MARK 8:27)

The nation of Israel had seen miracle-working prophets before Jesus appeared on the scene. Moses, Elijah, and Elisha would have immediately come to mind. God had given each of these three men great power to perform miracles that served to confirm their identities as his chosen spokesmen. Fourteen centuries earlier, Moses, the greatest of the Old Testament prophets, had led the children of Israel out of bondage in Egypt to the land promised them by God, a land that they now inhabited but didn't control. And throughout their journey God had performed a number of mighty miracles through Moses, the most dramatic being the parting of the Red Sea. In characteristic, matter-of-fact fashion, the fourteenth chapter of Exodus describes how Moses stretched out his hand and caused the sea waters to roll back, allowing the Israelites to cross over on dry ground. When he raised his hand again and stretched it over the waters, the sea "went back to its place," carrying the pursuing Egyptians to their watery grave.

Hundreds of years later, the prophets Elijah and Elisha had enjoyed similar ministries in which God performed many miraculous works through them. God had given to others, such as Joshua, the chosen successor of Moses, direct revelation that they would be the agents through whom he would perform miracles of both blessing and judgment. Still others along the way had proven the divine nature of their missions by uttering prophetic messages to the nation, some of which were fulfilled only after their deaths. Throughout the centuries, God had used men of various backgrounds and temperaments to deliver his message of redemption and judgment, and some had done so by way of both prophecy and miracle. No, the presence of such men in the life of the nation was nothing new, even if it had been some time since the last one had appeared on the scene.

But only a year or two into his public ministry, this One who was called Jesus was proving to be in an altogether different league. Traveling from town to town with a band of twelve disciples whom he had personally chosen to be his closest intimates and witnesses to all that he said and did, Jesus quickly distinguished himself from all of those who had preceded him. Rather than teach as the Rabbis did, he taught as One who possessed the very authority that the Word of God claimed for itself. Whereas Moses and the other Old Testament prophets had prefaced their God-given proclamations with "Thus says the Lord," Jesus introduced his statements with, "I say to you." Moreover, his teaching primarily concerned expounding upon his own person and mission, and that was anything but the normal pattern. More than a few of his fellow countrymen must have found themselves wondering whether this Jesus could possibly be the prophet of whom Moses had prophesied and of whom God had promised to hold accountable anyone who didn't listen to his words (Deut. 18:15–19).

But there was more. In the presence of his disciples, Jesus spoke of God—and of his own personal intimacy with him—in a way no one had ever done before. Indeed, none would have ever dared to speak in such a way. It might have been easy to dismiss such language as presumptuous or irreverent by someone else, but on the lips of Jesus it seemed both natural and genuine. Clearly, this was no ordinary prophet.

What about the reports that Jesus had raised several persons from the dead? Perhaps someone might argue that while that was an interesting fact, Elijah and Elisha had both done the same thing during their ministries. Indeed they had, but they had done so only with prayer to God and through personal contact with the bodies of those whom they had raised. Jesus, on the other hand, healed from a distance and raised Lazarus from the grave with a mere verbal command to "come forth."

Moreover, by this time Jesus had not only performed scores of miracles that showcased his compassion and power, but he claimed the right to forgive sins, a prerogative that—as everyone well knew— was reserved for God alone. And to top it all off, he hailed from the town of Nazareth! Had anything good ever come out of *that* place?

And so it was, with all of Palestine abuzz over his activities and teaching, that Jesus arrived in the region of Caesarea Philippi with his disciples in tow. It's there that he asked them the question that's the subject of this introductory chapter. No doubt aware of what some were saying about him, Jesus took this perfect opportunity to test the understanding of his disciples concerning himself and to give them more light in the process of doing so. The story, which is found in all three synoptic gospels (Matt. 16:13–16; Mark 8:27–30; Luke 9:18–20), relates that Jesus asked his disciples to tell him, "Who do men say that I am?" Without hesitation, the disciples informed Jesus that some of the people were saying that he was John the Baptist (who had by this time been beheaded by Herod Antipas), some were saying that he was Elijah, while still others were thinking him to be one of the other Old Testament prophets whom God had brought back from the dead.

But after receiving the disciples' response, Jesus asked them the even more pertinent question, "But who do you say that I am?" Simon Peter, the leader of the twelve, immediately replied, "You are the Christ" (Mark 8:29). Matthew's recorded answer of Peter's statement is even more explicit: "You are the Christ, the Son of the living God" (Matt. 16:16). All three gospel accounts tell us that Jesus then informed his disciples that they weren't to reveal this fact to anyone just yet, for they themselves were still in need of further instruction regarding the implications of this fact. And what were the implications that attended the revelation of Jesus as the Christ (the Greek word translating the Hebrew word *Messiah*, which means "Anointed One"), for whom the nation had so long anticipated? Just these—that he must "suffer many things, and be rejected by the elders and chief priests and scribes, and be killed, and after three days rise again" (Mark 8:31).

One can only imagine the startled reaction of Jesus' disciples to such news. The revelation that the long-awaited Messiah, the One for whom these same disciples had left everything behind to follow, would be rejected and put to death by the very people to whom he was sent to proclaim the good news of his arrival must have shocked them profoundly. Indeed, Peter's reaction (recorded for us in Matt. 16:22) proves that to be the case. They no doubt had imagined their quest ending in something far more glorious than rejection by the religious authorities and death at the hands of their Roman overseers. But according to Jesus, that was precisely what the future held for them.

The problem was that the disciples' thinking at this point wasn't far removed from that of the general populace, at least with respect to Jesus' mission. They had been with him long enough to know that he was neither a resurrected John the Baptist nor a reincarnated Elijah. In fact, they knew that he was the Christ. But they didn't yet fully understand that his ultimate purpose for being born was to give his life as a ransom for many. The full realization of that fact lay sometime in the future.

Part of the reason that the people at large (and undoubtedly some of Jesus' own disciples) were confused about Jesus' identity was that he didn't necessarily match their expectations of what the Messiah was supposed to be. From all indications, many of those who lived in first-century Palestine expected the Christ to be a great military figure who would deliver them from the yoke of Roman occupation and restore the nation to its rightful place as an independent theocracy. But Jesus spoke about peace and of the people's obligation to pay taxes to a civil government that they nevertheless despised.

More importantly, his teaching dealt with more than just earthly matters. Jesus was just as concerned with preparing the people for the life to come as he was with the life lived in the here and now. His was hardly the rhetoric of a military leader or social revolutionary intent on overthrowing the existing power structure and replacing it with a new one. On the contrary, the change that he sought was a heart change within each person that he came into contact with. Jesus called the people to a revolution all right, just not the kind that many of them had been hoping for or expecting.

As a result of this gap between the people's expectations and the reality of Christ's mission, it was only natural that they would fall into the trap of mistaking the real thing (Jesus) for something only preliminary (John the Baptist, Elijah). Even John the Baptist, the one who was sent to announce the arrival of the Messiah, experienced a moment of doubt regarding whether Jesus was the end for which all Israel had been waiting. As he languished in prison, perhaps surprised that his own ministry of preparation seemed to be coming to such an ignominious end, John sent representatives to Jesus to ask him, "Are You the Coming One, or do we look for another?" Jesus' answer to John's disciples is profoundly instructive: "Go and tell John the things which you hear and see: the blind see and the lame walk; the lepers are cleansed and the deaf hear; the dead are raised up and the poor have the gospel preached to them. And blessed is he who is not offended because of Me" (Matt. 11:3–6).

Be assured that John got the message loud and clear. As someone who knew his Old Testament, he would have recognized Jesus' list of miraculous works as those contained in Isaiah's prophecy concerning the future Messiah (29:18; 35:4–6; 61:1). Jesus was indeed the One to whom John had been sent to point the way. There was no need for him, or anyone else, to look for another.

But if John got the message, there were still many in Palestine who failed to do so, even though the prophecy from Isaiah demonstrates that they should have. While some did indeed come to recognize Jesus as the Messiah, many others denounced him as a charlatan or magician. Some of his enemies even said that he was an instrument of the devil (if not the devil himself). And while a few attempted to offer him respect by addressing him as Rabbi, in many cases that was as far as they were willing to go in their view of his significance. The end result, as we know only too well now, is that many of these same people were amongst the throng who cried out, "Crucify Him" on that first Good Friday nearly two thousand years ago.

Unfortunately, the situation in our own day isn't too dissimilar from that which existed in first-century Palestine. Despite the benefit of possessing the completed revelation of God, including his testimony to the person and work of Christ in the New Testament, people still say a lot of wrong things about who he is. Those who are willing to speak favorably of him in public will often grant that he was a great moral teacher or even a prophet (at least in some modern sense of the word). But, like many of the first-century Jews who called him Rabbi, they usually mean to limit his significance and identity to those designations and to go no further. Certainly they wouldn't deign to call him the only begotten Son of God. And for many others in our day, they aren't even willing to grant the favorable descriptions above. For them, there is nothing great about Jesus Christ or his teachings.

Of course, it shouldn't surprise us when the world at large speaks in such a way of Christ. While he was on earth, Jesus told his disciples that the world hated him because he testified of it "that its works are evil" (John 7:7). But if we're honest about it, we would have to admit that far too much of the world's thinking has infiltrated the confines of the visible church in our age. The Christ who is proclaimed from many a pulpit, and taught in a great many seminaries today, often bears little resemblance to him who is set forth in Scripture as the King of kings and Lord of lords.

Even among those of us who would never sit under preaching that denied Christ's divinity or that set him forth as only one way among many to the salvation offered by God, must come to grips with the reality that too often the portrait of Christ that exists in our minds is decidedly less majestic than the one that Scripture paints for us. The great Swiss Reformer John Calvin used to say that our minds are "idol factories," by which he meant to convey that we're particularly prone to conjuring up false images of Christ in our minds, perhaps ones better suited to our modern sensibilities, or demythologized, or rendered politically correct. But the Bible makes it clear that all such sanitized conceptions of Christ are sinful attempts to escape the reality of who he is and ultimately amount to idol worship.

The purpose of this book is to correct such deficient thinking about Christ, particularly among Christians, and to replace our false conceptions of his person and work with one befitting the Creator of the heavens and the earth, who upholds all things by the word of his power (Heb. 1:2–3). To that end, each of the twenty chapters seeks to expound upon a truth statement drawn directly from Scripture that touches upon the subject at hand. Those familiar with the Bible will appreciate that there are literally hundreds of truth statements about the person and work of Christ, any one of which could have been the subject of a separate chapter here. But the twenty statements that are included were chosen because they meet two criteria.

First, they fall into one of several different categories of statements about Christ that benefit from elaboration or clarification. Basically, there are three different kinds of statements here: (a) those that are either frequently misunderstood by Christians today or are among the most susceptible to being misunderstood, particularly when looked at in isolation from the rest of Scripture; (b) statements that are clear enough in their own right, and not so much subject to misunderstanding, but whose implications for Christianity aren't as well known or appreciated as they should be; or (c) in one or two cases, the biblical statements are under attack by some within the church who argue that such beliefs are divisive or no longer essential to the Christian faith.

Second, when considered together, these twenty statements furnish us with a relatively comprehensive portrait of the person and work of Jesus Christ, while hopefully avoiding unnecessary duplication. Some important aspects of Christ's life and work, such as his ascension into heaven at the end of his earthly sojourn, were obvious candidates for inclusion but weren't chosen for separate treatment because they aren't particularly controversial or misunderstood teachings and because they receive at least some attention under other headings. In the end it's hoped that one who has absorbed and mastered the twenty statements about Christ set forth here will have a well-developed and thorough understanding of his person and work.

The Christ who is set forth in these pages bears little resemblance to the puny caricatures of him that are common today. In reading this book, you'll be confronted with the Christ who was without blemish, but who was nevertheless "made perfect" by his earthly sojourn; by the Christ who cried out to the Father for deliverance from the sufferings of the Cross, but who himself upholds the world and is the victim of no man; by the Christ who was a friend of sinners, but who thoroughly detests sin and all its effects; by the Christ who is as human as you or I, but who is also fully God; by the Christ who was born of a virgin, but who has existed eternally; by the Christ who is King of the Jews, but whose Kingdom isn't of this world; by the Christ who employs people in his providential care of the universe, but is dependent upon none; and by the Christ who is Savior of the world, but who is also Judge of those who reject him. In short, what this book attempts to set forth is the Christ of the Scriptures. And he is glorious indeed!

In *Teaching for Spiritual Growth*, Perry Downs tells of a pastor who was invited to speak to his church's first grade Sunday school class. The pastor told the class, "I am thinking of one of God's creatures. It lives in the trees and gathers acorns for the winter. It has a large bushy tail and is grey." Then he asked the class, "Who can tell me what I'm thinking about?" After a long and uncomfortable silence, the pastor finally called upon one of the young boys in the class to give the answer. The boy replied, "I know the answer is Jesus, but it sure sounds a lot like a squirrel!"[1]

This story illustrates how Christians (both children and adults) can be taught to parrot answers but not think too deeply upon the subject at hand, even if that subject is the Lord of the universe. As Christians, we understand that Christ is the answer to our deepest need, but do we know how and why that is the case? Do we know what it is about Christ that makes him uniquely qualified to be our Savior? And do we understand how it is that the work that he was sent to do accomplishes our redemption, which is not only our deepest need but our only hope? All too often these days it seems as if the answer to these questions is a negative one.

But we have been called to a higher standard. The writer of the epistle to the Hebrews urges his readers to go on to perfection by partaking, not only of milk, which is fit for infants, but of the solid food that marks out those who "by reason of use have their senses exercised to discern both good and evil" (Heb. 5:12–6:1). Surely this "solid food" involves those teachings of Scripture that most fundamentally touch upon our relationship to God and our worship of him. And the most fundamental of those teachings is that we must come to understand, just as Peter did, that Jesus is the Christ, with all of the implications that attend such a confession—and they are many.

In his second epistle, the apostle John writes, "Whoever transgresses and does not abide in the doctrine of Christ does not have God. He who abides in the doctrine of Christ has both the Father and the Son" (2 John 9). Clearly, then, there is a "doctrine of Christ" that we must believe in order to be saved. Thankfully, John hasn't left us in the dark concerning those things in which this doctrine consists. We have his gospel account and his first epistle to draw upon, both of which are concerned with setting forth Christ in all his radiant glory.

Of course, it must also be pointed out that not all of our false conceptions or misunderstandings of Christ are equally serious, but some do endanger the soul and disqualify those who hold them from attaining the prize that awaits the faithful disciple of Christ. At the same time, we must not allow ourselves to think that just because we understand and confess the most vital components of the doctrine of Christ, we may dispense with the rest as unnecessary or superfluous. While it may be true that certain aspects of Christ's life and work are more important than others, no aspect is unimportant or unprofitable for our spiritual edification (cf. 2 Tim. 3:16). If we would give Christ his due, then we must know who he is. We cannot worship him rightly if we aren't thinking of him rightly, for our worship must be in spirit and truth (John 4:24).

Thinking rightly of Jesus Christ, therefore, isn't just an intellectual exercise, reserved for those in the ivory towers of academia. On the contrary, each of us is called upon to contemplate the person of Christ rightly and thereby render to him the service of worship that he is due. Understanding what these twenty statements about Christ mean is essential for a proper appreciation of who he is and what he has done on our behalf. And that isn't primarily an intellectual enterprise but a devotional one. This book challenges us to think and act more deeply upon who Jesus Christ is and what he has done—and to have our lives changed in the process.

Part 1:

Thinking Rightly of the Person of Christ

1

He Is the Image of the Invisible God

(Col. 1:15)

Like most good histories, the Bible starts its narrative at "the beginning." Actually, we'll need to qualify that statement somewhat in the next chapter, but for the moment it will suffice. We might also add that we don't want to leave the impression with such a statement that the Bible is in the same league as any other history or that it simply borrowed the time-tested practice of starting at the beginning from other good histories that have been written throughout the ages. No, the Bible is the *first* history, not only with respect to chronology but primarily that it alone gives us the story of the origin of the universe and of all life that springs forth upon the earth. Most importantly, it is first among histories because it comes to us from the hand of God himself. It is *his story*, given to us for our benefit and for his glory.

The Bible's narrative of history begins with the beautifully simple affirmation that "In the beginning, God created the heavens and the earth" (Gen. 1:1). Though only ten words in length, this first sentence of Scripture is unrivaled by any other ever written for packing so much significant information into so brief a presentation. This sentence speaks of the beginning of human history—time as we know it—and it tells us that at a particular point in time past (designated "the beginning") God created all things that exist. God created the "heavens and the earth," which is another way of saying that he created everything in the universe. While the singular term *heaven* is normally used as a designation for God's eternal abode, the plural *heavens* is the Bible's term for everything separate from this earthly realm, including not only the vast material expanse of the universe but also the spiritual (nonmaterial) realm as well. Thus, Genesis 1:1 makes it clear that all things that exist, whether material or spiritual and whether living or inanimate, owe their existence to the creative activity of God.

The Bible then singles out Earth for special mention within the created order because Earth is the central focus of God's creative and redemptive work. God formed each of the other planets in our solar system, and every other planet and star in every other galaxy outside of our own, but it's here on Earth that He chose to bring life into existence and even to create a being (man) who would bear "His own image" (Gen. 1:27). The first two chapters of Genesis go on to give more details regarding this creative work of God.

However, it's not the creation that concerns us here, but the Creator. Genesis 1:1 is a remarkably terse statement, especially with respect to this Creator. It simply informs us that it was God who brought all things into existence. There's no preceding philosophical discussion or defense of his existence, nor are we given any additional details concerning his identity at this point. But even in that very first reference to God in the opening sentence of the Bible, we're given a glimpse into the complex nature of his being, even if our English Bibles are unable to convey that complexity to us. That's because Old Testament Hebrew has two distinct terms that are rendered as *God* in English: *El* and *Elohim*. The latter term is essentially a plural form of the former but was never translated as "gods" when used in reference to the God of the Bible. Why? Because the Bible uniformly testifies to the singularity and uniqueness of God (see, e.g., Deut. 4:35; 6:4; 32:39; 2 Sam. 7:22; Isa. 44:6; Zech. 14:9; John 5:44; 17:3; 1 Cor. 8:4–6; 1 Tim. 1:17; James 2:19).

There is but one God who is Creator of the heavens and the earth. That is the consistent witness of the Scriptures, both Old and New Testaments. The most celebrated expression of this fact is the Shema, the prayer found at Deuteronomy 6:4 that the children of Israel were to recite when rising in the morning and going to bed at night: "Hear O Israel: The Lord our God, the Lord is one!" This explicit monotheism contrasted sharply with the beliefs of the people groups surrounding the Israelites in the Promised Land, many of which held to the notion of a pantheon of gods who ruled the nations and often competed with one another for ultimate control.

Thus, we might expect that Genesis 1:1, the verse in which we are introduced to the God spoken of in the Shema, would contain the clearest and most explicit confirmation of his oneness that's available in Hebrew—the singular *El*. Instead, it's the plural form, *Elohim*, that we find in this opening passage of Scripture. At the same time, however, it's just as clear that when the term *Elohim* is used elsewhere in the Old Testament, it's applied to the same God who is the subject of the term *El*, the singular and unique Lord of all. When he is referred to in the third person, it's with the singular pronouns *he* (Josh. 24:19), *him* (Deut. 4:35), *his* (Isa. 52:10), and *himself* (Psalm 50:6). Similarly, when he refers to himself (with four exceptions to be discussed below), it's always with the first-person singular pronouns *I* (Ex. 20:2), and *Me* (Isa. 46:9).

What's important to understand about this phenomenon is that the Bible isn't being schizophrenic in using these two seemingly contradictory terms for the same being, God. Rather, the author of Holy Scripture, God himself, is telling us something important about himself. And it's that complex nature of his person that Genesis 1:1 hints at in only the most rudimentary manner. But, when we take the rest of Scripture into account, that verse demonstrates itself to be just one of the many different ways that the Bible emphasizes, and brings to light, a single over-arching truth: God is a triune being.

The Trinity

There's no tenet more fundamental to Christianity than the doctrine of the Trinity, since it speaks to the identity of the God whom we worship. It's a simple fact that we cannot worship One whom we don't know. Thus, God's self-disclosure to humans is relationally-focused; it's given for the purpose of our coming to know him and having life in such knowledge. We must come to know who he is if we would be his people. And we cannot know who he is without going to his Word, where he gives us that disclosure.

Yet, contrary to the fanciful theories of some who write and produce best-selling books and movies, belief in the triune nature of God didn't spring into existence at the Council of Nicea in AD 325. Rather, the confession that God exists as Father, Son, and Holy Spirit is found in unequivocal form in the New Testament. Even before the New Testament was reduced to writing, Christians were being baptized in the threefold name, as they had been commanded to do by Jesus himself (Matt. 28:19).

Moreover, it's important to keep in mind that the triune God of the New Testament is the same God who is disclosed in the less explicitly Trinitarian language of the Old Testament. Thus, the Old Testament saints were saved by faith in the same triune God as we are today. The extent to which any of them understood the depths of the triune nature of God is unknown. But it's clear that, in this age subsequent to the incarnation of Jesus Christ, wherein God spoke most forcefully on the subject, we're without excuse for not recognizing and confessing this indispensable tenet of the faith. Indeed, some argue that the very fact that the apostles didn't feel compelled to expound at length on this doctrine in their canonical writings is proof that the Jews in first-century Palestine had more of an appreciation for it than we tend to give them credit for (notwithstanding their refusal to believe that Jesus is who he claimed to be).

Briefly stated, the doctrine of the Trinity holds that there is one God in being or essence who exists in three distinct persons, namely the Father, Son, and Holy Spirit. In the next chapter we'll expand this basic affirmation to give a more precise and complete definition of the doctrine.

The biblical evidence for the doctrine of the Trinity is varied and plentiful, but we intend to only scratch the surface of that evidence with our presentation here. Nevertheless, there are two very important strands of evidence for the doctrine found in the Old Testament. The first comes in the form of the four separate passages (to which we made mention above) that are the exceptions to the general rule that God always used the singular pronouns *I* and *Me* when referring to himself in Scripture. The four passages appear below:

> Genesis 1:26—Then God said, "Let Us make man in Our image, according to Our likeness."

> Genesis 3:22—Then the Lord God said, "Behold, the man has become like one of Us, to know good and evil."

> Genesis 11:6-7—And the Lord said, … "Come let Us go down and there confuse their language, that they may not understand one another's speech."

> Isaiah 6:8—Also I heard the voice of the Lord, saying: "Whom shall I send, and who will go for Us?"

What is remarkable about this group of passages is that each one records an incident wherein God (the Father) speaks in heaven but not, as is the usual case, to men on earth. Rather, he directs his words to someone else present in the heavenly realm and uses the plural pronoun *Us* to associate that other person(s) with himself. Thus, it seems that what we are privy to in these passages is nothing other than intra-Trinitarian speech—God the Father speaking to one or both of the other persons of the Trinity!

Some who oppose the doctrine of the Trinity (and a few who don't) have tried to minimize the significance of these passages by arguing that God is speaking to the angelic beings in heaven. But that theory seems unlikely, for a number of reasons. First, the angels are never said to be involved in the act of creation, as Genesis 1:26 would require. Indeed, the very next verse (vs. 27) explicitly ascribes that work referred to in verse 26 to God alone. Second, the use of the word *Our* in Genesis 1:26 also rules out that theory, since man is the only creature said to be made "in God's image." And finally, the work of confusing the language of the people referred to in Genesis 11:6–7, similar to the case above in Genesis 1:26–7, is in the next two verses ascribed to God alone.

But even if we were to make allowance for the possibility that the four passages above record the words of God speaking before a heavenly council that included the angels, there's one additional passage from the Old Testament about which it's impossible to deny the intra-Trinitarian nature of the recorded conversation. That passage is Psalm 2:7, which records the words of the Father ("the Lord") saying to his Son, "Today I have begotten You." Hebrews 1:5 states explicitly that the Son being referred to is Jesus Christ, the only begotten Son of God. And in verse 8 the author of Hebrews states clearly that this Son is divine; he is God. Thus, at least through the lens of the New Testament, we're able to affirm that the Old Testament contains an irrefutable testimony to the plurality of persons in the Godhead. In fact, there are a host of other Old Testament texts that testify to the plurality of persons, but we reserve them as a class for a later chapter.

The other interesting piece of evidence involves the Hebrew wording of the Shema, the prayer affirming God's oneness that we mentioned earlier ("Hear O Israel: The Lord our God, the Lord is one!"). What is fascinating about this passage is that the word that God caused Moses (the writer of Deuteronomy) to use for *one* isn't the one we would expect him to use if he were intending to stress the absolute oneness or singularity of God. This is so because there are two main Hebrew words that are normally translated as *one* in the Bible, *echad* and *yachid*. The latter term signifies an absolute numeric one and is sometimes translated as "only" to stress the fact of something or someone's solitariness or uniqueness. On the other hand, *echad* is more often used to refer to something that's one in a unified sense. For example, the word is used in Genesis 2:24 to refer to the way in which a man and woman become "one flesh," and in Numbers 13:23 to refer to a single cluster of grapes. Thus, it refers to what we might characterize as a compound unity. And it's this word *echad* that's used in the Shema.

Nevertheless, what's only hinted at in the Old Testament is made explicit in the New. It is there that we find the threefold name of God—Father, Son, and Holy Spirit—invoked by Jesus and the apostles, and the distinct personhoods of all three affirmed throughout. The Father and Son converse with one another in prayer (John 17), and the Son promises to send the Holy Spirit into the world after he returns to heaven (John 16:7–14). Indeed, we may say that the New Testament is the record of God the Father's full unveiling of the person and work of both the Son and the Holy Spirit. It's in the incarnation of his Son that God speaks most clearly to the doctrine of the Trinity. And because the identity of the Son is disclosed to us as none other than Jesus, this leads us to our first affirmation that flows from calling him the Christ: he is God incarnate.

The Deity of Christ

Though the doctrine continues to have its detractors amongst non-Christians, the biblical evidence for the deity of Christ is overwhelming. The evidence consists in a number of strands, and what follows is only a sampling of that evidence. First, there are passages that explicitly affirm the Son's divine identity. A few examples include Isa. 9:6 ("Unto us a Son is given ... And His name will be called ... Mighty God"), Matt. 1:23 ("'the virgin shall ... bear a Son, and they shall call His name Immanuel,' which is translated, 'God with us.'"), John 1:1 ("the Word was God"), John 20:28 ("And Thomas answered and said to Him, 'My Lord and My God'"), Acts 20:28 (God purchased the church "with His own blood"), Rom. 9:5 (Christ is "over all, the eternally blessed God"), Phil. 2:6 (Christ was "in the form of God"), Col. 1:15 ("He is the image of the invisible God"), Col. 2:9 ("For in Him dwells all the fullness of the Godhead bodily"), Tit. 2:13 (Christ is "our great God and Savior"), Heb. 1:3 (Christ is "the brightness of [God's] glory and the express image of His person"), Heb. 1:8 ("But to the Son He says: Your throne, O God, is forever and ever"), 2 Pet. 1:1 ("our God and Savior Jesus Christ"), 1

John 5:20 ("we are in Him who is true, in His Son Jesus Christ. This is the true God and eternal life"), and Rev. 1:7-8 (Christ is "the Alpha and the Omega ... the Almighty").

Second, there are passages that ascribe various titles and/or works of God to the Son. These include: "the Lord" (1 Cor. 1:3), the "Lord of Glory" (1 Cor. 2:8), the Creator (Col. 1:16), the Judge of all mankind (2 Cor. 5:10), and the "power of God and the wisdom of God" (1 Cor. 1:24).

Third, there are passages that describe the powers or traits of the Son in terms reserved for God. Included in this category are verses that describe Christ as sinless (1 Pet. 2:22), as knowing the hearts of all men (Acts 1:24), as our "righteousness and sanctification and redemption" (1 Cor. 1:30), as the One who "lives" in believers (Gal. 2:20), as the One who gives strength to believers to do all things (Phil. 4:13), and as superior to the angels (Heb. 1:4–14).

Finally, there are passages that disclose the prerogatives or titles claimed by Christ himself while incarnate on the earth. Examples include Son of God (John 9:35–37), Son of Man (John 3:13), judge of all (John 5:22), light of the world (John 8:12), Lord of the Sabbath (Luke 6:5), the sender of the Holy Spirit (John 16:7), the giver of eternal life (John 10:28), David's Lord (Mark 12:37), Thomas's Lord and God (John 20:28), fulfiller of the law (Matt. 5:17), forgiver of sins (Luke 7:48), the door to salvation (John 10:9), the resurrection and the life (John 11:25), the way, the truth, and the life (John 14:6), he of whom the Old Testament spoke (Luke 24:44), he who does the works of God (John 9:4), he who is to be worshiped (Matt. 14:33), he who existed before Abraham (John 8:58), he who is one with the Father (John 10:30), he in whom we have seen the Father (John 14:9), he who is not of this world, but from above (John 8:23), he who came from and will return to the Father (John 16:28), and he who has been given all authority in heaven and on earth (Matt. 28:18).

To these groups of passages we may add the circumstances and facts of his birth, his resurrection from the dead, his ascension into heaven, and the fact that he is said to be seated at the right hand of the Father in heaven (Col. 3:1). It's also significant that the New Testament writers frequently pair the Father and Christ together in their prayers and greetings (2 Thess. 2:16; 1 Pet 1:1; 1 John 2:1).

Perhaps the single most significant passage in the New Testament concerning the identity of Christ is the opening verse of John's gospel, for it brings us back around to where we started this chapter—"the beginning." This well-known verse reads, "In the beginning was the Word, and the Word was with God, and the Word was God." Since "the Word" is John's introductory title for Jesus Christ, this verse tells us in the most explicit of terms that Christ is God and that he was also with God (the Father) "in the beginning" (at creation). In other words, it's one of the clearest proof texts for both the deity of Christ and the Trinity.

These two interrelated doctrines form the bedrock upon which the Christian faith is built. They provide tremendous comfort and assurance to the Christian, since it's because of Christ's divinity that we may rest confidently in the fact that what he promised to his people will come to pass. And it's because of his divinity that he was able to fulfill the requirements of God's law on our behalf, providing the way for reconciliation between us and him.

Did Christ promise to give eternal life to those who place their trust for salvation solely in him? Then you may be sure that it will come to pass. Did he likewise promise to raise those same people up on the last day? Then it's already a settled fact, which only awaits that future day for its actual fulfillment. The world may scoff and choose to say otherwise, but this fact is undeniable—it's right to worship such a One as this.

Colossians 1:15 says that Christ is the "image of the invisible God." The second person of the Trinity left his heavenly abode and assumed human form, becoming the visible image of God. But in so doing, he didn't lose his divinity. He was (and is) just as much true God after assuming flesh, and being born in a stable as he was prior to that day. One who doesn't have a firm grasp of this basic article of the faith will be hard pressed to make sense of much of what the New Testament has to say about Christ. On the other hand, with this understanding in mind, the pieces of the puzzle come together nicely, leaving us with a beautiful portrait of the One who has become for us the visible face of God.

In the next chapter we'll elaborate further on these two doctrines and deal with some of the misunderstandings that have arisen with respect to them. But before continuing with our study it bears noting that many of the errors in thought that we'll seek to correct later in this book don't rise to the level of soul-endangering heresies. They may denigrate the work of Christ in some unfortunate way or cause one's theology to be confused at various points. But they don't, in and of themselves, prove the one who holds them to be an unbeliever. We cannot say the same thing with respect to the subject of this chapter, however. It's not enough to say that he who thinks of Christ as anything less than God doesn't think rightly of him. We are compelled by Scripture to go even further than that. We must affirm that the persons who don't embrace Christ as God are not Christians. They may have warm feelings for the Jesus that they have conjured up in their mind, but they don't worship God in either spirit or truth, for they haven't believed his testimony concerning his Son (1 John 5:10; John 3:18). It is only in confessing, as Peter did, that Jesus is "the Christ, the Son of the Living God," that we receive the same assuring response from our Savior: "Blessed are you…for flesh and blood has not revealed this to you, but My Father who is in heaven" (Matt. 16:17).

2

He Is the Only Begotten Son

(JOHN 3:16)

Anyone who has ever tried to explain the Trinity—and the interrelationship of Father, Son, and Holy Spirit—to a young child, knows how difficult it can be. I recently had such a conversation with one of my young daughters. When I finished my basic explanation of the three-in-one nature of God, she quietly nodded her agreement and responded, "That's pretty hard to understand." Of course, I quickly proceeded to tell her that it was hard for me to understand as well, indeed, that it was impossible to completely comprehend it. As finite beings, we'll never be able to plumb the depths of the Infinite.

Unfortunately, for too many people, the recognition of this reality produces a tendency to avoid the subject altogether. In his book *The Forgotten Trinity*, James White offers this perceptive comment on the current state of the church's attitude toward the doctrine:

It's the topic we won't talk about: no one dares question the Trinity for fear of being branded a "heretic," yet we have all sorts of questions about it, and we aren't sure who we can ask. Many believers have asked questions of those they thought were more mature in the faith and have often been confused by the *contradictory* answers they received. Deciding it is best to remain confused rather than have one's orthodoxy questioned, many simply leave the topic for that mythical future day "when I have more time." And in the process, we have lost out on a tremendous blessing.[1]

The difficulty we face in this task goes beyond our own finite ability to understand and is compounded by the fact that our human language is simply unable to accommodate or account for various biblical terms in a way that transcends our own preconceived notions and prejudices. Words such as *begotten*, *Son*, and *firstborn* convey to us a meaning that isn't always present in the Bible's usage of these terms. Even the word *person* presents us with difficulties in perception, as we naturally tend to associate the word with human beings.

But despite these hurdles, or perhaps because of them, it's both necessary and beneficial to wade further into these deep waters. And this for two very important reasons. First, it's when we begin to talk about Christ as the "only begotten Son" that many Christians stumble in their understanding of his person. Doesn't saying that he was "begotten" at some point in time mean that he hasn't always existed? Doesn't the term "Son" by nature convey a certain inferiority to the One designated as "Father"? And if that doesn't seal it, certainly designating the Son as the second person of the Trinity must do so, right? These are all valid questions that someone must deal with before truly appreciating and understanding what we mean by this doctrine.

The other reason for delving further into this study is that, as White noted above, there's great blessing in doing so. God displays his glory in his very being, and the more we become familiar with, and appreciate, the complexity and beauty of his nature, the more we should be inclined to lift him up in praise and worship. God reminded the Israelites of old of his incomparability by telling them that there was no one to whom they could liken him (Isa. 40:25). But rather than being a call to dispense with efforts to know him more intimately, this statement is designed to produce just the opposite effect. It's in being constantly aware of the wonder of God's nature that we overcome our own natural tendencies to compare God to anything or anyone else. It's through such reflection that we realize that he's simply too exalted to be compared to anything in the created order or reduced to a mere idol of our making. Thus, our inability to understand exhaustively the subject matter with which we deal here shouldn't deter us from looking into what Scripture has to say about it. We're determined to go as far as Scripture allows, and no further. And because God's Word always accomplishes what it sets out to do, such efforts will always receive his blessing.

In this chapter we'll round out our discussion of the doctrine of the Trinity and seek to correct some of the misconceptions (and downright heresies) surrounding it that have arisen over the centuries.

Three Persons in One Essence

The basic definition that we gave of the triune nature of God in the last chapter is that he exists as three distinct persons—Father, Son, and Holy Spirit—in one being or essence. This means that we affirm that there is but one God, while at the same time affirming that the Father is God, the Son is God, and the Holy Spirit is God. They aren't three separate Gods, but three distinct persons within the Godhead or single being of God. Thus, the Father, Son, and Holy Spirit aren't different manifestations, or modes, of God's being who appear on the biblical stage at different times. Rather, they're distinct persons, each of whom exists at the same time as the other two. And, if that weren't complex enough, we affirm that each of these three persons may lay full claim to the divine title and prerogatives, even though none of the three, in his individual capacity, represents the entire divine being whom we call God.

The care that we take in expressing the doctrine of the Trinity may seem silly to some, but we believe it to be dictated by Scripture itself and thus absolutely necessary to safeguard what it discloses to us about the nature of God. The history of the church demonstrates that when a person or group defines the doctrine carelessly or without taking all of the biblical data into account, they invariably end up falling into one of the many heresies that have arisen in this area of theology going back to the days of the apostles. Indeed, while the New Testament church from its infancy has proclaimed and celebrated the triune nature of God, it was only through its battles with heretical individuals and sects that the expression of the doctrine attained to the full-orbed beauty that we find in the Nicene and Athanasian Creeds of the fourth century.

Even today, with these creedal affirmations at our disposal, those of us who affirm a Trinitarian understanding of God often find that our conversation on this subject tends toward one of the opposite poles of tritheism or modalism. Tritheism emphasizes the separate persons of the Godhead to such an extent that it compromises the oneness of God. Whenever we find ourselves thinking of Christ as only one-third of God or we place his person in opposition to that of the Father and Holy Spirit in some manner, we have drifted off into this heresy. On the other hand, the heresy of modalism (also known as Sabellianism for one of its earliest proponents, Sabellius) emphasizes the oneness of God to the exclusion of the separate personalities of Father, Son, and Holy Spirit. Modalists don't deny that God is Father, Son, and Holy Spirit. But they deny that he's all three at the same time. The modalist sees God's disclosure of himself, and thus the perception of him by humans, taking the form (or mode) of the Father during the Old Testament period, of the Son during the days of Christ's incarnation, and of the Holy Spirit from the day of Pentecost to the present day. The God of modalism is unitary in existence and doesn't enjoy the intra-Trinitarian relationship of love for which we find abundant testimony in the New Testament.

Both of these ancient heresies are contradicted by the Bible, and so the early church rightly condemned them. The New Testament is just as explicit as the Old in affirming the oneness of God (see, e.g., Matt. 19:17; Mark 12:29; John 17:3; 1 Cor. 8:4; Eph. 4:6; 1 Tim. 2:5). God is always referred to in the singular; even Matthew 28:19 refers to baptism in the "name" (not names) of the Father, Son, and Holy Spirit.

At the same time, passages that make explicit distinctions among the persons of the Trinity render the modalist conception of God nonsensical. The prime example of such a text is the account of Jesus' baptism, which appears in all four gospel accounts (Matt. 3:16–17; Mk. 1:9–11; Luke 3:21–22; Jn. 1:32–34). The gospel writers tell us that immediately after receiving his baptism, Jesus saw the Spirit "descending like a dove and alighting upon him," at which point he heard a voice from heaven saying, "This is My beloved Son, in whom I am well pleased" (Matt. 3:16–17). There can be no doubt that the voice from heaven is the Father's. Thus, all three persons are present and involved at the same moment in time.

Another example occurs in John 15:26, where Jesus promises to send the Holy Spirit to the disciples after his departure. At first blush, such a statement might appear to support the modalist position that the Holy Spirit is the "mode" by which God makes himself known after the Son has left the scene. But just listen to the words of Jesus here: "But when the Helper comes, whom I shall send to you from the Father, the Spirit of truth who proceeds from the Father, He will testify of Me." How can such a statement by Jesus square with the modalist position? Jesus makes very explicit and concrete distinctions among himself, the Father, and the Holy Spirit. What sense does it make for him to say that he'll send the Spirit to them from the Father and that the Spirit will testify further of him (Christ), if they're all one and the same person? Furthermore, why in the world would Jesus have prayed to the Father, spoken of the Father's love for him (John 17:26), or spoken of having been sent from the Father in order to do the works that the Father gave him to do (John 17:4), if they aren't distinct from each other? How could Jesus the Son be seated at the right hand of the Father (Eph. 1:17–20) if he himself *is* the Father? Obviously, the modalist is unable to answer such questions.

Probably the two passages modalists most often appeal to for support of their position are John 10:30 and John 14:9. The first verse has Jesus saying, "I and My Father are one," and the second has him saying, "He who has seen Me has seen the Father." But neither verse supports the modalist position. As for the first, if Jesus had wanted to convey the message that he was the Father, all he had to do was say so. Instead, he carefully makes a distinction between himself and the Father ("I and My Father"). Rather, the point of Jesus' statement is that he and the Father are engaged in one unified work of redemption. There are no cross-purposes between the two of them; they're united in seeing to it that no one is able to snatch one of God's elect out of either Jesus' (v. 28) or the Father's (v. 29) hands. As for the second verse, Jesus' words came in response to Philip's request to "show us the Father." But in his response the Lord makes it clear that it was in the works that he was doing that the disciples were able to see the Father (vv. 10-11). As in the earlier verse, Jesus' language clearly distinguished his own person from that of the Father. The principal point of both verses is clear: the Father and the Son are not only one in purpose and intention, but in action as well.[2]

The other significant point is that both of these verses testify in the strongest of terms to the deity of Christ. No mere creature could ever make such declarations as we read here. Coupled with the assertion that we find at John 1:18 that "No one has seen God [the Father] at any time. The only begotten Son, who is in the bosom of the Father, He has declared Him," we may be certain not only that the Son is divine, as well as distinct from the Father, but that he is also able to "show us the Father" by all that he does and says, for it is he who "declares" the will and purposes of the Father.[3]

Having fleshed out the basic contours of the doctrine of the Trinity and what it says to us about Christ, we must add two more concepts to the mix in order to arrive at a complete understanding of this doctrine and its relationship to the Son. Those concepts are the co-eternality and co-equality of the separate persons of the Godhead. These two concepts aren't mere add-ons to what we have said thus far however. Rather, they're essential to a proper understanding of the doctrine and for making sense of the biblical record.

Trinitarian Co-eternality

In the last chapter, we stated that the Bible begins where most good histories do—at the beginning. But it's here that we qualify that statement somewhat, for we must be careful to not make the mistake of thinking that what the Bible describes as "the beginning" is anything other than the beginning of the created order. That is, what is described in Genesis 1:1 as well as John 1:1 is the beginning of time as we know it. But God isn't limited to the dimension of time. He has existed from all eternity. It was only through his work of creation that time came into existence. And if there was a beginning to time as we know it, there must have been something that preceded it, even if we're hard-pressed to call it a "time" prior to creation.

I realize this part of our discussion may seem a bit belabored to some readers, but this important distinction keeps us from falling into the trap of thinking that God himself had a beginning. Rather, he is the uncreated One, the One to whom all things, whether living or nonliving, owe their existence. As the only omnipotent One in the universe, he alone has absolute power to create and destroy, and nothing or no one is able to stay his hand. He alone is worthy of the worship that he himself demands from his creation. Thus, it's a contradiction to say that anything that's created can lay claim to being divine. The oneness of God rules out any such possibility. By definition, any created being, no matter how powerful or glorious, would be a contingent being, one who is dependent upon God for its own continued existence.

So what does this mean for us? It means that once we have proven the deity of Christ and his oneness with the Father, it becomes axiomatic that he too, like the Father, must be eternal. And what applies to the Father and Son likewise applies to the Holy Spirit, for if any of them came into existence through the creative work of God, then that person wouldn't be entitled to the divine name. We might also note that the proof works in reverse as well. That is, evidence for the eternality of the Son is also evidence for his deity, since there is only One who has eternal existence (Ps. 90:2).

Do we have any such evidence in the Bible? Indeed we do. For starters, the Old Testament prophecies concerning the One who would be the Messiah make it clear that he was to be One who was "from everlasting" (Mic. 5:2; Isa. 9:6). But the two best-known testimonies to the Son's eternality appear in John's gospel. In his prologue John tells us that the Word already existed at the beginning and that nothing that has ever been created was made "without Him" (John 1:1–3). Such a statement would be untrue if the Word himself had been a created being. The other passage appears at John 8:58, where Jesus utters the famous words, "Before Abraham was, I AM." Besides being a direct identification with the great "I AM" of the Old Testament (Yahweh), and thus an explicit testimony to his divine nature, this statement proves that Christ existed before the event of his incarnation. As John tells us in his prologue, there was indeed a time when the "Word became flesh" (John 1:14), but that Word didn't come into existence then, for he was without beginning.

What, then, are we to make of the various names by which the second person of the Trinity is known? In particular, what does it mean to call him "the only begotten Son"? To say that he is "begotten" seems to imply that he had a beginning, and to say that he is the "Son" (with or without the appendage) appears to imply the same thing. Over the centuries at least three ways of understanding this phrase have arisen. The first holds that the words refer to the eternal generation of the Son from the Father. The Son is "begotten" in the sense that his personal subsistence, not his divine nature, is generated (or brought forth) by the Father in eternity past, without any division, alienation, or change in the divine essence.[4] Similarly, the Holy Spirit is brought forth in eternity past, though he is said to proceed from both the Father and the Son.

The second understanding of the phrase is that it refers specifically to the incarnation of the Son. Those who argue for this reading of the term generally assign the begetting spoken of here to one of three different events in the life of Christ: (1) his physical birth; (2) his baptism in the River Jordan; or (3) his resurrection. There's at least some scriptural support for these last two choices. A.W. Pink argues for the second option on the strength of Hebrews 5:5, which quotes from Psalm 2:7 where the Father is recorded as saying, "You are My Son, today I have begotten You." Because the Hebrews passage is concerned with setting forth Christ's qualifications to be Mediator and High Priest of his people and because his baptism represents the event that most likely corresponds to his priestly installation ceremony, Pink believes that this ancient Psalm is God's prior pronouncement of Christ's fitness to fulfill the work that was assigned to him.[5] And it's this event that represented his "begetting." On the other hand, Paul links the same ceremonial pronouncement from Psalm 2 to Christ's resurrection in Acts 13:33, the third option above.

The final understanding of the phrase "only begotten Son" may be the one that is most popular today. Scholars such as James White argue that the phrase is a mistranslation of the compound Greek term *monogenes*. The first part of the term (*mono*) is obvious enough to us even in the English; it means "only" or "one." But the second part of the term (*genes*), which forms the rest of the phrase, is the source of the translation problem. It has traditionally been rendered as "begotten" because of its closeness to the term from which we would get the English word *generated*. But White and others believe that *genes* is more accurately related to our English word *genus*, which means "kind" or "species." Thus, the compound Greek term doesn't refer to begetting but to uniqueness and is more properly translated as "one and only," or "one of a kind."[6] Thus, Christ is the unique (or only) Son of God.

Regardless of which position one takes with respect to the meaning of the phrase, however, it is clear that when used in relationship to the Son, it doesn't have anything to do with being created or coming into essential existence. Acts 13:33 by itself is enough to dispel that notion. Indeed, it's interesting that the term *begotten* is used only four times in the New Testament in reference to humans (1 Cor.

4:15; Phlm. 1:10; Heb. 11:17; 1 Pet. 1:3), and in only the Hebrews reference does it refer to physical generation.

By the same type of analysis, the other terms used for Christ portray the preeminence or uniqueness of his person and in no way suggest a less-than-eternal existence on his part. Both Son of God and Son of Man reflect this preeminence over all things, the former relating primarily to his divine nature and the latter primarily to his human nature. In fact, Jesus himself attempted to teach the Pharisees that they must not read any unwarranted limitations into the term *Son* by pointing out to them that, although the Messiah could legitimately be designated by the title "Son of David," he was nevertheless David's Lord (Matt. 22:41–46)!

The same thing may be said with respect to the description that Paul gives to Christ in Colossians 1:15—"the firstborn over all creation." Recall that in the first half of that verse Paul refers to Christ as "the image of the invisible God." Paul uses the title *firstborn*, a term that was well known to the people of the Old Testament (see, e.g., Ex. 4:22), for its connotations of priority and superiority. Thus, he uses it not to imply any origination of the Son but to testify to his preeminence over all things since, as he tells us in the very next verse, they "were created through Him and for Him."

Finally, we note that the expression "second person of the Trinity" isn't a biblical title but one that we use merely to identify the Son as the One who is mentioned second in the triadic formula of Father, Son, and Holy Spirit. Thus, the Holy Spirit is referred to as the "third person of the Trinity," with the word *person* used to designate a distinct subsistence and identity. But the principle for which we contend here is simple: because the God of the Bible is an eternal Being, any person who is able to lay claim to the divine name must likewise be eternal.

Trinitarian Co-equality

Though no less important to the subject than co-eternality, the objections to the co-equality of the three persons may be dispensed with quickly, since the same line of argumentation and logic as we set forth above applies here. No person entitled to the divine name may be any less equal than the others, for by definition that would destroy the absolute unity that exists within the Godhead and substitute an ontological hierarchy of persons that finds no support whatsoever in Scripture. God doesn't share his glory with any others. To claim the name of Yahweh is to be identified as the One of whom "there is no other" (Deut. 4:39). And for us to worship one who couldn't lay such claim would be to violate the first commandment ("You shall have no other gods before Me"—Ex. 20:3). Thus, to say that the Son and Holy Spirit are God—to demonstrate the deity of each—is equivalent to proving the co-equality of each with the Father.[7]

We would be content to conclude our discussion of this topic right here except that one verse in the New Testament seems, at first glance, to contradict our thesis. Those who argue for Christ's being a lesser god, or no god at all, love to point to his statement in John 14:28 that "My Father is greater than I." To that statement we might also add the assertion that he made on multiple occasions to be doing "the Father's will."

What should we make of these two statements? Do they detract from the case that we've made thus far? Actually, one single passage from Paul's letter to the Philippians explains both of these statements in some of the most profound (and beautiful) words that Scripture has to offer:

> Let this mind be in you which was also in Christ Jesus, who, being in the form of God, did not consider it robbery to be equal with God, but made Himself of no reputation, taking the form of a bondservant, and coming in the likeness of men. And being found in appearance as a man, He humbled Himself and became obedient to the point of death, even the death of the cross (Phil. 2:5-8).

Paul's great Christ hymn, as it has come to be known, states in unambiguous language that Christ was "in the form of God," and "equal with God" prior to his incarnation, whereupon he "made Himself of no reputation" by taking up permanent residence in human flesh. And for what purpose did he do so? That he might "become obedient to the point of death." And this was done not for his sake, but for ours. The obedience he offered to God was the obedience that was our obligation to him, but which we ourselves were unable to offer. Thus, it is in performing the task assigned to him from all eternity that Christ the Son executes the Father's will. And it was in "taking the form of a bondservant" that he could say that the Father was greater than him.

In becoming incarnate, however, the Son didn't lose either his divine form or his equality with the Father. Rather, his divinity was joined to his new humanity (a subject we'll cover in some detail in the next chapter), and he voluntarily submitted himself to the Father's authority in order to undertake his new role as Mediator between God and man. It's also instructive that Jesus spoke about his Father being greater than him on the occasion of informing his disciples that he would soon be leaving them to rejoin his Father in heaven. Jesus wanted his disciples to understand that this was not only beneficial for them but also for him as well. Why? Because the Father is in heaven, a place much greater than their current abode. And it's in returning to heaven that the Son is again crowned with the glory that he enjoyed prior to becoming incarnate (John 17:5; see also 2 Cor. 8:9 and Heb. 2:9).

Jesus the Son isn't merely equal to the Father, he is of the same essence—the same *divine* essence. He and the Father exhibit such oneness of mind and purpose that Christ is able to say that "He who has seen Me has seen the Father." Thus, the Nicene Creed, developed in the fourth century in response to those who sought to strip Christ of his biblical title, stressed that the Son was "Very God of very God, begotten, not made, being of one substance with the Father."

With these last two pieces of the puzzle in place, then, we're in a position to offer an expanded and final definition of the Trinity, which we borrow from James White: "Within the one Being that is God, there exists eternally three co-equal and co-eternal persons, namely, the Father, the Son, and the Holy Spirit."[8]

Divine Community and Human Worship

Those of us who confess our faith in this triune God worship him as he has revealed himself to us. We pray to the Father for blessing and forgiveness of our sins; we trust in the work of the Son for our salvation and pray to the Father in his name; and we rely upon the work of the Holy Spirit to apply those same blessings to our lives. As Christians we claim the name of Jesus Christ, the Son, and proclaim him as our Savior. But we don't worship the Son at the *expense* of the Father or the Holy Spirit. Rather, we worship the triune God *through* the Son. It's the Son who gives access to God the Father, and it's only by loving and worshiping the Son that the broken relationship between God and man is mended (1 John 2:22–23).

The remaining verses of Paul's Christ hymn testify to this intra-Trinitarian focus upon the Son:

> Therefore God also has highly exalted Him and given Him the name which is above every name, that at the name of Jesus every knee should bow, of those in heaven, and of those on earth, and of those under the earth, and that every tongue should confess that Jesus Christ is Lord, to the glory of God the Father (Phil. 2:9-11).

It is for the glory of the Father that Christ is worshiped and adored. And to that we may add the concurrence of the Holy Spirit (John 16:13–15). The Son has been given the nations for his inheritance (Psalm 2:7–12), and the Spirit is in the process of bringing that promise to fulfillment. Thus, Christians may rest assured that their praises to Christ are met with divine approval and blessing. There is no competition for supremacy within the Godhead. All attention has been focused upon the Son, and the triune God is glorified through him.

The apostle John writes that "God is love" (1 John 4:8), by which he means that God is the highest representation, and very embodiment, of that self-sacrificial devotion toward others that seeks their welfare at all times. John understood only too well that the very essence of God is loving relationship, for he has existed in such personal relationship of Father, Son, and Spirit from all eternity. Yet John also tells us that God's greatest act of love consisted in this: that "in the beginning" he chose, out of his own good pleasure, to direct that love toward creatures of his own making, so that they too might know the love of the triune God; and that although they did not return the favor, God's love remained upon them, culminating in the supreme act of the giving of "*His only begotten Son*, that whoever believes in Him should not perish but have everlasting life."

3

He Is the Word Become Flesh

(JOHN 1:14)

Most of us at one time or another have seen the poem entitled "Footprints in the Sand," sometimes simply entitled "Footprints." These days the anonymous poem can be found on coffee mugs, napkins, clocks, and just about anything else that has enough space for the words. The poem tells the story of a man who dreamed that he was walking along the beach with the Lord, viewing scenes from his life as they flashed across the sky. After the last scene had passed before him, he looked back at the footprints in the sand and noticed that during the most difficult times of his life, there was only one set of footprints left behind. Bothered by his discovery, the man asked the Lord why he abandoned the man to fend for himself at the times when he needed him most. The Lord replied that the reason the man saw only one set of footprints in the sand during those times of trial and suffering was because "it was then that I carried you."

That story may be a familiar one, but there's another that sounds remarkably similar (albeit with a very different spiritual message) and that predates this one by almost two thousand years! In the earlier story, Jesus is walking along the beach, talking about the mysteries of the kingdom with one of his disciples. When the disciple decides to look back at the path they had been treading, he notices only one set of footprints—his own. And why is this so? Because according to those who were spreading this story, Jesus doesn't leave behind footprints, since he's pure spirit and only *seemed* to have a physical body.[1]

Those who were guilty of spreading such stories about Jesus in the early church were known as Docetics, from a Greek word that means "to seem." They were influenced by the concept of "dualism," which taught that spirit is good and matter is evil. The incarnation thus posed a real problem for them. They couldn't affirm that Christ was good if he had truly taken on human flesh, for matter is inherently evil. Thus, they solved the difficulty by arguing that Christ only *seemed* to be human to those who saw him during the days of his earthly sojourn.[2]

But the apostle John tells us that the Word became flesh—human flesh. And he does so in the most explicit terms, not only in his gospel account but in his first epistle as well. In common with the other gospel writers, John records the indignities heaped upon Jesus by Pilate and the Roman guard on the night of his arrest and trial. John tells us that Jesus' body was scourged by Pilate (John 19:1; cf. Matt. 27:26; Mark 15:15); that he had a crown of thorns placed upon his head (John 19:2; cf. Matt. 27:29; Mark 15:17); and that his body was taken by Joseph of Arimathea for burial after his death (John 19:38; cf. Matt. 27:58–59; Mark 15:43–45; Luke 23:52–55). However, John alone records that Jesus' side was pierced with a spear, at which point water and blood poured out, testifying to the fact that he was truly dead (John 19:34). He also recorded for us the account of Thomas placing his fingers into the nail holes and pierced side of Jesus (John 20:24–29).

But it's in his first epistle that John confronts the Docetic heresy head-on. The opening words that he uses in that letter are truly striking:

That which was from the beginning, which we
have heard, which we have seen with our eyes,
which we have looked upon, and our hands have
handled, concerning the Word of life—the life was
manifested, and we have seen, and bear witness,
and declare to you that eternal life which was with
the Father and was manifested to us—that which
we have seen and heard we declare to you, that
you also may have fellowship with us; and truly
our fellowship is with the Father and with his Son
Jesus Christ. And these things we write to you that
your joy may be full (1 John 1:1–4).

John emphasizes in this passage that those who were with Jesus
(the "Word of life") had not only seen him with their own eyes and
heard him with their own ears, but that they had handled him with
their own hands. And then, as if intending to make certain that no
one could possibly remain confused about what he was saying, a few
chapters later he adds this:

By this you know the Spirit of God: Every spirit that
confesses that Jesus Christ has come in the flesh is
of God, and every spirit that does not confess that
Jesus Christ has come in the flesh is not of God.
And this is the spirit of the Antichrist, which you
have heard was coming, and is now already in the
world (1 John 4:2–3).

John's message is unmistakable: Jesus is no mere apparition or
phantom, but the real thing—the Word of God in human flesh.
And as we shall see, this is no mere academic matter; it's one with
enormous practical significance. Indeed, for John it determines
whether one's theology is of God or "the Antichrist."

The Word

Before we consider the implications of the statement that "the Word became flesh," a more fundamental question presents itself: Why does John refer to Jesus as "the Word" in the first place? What exactly is he attempting to convey by the use of this title, one that no other New Testament writer uses in reference to Christ?

First, the Greek word that is used here in John 1:1 is *Logos*, from which we derive our English word *logic*. In Greek philosophical circles the term had come to mean a number of different things over the years but was most often used to refer to some kind of impersonal animating force or principle of the universe. John borrows the term and applies it to Christ in an obvious effort to direct his readers toward the *true* animating force of the universe—the God of Israel, who recently had become flesh and "dwelt among us" in the person of his Son (John 1:14).

But it's also likely that the Holy Spirit (through John) had other designs for using such a title. For one thing, as Louis Berkhof points out, it's more appropriate to say that the "Word became flesh" than that "God became man," since it wasn't the triune God who assumed human nature but the Son alone.[3] Perhaps more important, however, is the fact that it's John's wish to tell us something not only about Christ's person but about his office as well. And to speak of Christ as "the Word" ideally suits such a purpose. There are at least three distinct ideas contained in John calling Jesus "the Word."

1. The Wisdom of God

Because of the close connection between the concepts of logic and wisdom, it's quite possible that John uses this title (in part) to draw attention to the role that Jesus played in demonstrating, as well as possessing, the wisdom of God. Indeed, the apostle Paul makes this very point in several places in his letters to the various churches. Not only did he call Christ "the wisdom of God" (1 Cor. 1:24) "in whom are hidden all the treasures of wisdom and knowledge" (Col. 2:3), but he even says that Christ "became for us wisdom from God" (1 Cor. 1:30), a phrase reminiscent of the one under consideration here. Add to that the fact that *wisdom* is personified in Proverbs 8 in such a way as to lead many commentators to see a direct reference to the pre-incarnate Son, and the case seems stronger yet.

One of those who saw a connection between John's use of "the Word" and the "wisdom of God" was Stephen Charnock, a seventeenth-century English Puritan, who wrote:

> When the apostle speaks of "God manifested in the flesh," he speaks "the wisdom of God in a mystery" (1 Tim. 3:16).... Mysterious is the wisdom of God to unite finite and infinite, almightiness and weakness, immortality and mortality, immutability, with a thing subject to change; to have a nature from eternity, and yet a nature subject to the revolutions of time; a nature to make a law, and a nature to be subjected to the law; to be God blessed forever, in the bosom of his Father, and an infant exposed to calamities from the womb of his mother ... the creature with the Creator; he that made all things, in one person with a nature that is made; ... one with the Father in his Godhead, one with us in his manhood; the Godhead to be in him in the fullest perfection, and the manhood in the greatest purity; the creature one with the Creator, and the Creator one with the creature. Thus is the incomprehensible wisdom of God declared in the "Word being made flesh."[4]

One thing is certain: although Jesus "increased in wisdom" (Luke 2:52) during the days of his incarnation, he nevertheless possessed the wisdom of the ages, as his fellow countrymen were forced to admit time and again (John 7:15; Matt. 13:54).

2. The Creative Word

Because the opening verses of John's gospel speak of Christ as both "the Word" and as the Maker of all things, it's hard to imagine that the former term wasn't chosen by John to help his readers make the connection between the two. Genesis tells us that God spoke the universe into existence, and Psalm 33:6 says, "By the *word* of the Lord the heavens were made." John wants us to understand that Jesus Christ is the One who possesses that power to create all things. He is, as Paul tells us, the "power of God" (1 Cor. 1:24).

3. The Revealed Word

While it's likely that John uses the title "the Word" to draw attention to Christ as both the wisdom and the creative power of God, it's also likely that this third meaning, that of Christ being the *revealed* Word of God, is the one he intends to have primary force. In the same prologue, John tells us that it's the Word who has "declared" the Father to mankind. He also refers to Christ as "the true Light which gives light to every man" (v. 9) and says that the Word was "full of grace and *truth*" (v. 14). A few chapters later, John records the exchange that took place after many of Jesus' disciples turned away because of his teaching on election. When Jesus asked the Twelve if they too would turn away from him, Peter answered, "Lord, to whom shall we go? You have the words of eternal life" (John 6:68).

Thus, it's as the incarnate, revealed "Word of God" that Christ is set forth in John's gospel. It's Christ who brings to men the revelation of God in its ultimate glory—his very person. The words that he speaks are the words of God, because that is who he is. And he is God's final word to man (Heb. 1:1–3), for man needs no other than that which Christ has personally delivered.

The Pre-Incarnate Christ

When we piece together the various truths that John gives to us in his brief prologue, we learn a great deal about Christ. We learn that Jesus Christ is the Word, that he has existed eternally, and that he is God incarnate. We also learn that he has been active since eternity past in creating all things and in revealing the Father to men. And because John also tells us that no one has ever seen the Father, we're able to reach another conclusion that's supported by the rest of Scripture as well—it was none other than Christ the Son who appeared to the saints of old on those occasions where God presented himself in bodily form.

There are numerous examples of this in the Old Testament. The record of Abraham's visitor near Mamre in Genesis 18:1–19:24 clearly reveals him to be the Lord but one who was also distinct from the Lord (i.e., the Father). Jacob wrestled a man whom he only afterwards came to realize was God (Gen. 32:24–32). And God also appeared visibly to men under a number of different titles during that period, the most common of which was the "Angel of the Lord." The passages where those appearances are recorded sometimes alternate between identification of the visitor as the "Angel of the Lord" or simply as "Lord" or "God" (e.g., Ex. 3:2–6; Gen. 22:11–18; Judges 6:11–24), while at other times the "Angel of the Lord" is distinguished from the Lord in heaven (e.g., Zech. 1:12; 3:1–2), thus providing further testimony to the plurality of the Godhead. It's also instructive that *the* "Angel of the Lord" makes no further appearances after the close of the Old Testament. In the New Testament we're introduced only to *an* "angel of the Lord" (e.g., Matt. 1:20; Acts 5:19).[5]

All of this serves to confirm what we've already discussed—that Christ is, *and always has been*, the "image of the invisible God." Even before the "Word became flesh"—which is John's way of referring to the Son's permanent assumption of human nature—the second person of the Trinity was the visible face of God. Thus, it's possible to speak of the activity of the pre-incarnate Son of God, or even the pre-incarnate Christ, but it wouldn't be accurate to speak of the pre-incarnate Jesus, that being the name given to the child born in a stable at a certain point in time and whose human nature was thus united with the divine nature of the Son. Whatever similarities or resemblances the adult Jesus bore to the embodied Son of God who appeared to the Old Testament saints, Scripture doesn't tell us. But it was only upon his permanent assumption of human nature that the Son became Jesus Christ, the God-Man.

The God-Man

The church may have formally settled the matter of the Trinity at the Councils of Nicea and Constantinople in the fourth century, but questions regarding the nature of Christ continued for at least another hundred years. In addition to the Docetics, who denied Jesus' human nature, groups such as the Ebionites denied his divine nature. Then there were a whole host of groups who, while not necessarily denying one or the other nature outright, laid so much stress on one that the other was effectively excluded, at least in its fullness. The result was a Christ who was either fully divine and only partly human, or fully human and only partly divine.

But the church insisted that Christ was fully God and fully man. By virtue of his incarnation, he had become the unique God-Man, lacking in neither nature but possessing each to its fullest measure. When the matter finally came to a head at the Council of Chalcedon in AD 451, the church composed a creed, formalizing what it had always believed and laying out the following principles:

> 1. Christ is one Person, existing in two natures, the divine and the human.
> 2. Both natures are complete and undiminished by the union of them, so that Christ is "truly God and truly man."
> 3. Christ possesses "a reasonable soul and body."
> 4. Christ differs from other humans only in that he is without sin.

5. The union of Christ's two natures was accomplished "without confusion, without change, without division, [and] without separation," so that, while he remains one in person and subsistence, his two natures are nevertheless distinct, the characteristics of each being preserved, and in no sense becoming mixed or confused.

As with the doctrine of the Trinity, Christians readily admit that the doctrine of the dual nature of Christ is beyond complete human comprehension. But we also recognize that it's the clear and emphatic teaching of Scripture. That Christ was one in personality is demonstrated by the fact that he left no evidence of an I-Thou relationship in his inner life, such as we find within the triune God, where one of the persons addresses another.[6] Nor did he feel the need to qualify certain statements that he made that are applicable to one nature but not the other. For example, he didn't say, "As to my divine nature, before Abraham was, I am" or "As to my human nature, I thirst." Rather, both Christ and the writers of the New Testament speak of him in terms of the one person possessing both natures and are comfortable assigning to him whatever may be said of either nature. Thus, it's just as appropriate to say that Christ is eternal as it is to say that he died on the cross. Either statement may be made about him without qualification.

At the same, however, the Creed of Chalcedon cautions us against confusing the two natures. We may be able to assign to Christ (the person) whatever is true of either nature, as we did above, but we aren't able to do the reverse. That is, we may rightly say that Christ is omnipresent, but we may not say that Christ's human nature is omnipresent, for omnipresence is an attribute of divinity, not humanity. By the same token, we may not affirm that Christ in his divinity "increased in wisdom" or needed the bodily sustenance of such things as food and sleep, for they are applicable only to his human nature. Rather, we affirm that the divine Son of God *assumed* human nature but didn't thereby divest himself of anything in his divinity, nor were the two natures somehow fused or mixed into a third type of divine-human nature.[7] In the union, each nature retained its distinctive characteristics—the human nature wasn't divinized, and the divine nature was not humanized.

The Incarnate Christ and the Purpose of the Incarnation

The doctrine of the dual nature of Christ wouldn't be complete, however, without a discussion of how the two natures interrelated with each other during the days of Christ's incarnation. This is precisely where many Christians get tripped up. In applying the doctrine to specific biblical passages, we often fail to take into account what Scripture says about the nature of the incarnation in the first place. A prime example of where this tendency rears its ugly head is Mark 13:32, when Christ informed his disciples that he didn't know the time of his second coming. Some Christians, upon reading that passage, mistakenly reason that because omniscience is an attribute of deity and because Christ didn't know the hour of his own second coming, he must not have been fully God. But Paul said that in Christ dwelt "all the fullness of the Godhead bodily" (Col. 2:9). How are we supposed to put these two statements together? Was Christ omniscient or not?

For the solution to this apparent difficulty we refer back to the words of the Christ hymn of Philippians 2:5–11, which we discussed in the last chapter. After asserting Christ's divinity, Paul says that he nevertheless "made Himself of no reputation, taking the form of a bondservant, and coming in the likeness of men. And being found in appearance as a man, He humbled Himself and became obedient to the point of death, even the death of the cross" (vv. 7–8). There's probably no other passage in all of Scripture that so succinctly summarizes the theology of the incarnation as well as these two verses do. The relevant points for our discussion are that Christ "made Himself of no reputation," by taking on the form of a "bondservant," and becoming "obedient."

The first thing to notice is that Christ entered into this mission voluntarily. He "made Himself of no reputation" for our benefit. By entering into his mediatorial work on behalf of sinful people, he took on our form and became an obedient bondservant so that we might thereby gain life. However, in so doing, he didn't cease to be God, nor did he surrender any of the attributes of deity. Rather, he voluntarily submitted himself to carrying out the work of redeeming mankind, and that work brought with it a new, but temporary, way of doing things for the Son of God. In "making himself of no reputation" and coming in the likeness of men, Christ temporarily (1) veiled his divine glory so that men could see him and not be struck dead, (2) condescended to take on human flesh with all of its frailties and weaknesses, and (3) committed himself to reversing the curse that had fallen upon mankind, which involved a voluntary nonuse of some divine attributes in order to accomplish that objective.[8]

When this understanding of the nature and purpose of the incarnation is firmly grasped, we eliminate much of the confusion that occurs in interpreting specific biblical passages. Indeed, we see Christ in a whole new light—as One who had the power within himself to avoid the sufferings to which he was subjected but who chose the way of the cross for our sakes. In seeking to answer the question raised by Mark 13:32, Donald Macleod does a wonderful job relating Christ's nonuse of his divine attributes to the grand purpose of his incarnation:

> How does the omniscience of the *Logos* relate to the ignorance of the Mediator? Two things may be said.
> First, that as Mediator he was never ignorant of anything that he ought to have known.... As a finite creature there was much that Christ did not know, but as Mediator he knew all that he needed to know; or, more precisely, all that his church needed to know.... What it means is that the Father shared with him as much about the mystery of redemption as he needed to know. He received this knowledge in his capacity as the Great Prophet; he received it from the Father through the Spirit; and he received it not all at once, but gradually, the progress of the

revelation being determined by his own developing capacities and by the exigencies of the hour.... It is clear from Mark 13:32 that the time of the *parousia* was not revealed to Christ; and it is virtually certain that the reason why it was not revealed was that this was not something his people needed to know. It either had no bearing on Christian life and devotion, or the divine judgment was that such life and devotion would be better served by uncertainty on this issue than by precise information.

The other line of integration between the omniscience of the divine nature and the ignorance of the human is that just as Christ had to fulfill the office of Mediator within the limitations of a human body, so he had to fulfill it within the limitations of a human mind. Part of the truth here is suggested by the first of the three temptations in the desert: 'tell these stones to become bread' (Mt. 4:3). The essence of the temptation was that the Lord disavow the conditions of the incarnation and draw on his omnipotence to alleviate the discomforts of his self-abasement. He could have turned the stones into bread; and he could (perhaps) have known the day and the hour of his parousia. But the latter would have undone his work as surely as the former. Christ had to submit to knowing dependently and to knowing partially. He had to learn to obey without knowing all the facts and had to believe without being in possession of full information. He had to forego the comfort which omniscience would sometimes have brought. This, surely, was a potent factor in the dereliction (Mk. 15:34).... he suffers as the one who does not have all the answers and who in his extremity has to ask, Why? The ignorance is not a mere appearing. It is a reality. But it is a reality freely chosen, just as on the cross he chose not to summon twelve legions of angels. Omniscience was a luxury always within reach, but incompatible with his rules of engagement. He had to serve within the limitations of finitude.[9]

The Necessity of the Incarnation

The fact that Christ had to "serve within the limitations of finitude" is the fervent and consistent testimony of the writer to the Hebrews. More than any other New Testament author, he's concerned with setting forth Christ in all of his glory, both as the only begotten Son of God and as Jesus Christ, the only Mediator between God and men. Sin had broken the relationship between mankind and a holy God, and reconciliation demanded a mediator. And although it was man who owed the debt for his disobedience, he now lacked the power and ability to make satisfaction for his transgression. Only God, in his grace, could provide what man needed.

Thus, it was necessary for God himself, in the person of the Son, to be "made a little lower than the angels" (Heb. 2:9), that he, as a man, might make satisfaction for the debt owed to God. The writer of Hebrews tells us that "He had to be made like His brethren" in order that through his death "He might destroy him who had the power of death" and "make propitiation for the sins of the people" (Heb. 2:14–17). And being made like his brethren meant being able to stand in man's stead, which involved subjecting himself to mankind's "limitations of finitude," as Macleod explains. Both Christ and those whom he came to save needed to be of the same nature so that he might be able to call us his brethren (Heb. 2:11–13).

The Mediator had to be human. But he needed to be divine as well, for it was only by overcoming the limitations of human flesh—and reversing the effects of the curse that had fallen upon mankind—that his work could have the infinite value necessary to apply to all who would trust in him. Thus, the divine Word needed to become flesh.

Thankfully, Christ fulfilled that role perfectly and for the sins of his people made the propitiation that they weren't able to make for themselves. Because he "was in all points tempted as we are, yet without sin" (Heb. 4:15), his once-for-all sacrifice of his own body healed the breach between God and man (Heb. 9:26–28; 10:10). His flesh has now become the veil through which we pass into the holiest of holies and into the very presence of God, where Christ himself is now seated at the Father's right hand (Heb. 10:12, 19–20). In this manner, then, Christ has become the "author of eternal salvation" (Heb. 5:9) and the "Mediator of a better covenant," the first one having had no power to save (Heb. 7:11; 8:6–7).

The apostle Paul called the Incarnation "the mystery of godliness" (1 Tim. 3:16). That "God was manifested in the flesh" for our benefit, is a thought that is simply too high, and too glorious, for us to take in. And yet it is true! The Word became flesh and dwelt among us. He became the God-Man, who now continues to exist in two distinct natures forever, though his human nature has now been glorified and is thus free from the infirmities with which Jesus was forced to clothe himself during the days of his earthly life. Such a mystery is high indeed. But the God-Man of whom it speaks is higher yet, and worthy of all praise from those who are the objects of his gracious condescension. The late B.B. Warfield expressed such praise with the following words:

> The glory of the Incarnation is that it presents to our adoring gaze, not a humanized God or a deified man, but a true God-man—one who is all that God is and at the same time all that man is: on whose almighty arm we can rest, and to whose human sympathy we can appeal. We cannot afford to lose either the God in the man or the man in the God; our hearts cry out for the complete God-man whom the Scriptures offer us.[10]

4

He Was Born of a Virgin

(MATT. 1:23)

My family and I love Christmas. Not just the exchanging of gifts and other activities that accompany the celebration of Christ's birth on December 25th but the whole season of preparation that runs from Thanksgiving through Christmas. One of our favorite things to do is to drive through the neighborhoods in our community and admire the beautiful Christmas displays, some grand and some simple, that adorn many houses. There's a spirit of generosity and thankfulness that seems to permeate the whole season, and even many who aren't particularly religious are pleased to join in.

Of course, part of the reason that this is so is because the season has lost much of its religious significance for a large part of the general populace. For many, it has become little more than a time for family gatherings, office parties, and perhaps even some personal reflection on the impending year-end. But such reflection rarely extends to the real reason for the season. Non-Christians may tolerate the manger scenes and the ubiquitous Christmas carols, but the message that those things are meant to convey too often goes unnoticed by the vast majority of those who are exposed to them.

Although believers rightly decry the commercialization of Christmas for obscuring its deeper meaning, we must admit that even many Christians have little appreciation for the theological significance of the Christmas story. We may sing "round yon virgin mother and child," but do we give more than a moment's thought to what it means to speak of a virgin mother? More importantly, do we appreciate the fact that the child spoken of here, born in a stable because there was no room for him in the inn, is the same person who was prior to that, and is now once again, enthroned in the heavens with power and glory?

Christmas is the day that the Word became flesh. It's the day to which the Old Testament prophets pointed for thousands of years. The birth of Jesus in Bethlehem was the opening act to the series of events in his life that constitute his work as the Savior of his people. His human birth was necessary for that work. And as we will demonstrate in this chapter, it was just as necessary that the circumstances of that birth be of a miraculous nature—that he be "born of a virgin."

The Prophecies

The Christmas story, as we just intimated, has its true beginnings not in Bethlehem of Judea two thousand years ago but considerably earlier in the Garden of Eden. It was there, at the fall of the human race, that God gave the first promise of the gospel to Adam and Eve by pronouncing that a future Redeemer would crush the head of the serpent, the very same serpent that had just deceived them (Gen. 3:15). In that first of many Old Testament messianic prophecies we're also given a glimpse (however faint) into the special nature of that Redeemer, who is spoken of as the woman's "Seed." This unusual term finds no parallel anywhere else in the Bible, which uniformly uses the term *seed* as a designation for individuals descended from a particular male, whether it be Abraham, Jacob, or David (Heb. 11:11

is no exception to this rule). Thus, even at this earliest stage in biblical revelation—and most certainly as we look back through the lens of the New Testament—we detect something of the unique character of the One who was to have the task of crushing the serpent.

Of course, the rest of Scripture makes it clear that the promised Redeemer is Jesus Christ, the Word become flesh, whose birth in a stable in Bethlehem is the centerpiece of the Christmas story. But even though God graciously intervened in the face of Adam and Eve's transgression—by not only providing an immediate covering for their nakedness but for their sin as well—many generations of their descendants would have to wait for the complete fulfillment of that promise—the coming of the promised Redeemer in the flesh.

During those intervening years between the fall of Adam and Eve and the arrival of Jesus, however, God wasn't slack concerning his promise. Rather, he was preparing the world for Jesus' arrival. He was at work unfolding his plan of redemption and bringing to pass those things that would move salvation history toward its ultimate end. That perfect plan included the establishment of a nation that would bear his holy name and be a witness to his saving activity and purpose to the whole world. God's people, at least for a season, wouldn't be merely an invisible conglomeration of individuals spread throughout the world, with no way to communicate or fellowship with one another, but would comprise a distinct nation and people group, with God himself serving as their King.

When God finally moved to establish that nation several thousand years later, he did so by plucking a man named Abraham from his home in Ur (in modern day Iraq) and sending him and his family to the land that he had chosen for his people to eventually inhabit. And in the process God reiterated the promise given to Adam and Eve, while at the same time narrowing the scope of those from whom the Redeemer would be descended to Abraham's seed (Gen. 22:18; Gal. 3:16). Later on, after the children of Israel were forced to leave the Promised Land for a period of time, God led them back through his servant Moses, but it was God's mighty arm that guided and protected them all the way.

After another four hundred years passed, sometime around the year 1000 BC, the nation of Israel entered into its golden age. Under the reign of kings David and Solomon, Israel would become a major world power for close to a century and would construct a temple in Jerusalem as a centralized place of worship for all who called upon the Lord and were counted amongst his people. The nation that God had established then entered its most glorious period; she was envied and feared by her neighbors, and she possessed great wealth and honor throughout the ancient world.

Unfortunately, this state of affairs was rather short-lived. Around the year 922 BC, the kingdom split in two, with the Northern portion assuming the name Israel and the Southern portion becoming known as Judah. Indeed, by 740 BC things were beginning to look rather bleak for the children of the Exodus; neighboring countries were threatening Israel, and the nation was about to fall to the Assyrian Empire and be driven into exile.

It's into this situation that Isaiah, one of the most important of the Old Testament prophets, delivers a word from the Lord. And although he foretells of the future fall of both Israel and Judah, he also issues a word of hope. He speaks of a restoration to come and the salvation of Israel's remnant. And in the midst of his prophecy, Isaiah speaks of One who will be born in the future, One whose birth will be a sign to the whole world because of his identity, and One who will suffer for the sins of his people. This is what Isaiah writes in his prophecy:

> Therefore the Lord Himself will give you a sign: Behold, the virgin shall conceive and bear a Son, and shall call His name Immanuel (Isa. 7:14).

> For unto us a child is born, unto us a Son is given; and the government will be upon His shoulder. And his name will be called Wonderful, Counselor, Mighty God, Everlasting Father, Prince of Peace (Isa. 9:6).

These two passages speak of a sign that the Lord will give his people. The One who will come in the future will have a supernatural origin, by being born of a virgin, and his name will be Immanuel. If you've ever wondered why this passage doesn't identify the future hope of Israel as Jesus the Messiah but rather gives him the name Immanuel, then you need only look at the root meaning of the Hebrew word. *Immanuel* means "God with us," which is exactly what Jesus is. This is confirmed in the second passage, which tells us that his name will be "Mighty God." Moreover, James Boice believed that this passage also makes reference to the dual nature of Christ, since it speaks of a child being born (the human side) and a Son being given (the divine side).[1]

Only a few years after Isaiah uttered his prophecy, the prophet Micah spoke of this future ruler of Israel and of his eternal origin (his "goings forth are from of old, from everlasting"), thus further confirming the divine identity of the Redeemer. But Micah adds a new detail to watch for—another mark that helps to identify this future King; he would come forth from the insignificant town of Bethlehem in Judah (Micah 5:2).

Finally, as we close the book on the relevant Old Testament prophecies that foretold of the coming of the Messiah, we look at one more prophecy, this one from the prophet Jeremiah. A century after Isaiah and Micah delivered their prophecies, God sent Jeremiah to warn Judah of her impending judgment and exile. But in the midst of his prophecy he too issues a note of future hope. He speaks of One who will sit on the throne of David and will bring Israel and Judah together again:

> "Behold the days are coming," says the Lord, "that I will raise to David a Branch of righteousness; a King shall reign and prosper, and execute judgment and righteousness in the earth. In His days Judah will be saved, and Israel will dwell safely; now this is His name by which He will be called: THE LORD OUR RIGHTEOUSNESS" (Jeremiah 23:5–6).

Jeremiah not only speaks of a future restoration but he also gives us yet another name by which we may call this future ruler over the nation—THE LORD OUR RIGHTEOUSNESS. It's clear by now that the names that Scripture gives thus far for this future ruler are actually titles that describe his essence and identity. And it's equally clear that Jeremiah's use of this title for this future King adds to the groundwork that Isaiah lays by continuing to make it clear that this One to come will be no ordinary man. He'll not only be "God with us," but he'll also be One capable of supplying the very righteousness that we need but are unable to supply for ourselves. Thus, he'll be THE LORD OUR RIGHTEOUSNESS.

When we collect the identifying marks of the future King that the Old Testament prophets have given to us, we see that he'll be born of a virgin in a place called Bethlehem; he'll be of the line of David, the royal line of Israel; and most gloriously of all, he'll be a King like no other for he'll have an eternal origin as God in human flesh, the righteous One whose reign extends far beyond the borders of Israel or Judah, for he will execute judgment and righteousness over all the earth.

The Preparation

Without a doubt, this promised Redeemer was One for whom the children of Israel could wait with a great sense of excitement and hope. But it should be noted that between the time of the last of these prophecies and the fulfillment of them in the birth of Jesus another six hundred years would pass! An awful lot happened in the history of Israel between the time of those promises and the birth of the Lord in Bethlehem. There must have been times when the Jews felt as if God was slack in fulfilling his promises as they suffered through one subjugation after another by foreign powers. After the Assyrians and Babylonians came the Greeks, the Egyptians, and finally the Romans who occupied Palestine at the time of Jesus' arrival.

But something very important was taking place during these centuries. As we stated a few moments ago, the world was being prepared for the arrival of the Messiah. Not only was God systematically unfolding his plan of redemption within the nation of Israel, his chosen people, but he was also creating the ideal conditions for the gospel to go forth from the land of Palestine into the whole world. In the last several hundred years prior to Christ's birth, the Mediterranean world had become united by a common language (Greek), a comprehensive system of roads, and a relative peace that had never before prevailed in that part of the world.[2] The combination of these developments led to a much more favorable environment for the spread of the gospel to the Gentile nations outside of Palestine.

So there was good reason for God's delaying the sending of his Son to earth. And even though it was a long time between the prophecies of Christ's birth and the actual fulfillment of them, we may still find ourselves asking if God had really done enough to prepare the world for this great moment. After all of this preparatory work, had he still sent Jesus *too soon*? The question is prompted by the fact that the inhabitants of Jerusalem, Nazareth, and the other cities of Judea certainly didn't appear to be ready for the kind of King that Jesus turned out to be. They were looking for someone decidedly more militant in spirit. Perhaps it would have been better if God had waited a few more centuries to send his Son.

The problem with that analysis is that God's Messiah could only come from one nation, and that nation ceased to exist after AD 70, when it was completely destroyed by the Roman Emperor Titus and the Jews as a distinct people group were scattered to the winds for the last time. And this final subjugation had the effect of further hastening the spread of the gospel throughout the Roman Empire and beyond, so that within a few hundred years Christianity had become the dominant religion in the civilized world—just as God had planned all along.

And so it is that Christ's coming took place at the perfect time in order to accomplish God's purpose to send the gospel forth to all nations. The Jews' long wait for the Messiah was necessary, for as Paul tells us in Galatians, "God sent forth His son, born of a woman" only "when the fullness of time had come" (Gal. 4:4).

The Fulfillment

The Announcements to Mary and Joseph

In the opening chapter of Luke's gospel, we read that the angel Gabriel was sent to Nazareth to a virgin named Mary, who was betrothed to a man named Joseph, who was of the line of David. The angel told Mary that she had found favor with God and that she would conceive a child in her womb and bring forth a Son whom she was to call Jesus. When Mary inquired how this was possible, since she was a virgin, the angel answered that "The Holy Spirit will come upon you, and will overshadow you; therefore, also, that Holy One who is to be born will be called the Son of God." He added, "For with God nothing will be impossible," to which in a great show of faith Mary responded, "Behold the maidservant of the Lord! Let it be to me according to your word" (Luke 1:26–38).

Shortly thereafter, as Matthew's account informs us, an angel appeared to Joseph in a dream and told him to not be afraid to take Mary as his wife, since the child conceived in her womb was from the Holy Spirit. He too was commanded to give the name Jesus to the child, "for He will save His people from their sins." Matthew adds that Joseph did as he was commanded, taking Mary as his wife, and didn't "know" her until after Jesus was brought forth. And Matthew makes the point of telling us that this was done in fulfillment of Isaiah's prophecy, that Jesus was the promised Immanuel ("God with us") of old (Matt. 1:18–25).

Unlike most parents, Joseph and Mary didn't have the privilege of choosing a name for their child. The angel informed them that they were to call their son Jesus; there was no choice in the matter for them. But it couldn't be any other way, for no other name was suitable for the child that would be born to them. The name Jesus means "the Lord's salvation" or "the Lord saves," and it was the only appropriate name for someone who, as the angel informed Joseph, will save his people from their sins.

The Birth

The details of Christ's birth are found in Luke's account, where we learn that Joseph and Mary had to travel from their hometown in Nazareth to Bethlehem to enroll in a census ordered by Caesar Augustus. And in God's providence, it was while they were there to be registered that Jesus was born, in a stable with a manger, because there was no room for them in the town's inn (Luke 2:1–7). Jesus' birth demonstrates how God uses human agents to bring about the work that he has ordained. Caesar may have thought he was doing as he pleased in calling for a census to be taken, which required each citizen of Palestine to return to the city of his or her birth. But it was the Lord who was engineering the circumstances. It was the Lord who was seeing to it that Joseph and Mary would be in the appointed place (Bethlehem) at the appointed time of Mary's giving birth.

Angels and Shepherds

Angels not only delivered the message of Christ's coming birth to Mary and Joseph beforehand, but they also made announcement of the birth after it had taken place. On the night of Jesus' birth an angel appeared to a group of shepherds who were tending their flocks in the fields outside Bethlehem. The angel told them not to be afraid, for "I bring you good tidings of great joy which shall be to all people. For there is born to you this day in the city of David a Savior, who is Christ the Lord." This angel was then joined by a multitude of the heavenly host, who praised God and sang, "Glory to God in the highest, and on earth peace, goodwill toward men" (Luke 2:8–14).

When the angels returned to their heavenly abode, the shepherds made haste to go and see for themselves what great thing had transpired. After finding the infant child where the angels said he would be, we are told that the shepherds went and "made widely known the saying which was told them concerning this Child" (Luke 2:15–20). In this manner, then, the world was beginning to be made aware of the arrival of the long-promised Messiah.

As for the shepherds, they were given the privilege of having the birth of Jesus announced directly to them by the heavenly host; of being able to see the newborn Babe lying in the manger; and of being able to make widely known the great things that they had been allowed to see and hear. And what is so paradoxical about this fact is that shepherds were near the bottom of the social class in Judean society. They were looked down upon, and viewed as completely insignificant people.[3] Yet God allowed them to have a blessed role in this story. And it demonstrates the fact that the gospel is for all such people. Just as the angel had said—the announcement that he brought was "good tidings of great joy which will be to all people."

It is also worth pointing out that the angel who spoke to the shepherds did not tell them to go and find Jesus; he merely gave them a sign by which they could identify the child ("You will find a Babe wrapped in swaddling cloths, lying in a manger"). But the passage tells us that they not only undertook "with haste" to locate the infant Jesus, but after they had done so, to make widely known the news which they had heard and seen. Thus, they risked disbelief and ridicule in sharing what they had found with others, since the society in which they lived did not even consider them worthy witnesses in a court of law. Of course, this was just one of the ways in which God, through the Incarnation of Christ, was turning the world upside down, demonstrating the folly of human wisdom, and, in the process, reminding us all that salvation is a work of his grace alone.

The Wise Men

The final aspect of the Christmas story involves the pilgrimage of the "wise men from the East." Following a star that alerted them to the fact that the time had arrived for the Messiah's birth, they traveled from their homeland to find the young child Jesus, probably some months later. After stopping in Jerusalem to find out where the birth of the Messiah was to take place, they once again followed the star until it led them to the very house where Jesus was now living. It was there that they presented the young child with gifts of gold, frankincense, and myrrh (Matt. 2:1–12).

The story of the wise men's participation in the Christmas story serves to further illustrate the change that was taking place in the world with the arrival of Jesus. The wise men were at the other end of the social scale from the shepherds, so it demonstrates that indeed the gospel is also for the wealthy and powerful.[4]

But the greater lesson in this part of the story has to do with the fact that the wise men came all the way from the East (most likely Persia) to seek out the Lord Jesus. They were Gentiles, seeking out the One whom they knew would be called the "King of the Jews." Yet notice how the chief priests and scribes reacted to the news. They weren't even interested enough to send a representative of their own down the short road to Bethlehem to investigate the claims of the birth of their Messiah for themselves.[5]

But these Gentiles were. And it demonstrates once again the fullness of the time, for God was now opening up the way for the entire world to be confronted with the gospel. And these three kings were the first Gentiles to make the pilgrimage. Though they were kings themselves, they came looking for the only One in history about whom it can be said he was actually *born* a King.[6]

The Necessity of the Virgin Birth

Christmas may still hold a great deal of sentimental value for most people, but I fear that the doctrine of the virgin birth has fallen into serious neglect in recent decades. It is not that the fact of the birth is no longer taught and preached on, for it is invariably a part of the retelling of the Christmas story that occurs in some form in most churches every December. Rather, it is the *doctrine* that has fallen on hard times.

In the first place, it must be recognized that there are many churches today that will gladly read the Christmas story in their services, while privately (and in some cases, even publicly) scorning the notion of a virginal birth. For them, the idea is simply too unsophisticated for their supposedly "modern" sensibilities, and thus it is discarded as a mere fiction invented by the apostles to make the Christmas story more interesting.

Such thoughts need not detain us here, however, for it should be obvious that those who are not willing to embrace the historicity of the virgin birth due to its miraculous nature will not be able to make it past the opening verse of the Bible. Anyone who understands that God created the universe out of nothing will have no difficulty accepting that he can also cause a virgin to give birth. But those who will not embrace the fact of the virgin birth do not fail to do so because it is too fantastic to be true, but because they do not believe in the God for whom "nothing is impossible."

On the other hand, even in some Bible-believing churches where the historicity of the virgin birth is not disputed, the doctrine is often neglected, either out of sheer ignorance or lack of appreciation for its theological significance. It certainly doesn't garner the attention that it deserves. But it is no side issue, as if the birth of Christ could have taken place in any other manner, given the state of man and the nature of God. Instead, the virgin birth was necessary for at least two important reasons.

A True God-Man

First, it was necessary in order to produce the true God-Man. One nineteenth-century commentator stated the matter in this way:

> If the pre-existent Son of God became incarnate by ordinary generation we could not escape the conclusion that a human individual person was begotten. The Incarnation would then not be a real Incarnation, but an inhabitation of Jesus by the Son of God, with two distinct personalities, that of the pre-existent Son of God and that of the begotten son of Joseph.... Only a God-man who had taken human nature into organic union with himself and so identified himself with the human race as to become the common man, the second Adam, the head of the race, could redeem the

race. The doctrine of the Virgin Birth gives such a God-man. Natural generation could not possibly give us such a God-man.[7]

Just as the first Adam's entrance into the world was wholly supernatural, so must be that of the last Adam, Jesus Christ. Every description or title used of Jesus in the birth narratives presupposes his supernatural origins: "of the Holy Spirit" (Matt. 1:20); "God with us" (Matt. 1:23); "Son of the Highest" (Luke 1:32); "Holy One who is to be born" (Luke 1:35); "Son of God" (Luke 1:35); "Savior" (Luke 2:11); and "Christ the Lord" (Luke 2:11).

Though it was necessary that Christ share in the common humanity that came from Adam, it was just as necessary that he be born of God and not of the will of the flesh (John 1:13). Because the birth of the Savior was God's answer to humanity's predicament, Christ's entrance into the world by way of a purely natural (human) generation wouldn't have demonstrated the truth that salvation is all of grace. Thus, Scripture informs us that God didn't merely make provision for the eventual birth of his Messiah, but he prepared a body beforehand for him (Heb. 10:5) so that it might be of his production, not man's (Heb. 8:2; 9:11).

It's a testimony to the importance of this doctrine that so many of those who oppose the Christian faith attack it so vociferously. Not being able to tolerate a supernatural Christ and understanding how indispensable his Virgin Birth is to that identity, they sling their poisonous arrows at it with all their might. But it's all to no avail, for Scripture has spoken in no uncertain terms on the subject. And we need the Christ who is offered to us there, not the one of their making. We need the true God-Man set forth in Scripture to deliver us from our sin and misery.

A Sinless God-Man

The second reason that the Virgin Birth was necessary is so that the sinlessness of Christ could be preserved. If Christ was to be our spotless sacrificial Lamb, then he had not only to live a perfectly righteous life, but he also had to enter our world free from the taint of original sin, the unfortunate affliction of all who are descendants of Adam. Only One who didn't share in Adam's sin could provide the redemption we need. It was necessary that he be "holy, harmless, undefiled, [and] separate from sinners" (Heb. 7:26).

Some commentators point out that there's no passage of Scripture that explicitly declares that it's through the male seed that original sin is transmitted from one generation to the next. That may be so, but it's difficult to see how the Bible's teaching on original sin can be squared with any other understanding. If sin isn't transmitted through the male parent, then it seems strange that Paul would attribute the fall of the human race and its subsequent effects to Adam and not to Eve, who was first to eat of the forbidden fruit (Rom. 5:12–21). It also helps to explain statements such as that found in Exodus 34:7, where God says that he visits the iniquity "of the fathers" upon the children and the children's children. And it fits in perfectly with the prophecy of Genesis 3:15 and its reference to Christ coming from the seed of the woman.

At any rate, though I'm aware of the circularity in reasoning here, the fact of the Virgin Birth itself provides the best evidence for such an understanding. For the true God-Man to be truly God, he must be free from the taint of sin, and it's difficult to see how that could have been accomplished if his birth hadn't been as supernatural as his being. Since Scripture clearly states that all who are born into this world are infected with sin (Job 25:4), only a supernatural birth could avoid the consequences that attend natural human generation. There must, of necessity, be a discontinuity between fallen, sinful man and the Word become flesh if he is to be our spotless Lamb. And nothing seems more suited to account for that difference than the Virgin Birth itself. Clarence Macartney was one commentator from the last century who saw the issue in those terms, and he has beautifully described the implications of dispensing with the Virgin Birth in the following manner:

All the rivers of Christian theology become one great life-giving stream in the Cross of Christ. But if Jesus were the son of Joseph and Mary, then He was not free from the taint of sin, He was not separate from sinners. You have left in that manger-cradle at Bethlehem the Child who may become a world's great prophet, leader, dreamer, reformer, but Jesus, the Savior, the Redeemer, is gone! Christ is lost to humanity! Wise men of the East, take back your gifts which you have laid at his cradled feet, for the child is not the King of Heaven and Earth. Shepherds, standing in silent awe in the lowly cavern where the young child lies, go back to your sheep upon the fields, for this world and its cares are the only reality! Angels, whose music comes floating down from heaven's gates, silence your sweet songs and leave mankind to the grim music of its sobs and moans and curses and blasphemies. Star of Bethlehem, tender dayspring from on high, go out and leave this world in the blackness of darkness, forever groping in endless cycles with its lusts and its illusions, for Jesus is not that Holy thing which shall be called the Son of God, and shall save us from our sins. He was born of flesh, and of the will of man, not of the will of God. Our Christ is gone, and with Him dies the hope of humanity.[8]

Mary: The God-Bearer

Our discussion of the Virgin Birth wouldn't be complete without briefly touching upon the relationship of Mary to the birth of Jesus and her role in the Christmas story. The church has always recognized the extraordinary role that Mary played in the Incarnation as the one chosen by God to bear the Christ-child. She was indeed "blessed among women," and the "highly favored one" (Luke 1:28).

In the debates that erupted in the early centuries of the New Testament era over the precise nature of the Incarnation, the issue of whether or not Mary should be designated with the Greek term *theotokos* arose. Essentially, the term means "God-bearer," and it had begun to be used as a way of affirming that the child Jesus to whom Mary gave birth was none other than the divine Son of God. Thus, it wasn't intended primarily as a reference to the privilege or identity of Mary but as a way of testifying to the reality of the Incarnation. Designating Mary as God-bearer, it was felt, helped to safeguard that fact against heresies that tended to separate Jesus into two distinct persons, one human and one divine. The beauty of the term was that it carefully avoided the inaccuracies inherent in the unfortunate modern term "Mother of God" by saying only that Mary bore the already preexistent Word in her womb while stressing that the person to whom she gave birth was none other than the divine Son of God, whose human nature was derived from hers.

Two ecumenical councils of the fifth century affirmed the use of the title God-bearer, and the Chalcedonian Creed of 451 officially enshrined it with the qualifying phrase that Mary's role as God-bearer was "as regards [Jesus'] manhood." Thus, the title was a good one as far as it went. But there's little doubt that use of the term also helped to accelerate the tendency toward Mariology that picked up steam in that century. As Macleod noted, "Although to the theologians *theotokos* was a statement about Christ (affirming his divine identity), to the populace it was a statement about the Virgin Mary, just as it is today."[9] In conclusion, we may say that while the title God-bearer is accurately applied to Mary, the mother of Jesus, it should be used with caution to distinguish it from the misleading and inaccurate designation Mother of God.

When the wise men visited the home of Mary and Joseph in Bethlehem, they presented to young Jesus three gifts that they had brought with them on their journey from the East. The gold was symbolic of his royal power; it was a tribute to a king. The frankincense, which was used in the temple worship, probably had a double significance; it symbolized not only his divine nature and identity as the Son of God but also brought to mind the practice of mixing it with the oil to anoint the priests of Israel who served in the temple. Thus, it also pointed to Christ's role as our Great High Priest. And the myrrh, which was a fragrant spice used in burial, spoke of his death. Jesus was indeed born to rule over all the earth; he was born the King of kings. But he was also born to die. The purpose for which he came was to give his life as a ransom for all those whom God would call unto himself.

We can only speculate about how much of this Mary understood at the time of the wise men's visit. Did she appreciate the significance and implications of the Magi's gift of myrrh to her infant son, who had as yet experienced only brief days or months of life? Mary's conception may have been miraculous, but undoubtedly she was like any other mother who loved her child deeply and wanted only the best in life for him. So we can appreciate how she may have felt at seeing the last of these three gifts presented to her young Son.

But we can also surmise that at the same time she was comforted by the knowledge of the promises of God—promises she had received only recently from the angel Gabriel as well as the promises that he had delivered through his prophets centuries earlier. The restoration that Isaiah, Jeremiah, and others had spoken of has come; it has happened in the life and person of Jesus Christ. Nowadays, when we sing "O Come, O Come, Emmanuel," we understand that Emmanuel has already come, and through his death and resurrection he has ransomed captive Israel. We who bear his name and have placed our hope and trust for salvation in him alone have become a part of that ransomed people.

This is the truth that we celebrate at Christmas. The complete Christmas story begins in a stable but ends in the throne room of heaven. It's an account of the fulfillment of God's promises. We still await the ultimate restoration, when Christ will return and institute judgment and righteousness in all the earth. But the accomplished work of his first coming (which we'll soon explore in detail) is the guarantee that the day of full restoration is drawing near. And this is cause for celebration—not just on December 25th, but every day of the year.

5

He Is the Same Yesterday, Today, and Forever

(HEB. 13:8)

Given all that we've said about Christ in the prior four chapters, it might seem incongruous to likewise affirm the statement above. When we consider what took place at the incarnation—the Son's permanent assumption of human flesh, his voluntary submission to the Father, and the significant changes wrought by his work—it's difficult at first blush to see how such a statement can be squared with the biblical data. Nevertheless, the writer of Hebrews not only wants us to understand that such an affirmation is true, but he wants us to find great comfort in that fact.

More than any other book in the New Testament, Hebrews sets forth a complete picture of the person and work of Christ. As a result, it will provide us with a great deal of material in future chapters. This particular passage about Christ is especially appropriate for completing our study of his person and for leading us into the discussion of his work, since it speaks to both subjects simultaneously. To say that Jesus Christ is always the same is to affirm something quite wonderful not only about his essential nature but also about his mediatorial work on our behalf. And the observant Christian is able to derive comfort from both aspects of this vital truth.

One of those who appreciated the apparent difficulty posed by this passage of Scripture was Arthur W. Pink. In his commentary on this verse, he writes:

> Were we to take this declaration absolutely it would involve us in inextricable difficulties. Ponder its terms for a moment. Did your Lord undergo no radical change when He became incarnate? Did He experience no great change at His resurrection? During the days of His flesh, He was "The Man of sorrows:" is He so now after His ascension?—one has but to ask the question to perceive its absurdity. This statement, then, is to be understood with certain limitations; or rather, it is to be interpreted in the light of its setting.[1]

Pink's observation demonstrates the potential for misunderstanding posed by a biblical text such as the title to this chapter. Imagining a Christ who was unaffected by the Incarnation, with the great changes that took place during that period of his existence, can lead to all sorts of erroneous conclusions. But when we interpret the statement in its setting, as well as the rest of Scripture, it becomes quite valuable to us. When we do this, we can identify at least three distinct senses in which Christ is unchangeable: (1) in his divine nature; (2) in his offices (i.e., his work); and (3) in his doctrine.

The Same in His Divine Nature

One of God's attributes is his immutability or unchanging nature. This doesn't merely mean that he forever remains the same in his essence as a spirit, for example, but that all of the other attributes that rightly belong to him as divinity are likewise not subject to change or divestment by him. God's omnipotence, his omniscience, his holiness—each of these attributes, as well as others, is subject to the immutability that characterizes God's nature. If God could ever be found to not be in possession of any of these attributes, he would cease to be God. Of course, this is impossible (Mal. 3:6), and for that reason God is said to be immutable.

The doctrine of immutability is just as applicable to Christ, God the Son, as it is to the Father and the Holy Spirit. And the reality of the Incarnation doesn't detract from that affirmation one bit. Though the Incarnation changed the way God the Son manifests himself to us, it didn't alter his eternal, divine nature in the slightest. At the Incarnation, Christ united human nature with himself, but in so doing he experienced no change in his essential nature as God. His divine nature is ever the same. It's with this limitation, as Pink calls it, that we understand the thrust of the passage.

However, it's probably legitimate to go even further. Since humans are made in the image of God, we're warranted in saying that Christ possessed prior to his incarnation even those attributes that belonged to humanity in its originally created state (except for flesh and blood). Thus, he assumed our physical limitations for a time, but in so doing he neither added to, nor took away from, any aspect of his essential personhood. Stephen Charnock expresses this idea well:

> He took the "form of a servant," but he lost not the form of God; he despoiled not himself of the perfections of the Deity.... The glory of his divinity was not extinguished nor diminished, though it was obscured and darkened, under the veil of our infirmities; but there was no more change in the hiding of it, than there is in the body of the sun when it is shadowed by the interposition of a cloud.... Again, there could be no change in this union; for in a real change, something is acquired

which was not possessed before, neither formally
nor eminently: but the divinity had from eternity,
before the incarnation, all the perfections of the
human nature eminently in a nobler manner than
they are in themselves, and therefore could not be
changed by a real union.[2]

Earlier in his epistle (1:10–12), the writer of Hebrews quotes
from Psalm 102:25–27. In that passage, the Psalmist rejoices that
the Lord is both eternal (the earth and heavens will perish, "but You
will endure") and immutable ("they will be changed, but You are the
same"). The writer of Hebrews explicitly ascribes this affirmation
about Yahweh to Jesus Christ, thereby testifying to his deity and
immutability. Even after the Incarnation, he saw no contradiction in
making this claim, and neither should we. Jesus Christ is the same
yesterday, today, and forever. As God, he cannot be otherwise. It's of
Christ's very nature to be forever free from change.

The Same in His Offices

When we speak of the offices of Christ, we tend to refer to the three
main headings—prophet, priest, and king—under which the work
of Christ on behalf of his people is usually categorized. As a prophet,
Christ was God's final revelation to mankind, delivering the Word of
God directly to the people through his preaching and teaching. He
came bearing "the words of eternal life" (John 6:68), and the gospel
that he proclaimed (based in his own person) continues to be the
power unto salvation to all who believe. As a priest, Christ fulfilled
the Law to which we were subject and offered himself as an effectual
sacrifice in our stead. He continues his priestly work now by making
intercession on behalf of the saints. And as a king, Christ arrived on
the scene with sovereign authority over all mankind, commanding
them to "repent and believe" the gospel that he proclaimed. He now
rules all of creation (Matt. 28:18) from his heavenly throne, where
he's seated in glory at the right hand of the Father.

In addition to this threefold office of Christ, however, we may also speak of his office as Mediator of the new covenant. But while it's possible to make a distinction between this title and any one of the other three, the term is largely an all-encompassing one, referring to the work of reconciliation that Christ continues to perform on behalf of his people. Thus, it's not so much a separate office from the threefold one of prophet, priest, and king as it is a shorthand way of referring to all that is contained within the accomplished work of all three offices (with an obvious emphasis upon the priestly aspect of his work).

Regardless of which office we are specifically referencing, however, the point is the same: Jesus Christ's work of saving sinners will continue unabated until all for whom he died are brought into his kingdom. And the way in which he carries out that work remains unchanged from the beginning. His priesthood is unchangeable because, unlike the priests in Old Testament Israel, he continues forever (Heb. 7:24). He has no successor, for he's not only the last of the prophets (Heb. 1:2) and kings (Heb. 1:8) but is now the *only* Mediator between God and men (1 Tim. 2:5). He still saves sinners through the "foolishness" of preaching (1 Cor. 1:18), and continues to receive all those who come to him in faith. Those that have done so may take comfort in the fact that he lives to make continual intercession on their behalf (Heb. 7:25) and will finish the work that he has begun in them (Phil. 1:6), ultimately bringing them to glory with him. This entire state of affairs remains unchanged—precisely because Christ himself is unchangeable.

The Same in His Doctrine

And not only is Jesus Christ always the same with respect to his divine nature and offices, but he's also the same with respect to the system of doctrine that he has laid down for us. Given the context of Hebrews 13:8, this is probably the primary sense in which the writer intends for us to understand his statement, although it's also true that the unchangeable nature of Christ's doctrine is merely an application that flows from the other two. Indeed, the second and third senses (his sameness in offices and doctrine) are very closely related, since both owe their certainty to the fact that Christ is God and therefore cannot vacillate in either his modes of working or the content of his teaching. Christ's divine nature, and thus his immutability, provides the guarantee that his work and doctrine will never change. They will be just as constant and unshakeable as he is himself.

To say that Christ is always the same with respect to his doctrine is to affirm that there is never any reason for us to "update" Christianity for the times. What was true with respect to the Christian religion in the first century is just as true for us today in the twenty-first. It's the same truth about Christ and the gospel that saves sinners. And it will be the same gospel until the last saint is brought into the fold. While we may wrestle with ethical questions that the first-century church never could have foreseen (such as human cloning and stem cell research), it's only the application of the unchangeable truth to specific situations that is new; the truth itself doesn't change. Nor do we need to adapt our teaching about Christ to any particular locale or cultural situation. Scripture doesn't present to us one Christ for the Romans, another for the Ephesians, and yet another for the Philippians. On the contrary, Christ transcends all time periods and all cultural and national boundaries. What is right belief and behavior in one time and place is right in all times and places—for Christ is the same.

Practical Considerations

In light of this truth, the writer of Hebrews offers a number of practical applications to his readers that are just as applicable to us today. His statement concerning the sameness of Christ is bracketed by exhortations to the Hebrew Christians to follow the faith of those who had spoken the (pure) word of God to them (v. 7) and to not fall prey to those who would carry them off with "various and strange doctrines" (v. 9). This is a particularly serious problem in our day, though it must be admitted that the phenomenon is hardly new. Following after strange doctrines was already a problem in the New Testament period, and it has continued more or less unabated throughout the history of the church. Closer to our own day, but still a century and a half ago, Charles Spurgeon could remark as follows:

> There is an itching, nowadays, after originality, striking out a path for yourself. When sheep do that, they are bad sheep. Sheep follow the shepherd; and, in a measure, they follow one another when they are all together following the shepherd. Our Great Master never aimed at originality; he said that he did not even speak his own words, but the words that he had heard of his Father…. Many young Christians, if they were to pretend to strike out a path for themselves, must infallibly fall into many sorrows, whereas by taking some note of the way in which more experienced and more instructed Christians have gone, they will keep by the way of the footsteps of the flock, and they will also follow the footprints of the Shepherd. God's people are a thoughtful people, and they are an imitative and humble people, willing to be instructed, and willing to follow holy and godly examples.[3]

Christ has not only given us a revelation from God that cannot be improved upon, but he has provided us with faithful forebears (the "great cloud of witnesses" mentioned in Hebrews 12:1) who have demonstrated the unchanging nature of the gospel message throughout all time periods and have thereby testified to the faithfulness of God. The entire letter to the Hebrews is designed to encourage Christians to stay the course in the face of persecution. The writer urges his readers to follow those who have come before by imitating their godly example and embracing the doctrine that they received directly from Christ. It's in so doing that we're able to "run with endurance the race that is set before us" (12:1) and to boldly say, "The LORD is my helper; I will not fear. What can man do to me?" (13:6).

We may fancy our own day and age as one of great upheaval and rapid change, but from a religious perspective the first-century Hebrew Christians were witnesses to the greatest set of changes that God ever introduced in his plan of redemption. More than any other book, Hebrews deals with the profound change in administration that God brought about by the substitution of the new covenant for the old. Not only had Judaism now been rendered obsolete, but also all of the ancient accoutrements of Old Testament religion (the ceremonial law, the Levitical priesthood, the sacrificial system, and the temple), had been supplanted by the finished work of Christ. In the midst of such radical changes, it was fitting for the writer of Hebrews to remind his audience that Jesus Christ, the head of the church in all ages, remains unchanged.[4] We too need to be regularly reminded of this fact, for it should bring comfort to all those who call upon his name to know that he is the same yesterday, today, and forever.

Part 2:

Thinking Rightly of the Work of Christ

6

He Was a Friend of Sinners

(Matt. 11:19)

An old familiar adage declares that "we are known by the company we keep." Like most clichés, there's a great deal of truth in such a statement. That is, after all, how they tend to become clichés in the first place. In this case, we do well to recognize the fact that the reputation of those with whom we associate will often be ascribed to us, whether such a characterization is fair or not. We also do well to admit that we're susceptible to being influenced in our behavior by those with whom we spend our time, which is why the Bible so frequently warns us to choose our friends wisely. Not only are there abundant warnings in Scripture not to keep company with immoral people (1 Cor. 5:9–13), but also the potential effects of not heeding such a warning are illustrated by the biblical saying that "evil company corrupts good habits" (1 Cor. 15:33).

But just as most clichés are generally based in truth and thus helpful, so it is that they're also subject to limitations and exceptions in application. And that's especially the case when we attempt to apply our human clichés to Jesus Christ, the unique Son of God. This was one of the many things that the Pharisees of Jesus' day failed to understand. The Pharisees were the party of strict religious adherents who, along with the scribes (the interpreters of the law), were the primary opponents of Jesus in his earthy ministry. These two groups were often lumped together for condemnation by Jesus (Matt. 23:25), because of their hypocritical judgment of others and the brazen manner in which they advanced their own self-interests above those of the people. Although a number of prominent Pharisees (most notably Nicodemus) would go on to become followers of Jesus, on the whole they were openly hostile to him and his claims to be the long-awaited Messiah.

In the ninth chapter of Matthew's gospel we read about one of the many confrontations that Jesus had with the Pharisees. The occasion was the calling of Matthew to be one of Jesus' disciples and the celebratory meal that accompanied that event. As Jesus and his disciples were dining at Matthew's house, we read that many other tax collectors (Matthew had been one) and "sinners" joined them at the table, which prompted an accusatory question from the Pharisees to Jesus' disciples as to why he would allow this to take place. How, they asked, could Jesus stoop so low as to "eat with tax collectors and sinners?" (Matt. 9:11). But when Jesus heard that the Pharisees had asked such a question, he told his disciples that it was precisely those "sinners" to whom he had been sent to offer salvation through his name.

A short time later, Jesus exposed the blatant hypocrisy of the Pharisees by pointing out the internal inconsistency with which they attempted to defame both John the Baptist and him: "For John came neither eating nor drinking, and they say, 'He has a demon.' The Son of Man came eating and drinking, and they say, 'Look, a glutton and a winebibber, a friend of tax collectors and sinners!'" (Matt. 11:18–19). There simply was no way for a man of God to win with the Pharisees. They would find some basis upon which to criticize him, no matter which path he chose. And that attitude merely betrayed the spiritual state into which they had sunk. Jonathan Edwards comments upon this passage:

So inconsistent were they with themselves that there was not such thing as a prophet's suiting them. They condemned the doing of that which at the same time they condemned the not doing of, and both they condemned with great bitterness, and virulent and contemptuous reproaches. This plainly showed that their objections against John the Baptist and Christ were but vain pretenses, and that the true reason why they disliked them was not the manner of living of either of them with respect to eating and drinking, but because they hated their persons and the business they came upon. When men have a prejudice against other persons they will be ready to find fault with everything in them, they will find our bad names for their virtues, and will reproach those things in them which they approve of and commend in others to whose persons they have a liking.[1]

The general hard-heartedness of the Pharisees stands in sharp contrast to the attitude of Jesus toward common people, those whom the Pharisees tended to refer to derogatorily as sinners. Jesus spent his time with such people, knowing that it was for the very purpose of saving sinners that he came into the world (1 Tim. 1:15) and that such work required him to go wherever sinners were to be found. Of course, Scripture is clear that *all* people are sinners and thus need the salvation that Christ's work secures. But the Pharisees represent the self-righteous attitude that is unable to recognize one's own need for Christ and relies instead on some man-made method of gaining acceptance with God, such as adhering to a strict set of (extra-biblical) religious regulations. Jesus, however, condemned any such system of works righteousness as sheer futility (Matt. 5:20) and called upon sinners to repent and believe the gospel—a gospel that found its fulfillment in the work that he undertook on behalf of sinners everywhere. As we begin our discussion of that work, and as we proceed through the chapters to come, it behooves us to keep in the forefront of our minds this foundational truth—Christ Jesus came into the world to save sinners.

Jesus' Interaction with Sinners

Of course, when the Pharisees branded Jesus with the title "friend of tax collectors and sinners," they didn't intend it as a compliment. The general populace in Judea despised tax collectors because they collected levies on behalf of the occupying Roman government, often taking advantage of people in the process. By identifying Jesus with them and with sinners in general, the Pharisees sought to impugn his character and turn people against him. They hoped to tar Jesus' reputation by insinuating that his association with such people was proof that he had a similar moral disposition. "After all," they undoubtedly argued, "if it's legitimate to say that we're known by the company we keep, or that 'birds of a feather flock together,' then you may draw your own conclusions about this one named Jesus of Nazareth."

But the Pharisees misjudged Jesus on every score. They understood neither the nature of his person, nor the complexion of his work. Whatever accuracy such clichés may have when applied to the rest of us, they have no validity whatsoever in commenting upon the person of Jesus Christ, who was every bit as much the spotless Lamb of God after his encounters with sinners as he had been before. He remained free from the stain of sin despite his close and constant interaction with sinners of every stripe. Rather, it is *they* who were changed by coming into contact with Jesus, the friend of sinners!

Because he was a discerner of men's thoughts, knowing what was in them before they uttered a word, the record of Jesus' interactions with individuals in the New Testament presents a complex picture of how he chose to confront sinners with the gospel. No single pattern can account for the way he dealt with the diverse set of persons with whom he came into contact. Rather, he dealt with each as the circumstances called for and in accordance with his own divine wisdom. At times he could be abrupt and sound almost callous

(Matt. 8:22), while at other times he was the epitome of patience and sensitivity. But in each case, his aim was identical: bring persons to an awareness of their sin and their need for saving grace. When we examine the record of the New Testament, we're able to discern the following five general principles that characterized Jesus' interaction with sinners:

1. The Marginalized and Downtrodden Were Attracted to Jesus' Ministry

In large measure, those whom the scribes and Pharisees derisively termed "sinners" were the marginalized and downtrodden masses of Israelite society. They tended to be poor or diseased and very often felt the sting of being treated as less than human by the religious authorities in Jerusalem. Jesus told his disciples that the scribes and Pharisees laid heavy burdens on men's shoulders but wouldn't lift a finger to help those in need (Matt. 23:4). As a result, Jesus was moved with compassion for the multitudes "because they were weary and scattered, like sheep having no shepherd" (Matt. 9:36). Those who were supposed to be tending to the needs of the flock in Israel were the ones most responsible for making life unbearable for all but the privileged few, piling on burden after burden through their man-made religious regulations and judging others with a harsh and hypocritical spirit.

Is it any wonder, then, that it was from this same mass of everyday people that Jesus gained his greatest number of followers? While the scribes and Pharisees were busy berating the populace for innumerable violations of their extra-biblical laws, Jesus was out on the highways and byways of Israel saying, "Come to Me, all you who labor and are heavy laden, and I will give you rest. Take My yoke upon you and learn from Me, for I am gentle and lowly in heart, and you will find rest for your souls" (Matt. 11:28–29). The marginalized and downtrodden of Israelite society were as attracted to Jesus and his ministry of mercy as they were repelled by the ministry of death preached by the scribes and Pharisees. Jesus, who wasn't a member of the religious elite in Jerusalem, preached rest for weary souls, and he made it clear that his ministry involved preaching the gospel to the poor, who were otherwise ignored by those who should have been tending to their spiritual needs. Thus, the people had found a true friend in Jesus, for in this way he was indeed one of them.

2. Jesus Respected People but Was No Respecter of Persons

In his interactions with people, Jesus always treated them with respect. He recognized the inherent dignity that they possessed as creatures made in the image of God, and he conversed with them in a manner that was befitting that reality. Though he had the right to demand worship from all whom he encountered, he invariably settled for something far less. Having voluntarily made himself of no reputation, he didn't press his rights upon people but humbly identified with them. Thus, he showed his concern for others by listening to them, sympathizing with them in their losses, and even by ensuring that they were properly fed.

At the same time, Jesus showed no partiality to people on the basis of their social or economic standing or even on the basis of their national identification (though we'll qualify this statement somewhat in a later chapter). As the apostle Peter put it in a slightly different context, Christ was no "respecter of persons" (Acts 10:34, KJV; cf. Matt. 22:16). Rather, he treated all people, regardless of their station in life or ethnic background, as similarly situated and equally in need of the gospel that he preached. As a result, he ministered to Jew and Gentile alike, women as well as men, poor as well as rich.

3. Jesus Did Not Condone or Excuse Sin in Those He Encountered

In our day it has become quite common, perhaps even fashionable, to hear people pontificate about how Jesus supposedly overlooked sin during his earthly ministry and that this was in keeping with some higher principle of love that negates the specific condemnations of the law. Many who argue this way are careful to add that Christ himself didn't sin but that his purpose for coming into the world was not to judge others for their sins, only to save them. For this latter argument there is indeed plenty of biblical support (e.g., John 3:17; 12:47; but see also 3:18; 9:39).

But just because Christ's final judgment of sin lies in the future (2 Tim. 4:1), it doesn't follow that he was indifferent toward or tolerant of the sin that he observed. On the contrary, Jesus condemned sin in the most severe terms, especially as it manifested itself in the work of the scribes and Pharisees (e.g., Luke 11:37–52; Matt. 23:27, 33). He condemned entire cities for their sin (Luke 10:13), and confronted individuals with their sin in order that they might repent of it and turn to him in faith. The case of the woman at the well in John 4 is a prime example of one way that Jesus dealt with people caught in sinful lifestyles. Not only did Jesus very deliberately steer the conversation in a direction that allowed him to comment upon her sin, but it was in so doing that she was allowed to perceive that he was a prophet.

Without a doubt the favorite text of those who contend for a less judgmental Jesus is the story of the woman caught in adultery, which is found at John 8:2–11. The scribes and Pharisees brought to Jesus a woman accused of being an adulterer. In an obvious attempt to discredit Jesus in front of the people, they ask him what should be done to her, hoping to trap him into either denying the law of Moses (which directed that adulterers were to be stoned to death) or running afoul of the Roman authorities and the general populace by affirming a death sentence against her. In typical fashion, Jesus saw through the Pharisees' scheme and answered that whoever was without sin should cast the first stone, thereby putting an end to the whole charade. At this point Jesus remarked to the woman that since there was no one left to condemn her, neither would he.

It's this forgiving attitude toward the woman in John 8 that some have mistaken for laxity toward sin on Jesus' part. However, this notion ignores not only the bigger picture contained in the New Testament as a whole but also the remaining details of this particular story. Jesus did tell the woman that he wasn't condemning her for her sin, but he also commanded her to "go and sin no more." More important, however, by calling for the one who was without sin to cast the first stone, Jesus pointed out the sins of the men who had brought the woman there in the first place. Instead of using the occasion to focus on the sin of one single woman, Jesus used it to expose the sins of numerous individuals, each of whose refusal to cast the first stone amounted to a confession of sin on their part (see John 8:9). As A.W. Pink perceptively noted, "Christ's enemies had thought to ensnare Him by the law of Moses; instead they had its searching light turned upon themselves."[2]

4. Jesus Used His Encounters with Sinners to Call Them to Repentance and Faith

Jesus said that he had come into the world "to seek and to save that which was lost" (Luke 19:10). As a result, he didn't simply stand on a street corner in his hometown of Nazareth and preach the gospel, hoping that some curious souls would stop and listen to him. Rather, he left his home and looked for them wherever they could be found. He sought them in the marketplaces, at the synagogues, on the roads, and in their homes. He pursued them not only in his home province of Galilee but also in the provinces of Judea, Samaria, and even Perea, the land beyond the Jordan River. And he did so for the purpose of calling sinners to repentance and faith.

The deliberate manner in which Jesus sought out sinners is vividly illustrated in the account that gave rise to his statement that he had come to seek and save that which was lost. Luke 19:1–10 records the story of a man named Zacchaeus, who, because of the large crowd that had gathered, climbed into a sycamore tree to get a good look at Jesus as he was passing through the town of Jericho. When Jesus noticed him in the tree, he invited himself over to Zacchaeus' house, from where it was that Zacchaeus renounced his sin and became a follower of Christ from that day forward. This was the kind of thing that Jesus did regularly. He spent his time going into people's homes and neighborhoods, preaching the gospel of grace to them. For this reason he had no place of his own to lay his head. He was too busy seeking and saving people who were lost.

5. Jesus' Relationship with Sinners Was Unique

Perhaps it's unnecessary to point out that Jesus' relationship to sinners was unique. But I suspect that much confusion has arisen over the centuries precisely because some have read the gospel accounts without keeping this fact in mind. If we remember that Christ was "separate from sinners" (Heb. 7:26) in both his nature and deportment, we'll have no difficulty understanding how it is that he was able to spend all of his days with those who practiced lawlessness and yet not be infected with the same proclivity to sin. Recalling this fact will also allow us to see that when Jesus gathered together with sinners, it was a case of "birds of a feather flocking together" only in the most limited sense—that of sharing a common human nature. But with regard to the inclination to do that which God proscribes, Jesus was a "bird" of an altogether different flock.

Remembering Christ's uniqueness also provides insight into how it is that he could still have had compassion upon those who were not only different from him in such an important way but from whom he "endured hostility" (Heb. 12:3). How is it that the One who hates sin in all its forms is able to look upon those who have the filth and stench of it clinging to them and yet not feel anything but sheer contempt for them? The nineteenth-century commentator Adolph Saphir beautifully explains this paradox of Christ's love for sinners:

> This compassionate, loving, gentle, all-considerate and tender regard for the sinner can exist in perfection only in a sinless one. This appears at first paradoxical; for we expect the perfect man to be the severest judge. And with regard to *sin*, this is doubtless true. God charges even His angels with folly. He beholds sin where we do not discover it. And Jesus, the Holy One of Israel, like the Father, has eyes like a flame of

fire, and discerns everything that is contrary to God's mind and will. But with regard to the *sinner*, Jesus, by virtue of His perfect holiness, is the most merciful, compassionate, and considerate Judge. For we, not taking a deep and keen view of sin, that central essential evil which exists in all men, and manifests itself in various ways and degrees, are not able to form a just estimate of men's comparative guilt and blameworthiness. Nay, our very sins make us more impatient and severe with regard to the sins of others. Our vanity finds the vanity of others intolerable, our pride finds the pride of others excessive. Blind to the guilt of our own peculiar sins, we are shocked with another's sins, different indeed from ours, but not less offensive to God, or pernicious in its tendencies. Again, the greater the knowledge of Divine love and pardon, the stronger faith in the Divine mercy and renewing grace, the more hopeful and the more lenient will be our view of sinners. And finally the more we possess of the spirit and heart of the Shepherd, the Physician, the Father, the deeper will be our compassion on the ignorant and wayward.

The Lord Jesus was therefore most compassionate, considerate, lenient, hopeful in His feelings toward sinners, and in His dealings with them. He was infinitely holy and perfectly clear in His hatred and judgment of sin; but He was tender and gracious to the sinner… He looked upon sin as the greatest and most fearful evil, but on the sinner as poor, lost, and helpless.[3]

Jesus as the Great Physician

When the Pharisees grumbled about Jesus' association with sinners, he responded in the following way: "Those who are well have no need of a physician, but those who are sick.... For I did not come to call the righteous, but sinners, to repentance." With this statement, Jesus declares himself to be the Great Physician who alone can bring spiritual healing to those afflicted with the disease of sin. By saying that he didn't come to call the righteous to repentance, he didn't mean to imply that there were any such persons who didn't need the cleansing from sin that he offered. Romans 3:10 makes it clear that there is no one who is righteous apart from Christ's work. Rather, the statement may be interpreted as referring to one of two types of persons: (1) those who had already repented of their sin and had chosen to follow him, or (2) those who had such an exalted view of their own righteousness that they felt no need for Christ or the benefits that he offered—in other words, the self-righteous. Given the context of Christ's statement, it's likely that he had the second type of person in mind. And no single group of persons exemplified that attitude more than the Pharisees.

Earlier we looked at how the hatred of the Pharisees for both John the Baptist and Jesus led them to level inconsistent criticisms against both of them, accusing Jesus of sin for eating and drinking with sinners while accusing John of sin for doing just the opposite. And at this point it's easy to see once again how the Pharisees' sin blinded them to the inconsistency of their own arguments. As those who epitomized a self-righteous attitude—placing trust in their own righteousness while viewing everyone else as in need of a spiritual change of heart—one would think they would have welcomed Jesus' drawing close to the rest of the populace ("sinners") in order that he might heal them from the debilitating disease of sin.[4]

But of course, the Pharisees didn't really want others to be healed any more than they wanted to be healed from their own sin. Self-righteousness is threatened by the general improvement of others, since it's always based upon a relative standard of one's own making and not upon perfection, which is God's standard. Scripture makes it clear that God is not impressed by, or satisfied with, any person's self-righteous attainments. In the very best of persons, such works of righteousness are but "filthy rags" in his sight (Isa. 64:6). The

Pharisees, however, seem not to have appreciated or understood this basic biblical truth. And by trusting in themselves, they came to despise everyone else (Luke 18:9), especially Jesus Christ, whose perfection of character had the effect of bringing out in high relief their own ugliness.

Before leaving this discussion, one final note is in order. Just as Jesus' statement that he didn't come to call the righteous to repentance shouldn't be taken to imply that there are any who actually fit that description, so too we should be careful not to think that his metaphor of sinners being sick persons means that they're only in need of some inconsequential spiritual elixir to make them well again. On the contrary, the more common scriptural way of referring to unrepentant sinners is as those who are "dead in their trespasses and sins" and in need of spiritual rebirth (Gen. 3:3; John 3:3; Rom. 6:13; 11:15; Eph. 2:1; Col. 2:13). Thus, it doesn't do justice to Scripture to think of a believer as one who has simply moved up the ladder of spirituality from a previously lower position. Jesus, the Great Physician, doesn't merely bring sinners into a higher state of healthiness—he raises them from the dead!

The Privilege of Being Called a Friend of Jesus

When Jesus calls someone his friend, it's not because that person has distinguished himself or herself as one who is worthy of such a title. Rather, it's a testimony that Jesus has chosen, by an act of his sovereign will, to raise that person from spiritual death to new life in him. On the eve of his own death, Jesus told his disciples, "Greater love has no one than this, than to lay down one's life for his friends" (John 15:13). The greatest act of love ever performed was Christ's death on behalf of those whom he has chosen to call his friends. It was his death that secured their eternal salvation, and from the moment that one is empowered to place their trust in that work they are reckoned a "friend of God" (James 2:23).

The Safety in Calling Jesus a Friend

Christ's uniqueness is displayed not only in his personhood but also in the friendship that he has for his people. The friendship of Jesus for his people isn't merely of a higher quality or degree than are our human friendships; it's of a whole different nature. While our human relationships come and go, Christ's friendship for his people is unwavering and constant. Furthermore, it's not based upon anything that he sees within us. Christ befriends us in spite of our lack of lovable qualities and our own inconstancy.

And therein lies its beauty. Because it arises solely from an act of his sovereign will, not ours, Christ's friendship for sinners is safe. It will not—for it cannot—ever fade or be withdrawn. Here is the way in which one nineteenth-century preacher describes it:

> The absolute spontaneity of Christ's friendship for His people, though the feature which makes it indescribably precious, is almost beyond the reach of our conception. Human love is so conspicuously generated by the good qualities which first attract our admiration, that this love, which springs only from the exuberance of God's own goodness, baffles our reason. Yet this is the secret of its immutability. Founded only upon His own nature, and conditioned upon nothing but His own purposes and resources which are infinite, it must remain "from everlasting to everlasting," without "variableness, or shadow of turning."[5]

Each of these early chapters concerning the work of Christ is expressed in terms of the past tense (e.g., he *was* a friend of sinners, he *was* tempted) because they expound upon those aspects of his work that are primarily descriptive of his *earthly* ministry. Although later chapters deal with the realities that flow out of that completed work, for the most part they describe those aspects of his work that are ongoing or yet future. Nevertheless, it should be obvious that we could just as easily have used the present tense in the title of this chapter, since Christ did not cease to be the friend of sinners when he sat down at the right hand of the Father in heaven. His immediate physical presence amongst those on earth may have come to an end for now, but he is still the friend of sinners—those who, by the Spirit's work, have come to recognize their need for grace and have repented of their sin.

The Pharisees may have thought they were denigrating Jesus with the title "friend of sinners," but as Charles Spurgeon points out, "Many a tribute to virtue has been unwittingly paid by the sinister lips of malice."[6] Christians understand that Christ's acceptance of the title is cause for rejoicing. None of us has ever had a human friend like Jesus. And no human friend could ever do for us what Jesus has done. If he has befriended you, you may rest peacefully in the knowledge that, unlike your human friends, Jesus will never disappoint or betray you. His loving friendship will be the most constant fixture in your life. You are safe in calling him a friend, for he is the sure friend who will never let go of you.

7

He Was Tempted

(HEB. 4:15)

Most Christians, if they were honest with themselves, would probably admit that the title above makes them a bit uneasy. It's one thing to say that Christ was a friend of sinners. But it's another matter to say that he, like them, was tempted. Of course, the problem largely centers on the fact that we tend to mistakenly think of temptation as sin. Jesus, however, was tempted, and yet he remained sinless to the end of his life. Thus, it's our understanding of the content of temptation that needs revising, at least with respect to the way in which such language is used in reference to Christ.

And it's right here that the twin doctrines of Christ's person and work intersect in the most concrete of ways. We cannot rightly understand the statement "he was tempted" without first appreciating the way in which the nature of his person was involved in those assaults. The statement does raise a number of thorny questions: (1) How is it that a sinless One can be said to have been tempted? (2) Does the fact of Christ's sinlessness detract from his having fully experienced human nature? (3) Was it possible for Christ to sin? and (4) If Christ couldn't sin, does that detract from the reality of the temptations?

The goal of this chapter is to answer those questions, and in so doing, to demonstrate that there's nothing inconsistent in affirming that Christ was both sinless and tempted. Anyone who surveys the available literature on this subject, at least at the biblical commentary level, will discover that there's little discussion surrounding the issues involved here. Hardly anyone wants to devote more than a few lines of comment on this subject. While I acknowledge the complexity of the questions raised here, I'm also convinced that the difficulty presented by the affirmation that "Christ was tempted" isn't as pronounced as many seem to believe. A close examination of the biblical evidence will bear up that contention.

The Biblical Concept of Temptation

When we come to the subject of biblical teaching on the nature of temptation, it's critical to keep two distinctions in mind. The first is noted by J. I. Packer:

> The biblical idea of temptation is not primarily of seduction, as in modern usage, but of making trial of a person, or putting him to the test; which may be done for the benevolent purpose of proving or improving his quality, as well as with the malicious aim of showing up his weaknesses or trapping him into wrong action.[1]

This distinction relates to the ultimate source and purpose of the temptation and helps to explain why the Bible takes care to say that God tests his people (Gen. 22:1) but doesn't tempt anyone (Jas. 1:13). Rather, it's the devil who tempts men to evil; that is why he's called "the tempter" (Matt. 4:1, 3). God may see fit to test the faith of his people with various trials, and he may even bring them to the place where they may be tempted by the devil, as he did with Job and Jesus. But it's still the devil who attempts the seduction.

The second distinction is more subtle, though no less important. If the distinction above may be thought of as the thirty-thousand-foot view of temptation, the second way of discussing the idea is the ground level view. It involves the more practical sense in which we speak of the particular act of temptation. At this point it's possible to speak of a temptation either as the particular enticement offered to a person (such as fame or money) or as the struggle that takes place in the person so tempted (such as when we say that a person underwent a temptation to sin).

To bring the two concepts together, we may say that one is tempted *by* the devil (the source of the temptation) but tempted *with* riches (the instrument of temptation). However, it's possible to speak of a temptation having taken place without any personal experience of struggle on the part of the one offered the enticement to sin. In that case, the temptation consists solely in the offer or inducement. Thus, if I offer a beautiful painting to a blind man in return for some sinful action on his part, we may rightly call that a temptation to sin, even though it's difficult to imagine such an offer producing any real struggle to sin on the man's part. On the other hand, due to the innate sinfulness of man, most inducements to sin result in varying degrees of moral struggle in the one so tempted.

Finally, the relationship between temptation and sin is explicitly (if narrowly) treated in James 1:14–15. James says that "each one is tempted when he is drawn away by his own desires and enticed. Then, when desire has conceived, it gives birth to sin." James' words make a couple of things clear. First, temptation ordinarily involves being "drawn away" by our own desires to do something in response to the inducement. Second, such temptation isn't necessarily sinful in itself. Rather, it's only when our desire has conceived, or caused us to succumb to the inducement, that we end up sinning. In James' narrowly defined situation, we sin only when we act in accordance with our desires to do that which we have been enticed to do (presuming that which we're enticed to do is sinful).

Nevertheless, given the whole of Scripture it seems necessary to qualify this last statement in the following manner: although to be tempted isn't necessarily a sin, the desires that give rise to our being "drawn away" are very often sinful in nature. As a result, we can say that certain temptations are, in and of themselves, sinful, since they merely represent the expression of a sinful desire. In those cases, the desire has already been fully conceived (to use James' language). Jesus' teaching on the sins of the heart seems to accord with such a view.

And it's precisely because we understand this truth that we have such great difficulty with the statement that "Jesus was tempted." The cure for our unease, however, comes from rightly discerning the nature of the temptation under consideration. We're justified in saying that some temptations are inherently sinful. But we're just as certain that some others are not.

A couple of real-life examples can demonstrate the distinction among various types of temptation. First, imagine a situation where I'm tempted to steal something from my neighbor but I ultimately resist the temptation to do so. If we define the temptation as the act of my giving serious consideration to swiping my neighbor's possession, then we would have to affirm that the temptation itself was sinful. At a minimum, I'm guilty of the sin of covetousness. But if we take Jesus' teaching on sin seriously, we have to say that I'm guilty of the actual theft even if I resisted doing that which would have made me guilty in the eyes of the civil law.

On the other hand, we may experience a temptation to do something that's morally innocent. A person on a diet may be tempted to take an extra piece of pie with his or her meal, but unless that desire represents an act of gluttony, there's no moral failing even in the act of succumbing to the temptation. Finally, it is possible to imagine someone having a completely benevolent or innocent desire to do something, the doing of which would nevertheless be sinful. Such cases seem to line up most closely with James' definition, where the temptation itself is not sinful, for it has not yet "given birth to sin."

With apologies to the reader for that protracted (but important) piece of analysis, we may finally state the principle for which we are contending: whether a temptation is inherently sinful or not depends upon the circumstances of the case. A number of factors should be considered, including the source of the temptation, the nature of the desire, the extent to which one acts upon the desire, and even, as we shall discover, the identity of the one undergoing the temptation. With this principle firmly in mind, we are now in a position to evaluate the temptation experiences of Jesus Christ to see how they fit into this general framework.

The Nature of Christ's Temptations

First, it's accurate to say that Christ's entire earthly life was one continuous confrontation with human sin. The Son of God's humiliation involved his coming in the likeness of sinful men and having to endure the indignities that sinful human beings inflict on one another. But those indignities were greatly magnified when they were heaped upon the One who is holy and pure. As the friend of sinners, Jesus dealt patiently with those whom he had come to save, but his attitude toward ubiquitous sin was nothing but pure revulsion, which he expressed verbally on numerous occasions (Matt. 15:7–8; 16:23; 23:37; John 2:13–16; 8:44; 9:41; 19:11).

And even though Jesus was confronted by human sinfulness in all its forms, the New Testament never indicates that he ever struggled with enticements to sin that undoubtedly came his way daily. The Bible doesn't record a single instance of Jesus even considering to commit any of the sins that plague us, such as lust, greed, and selfishness. And that must be the case, since, as we've already pointed out, such consideration amounts to sin.

Rather, the enticements to sin were all external to Jesus. That is, they didn't arise from his internal desires but were presented to him by the tempter himself or by sinful human beings and were immediately rebuffed by him. Jesus had no "law of sin" that resided in his members (Rom. 7:23) and that could possibly tempt him to commit a sinful act.[2] Understanding this is critical for rightly comprehending what is meant by the statement that "Jesus was tempted."

We typically refer to only two experiences in Jesus' life as temptations, and both of them help to illustrate the matter under consideration here. The first was the temptation by Satan at the beginning of Jesus' earthly ministry, and the second was his temptation to turn away from the Cross at the end of that ministry.

The Temptation in the Wilderness

Immediately after undergoing his baptism by John in the Jordan River, Jesus was led by the Holy Spirit into the wilderness for the express purpose of being "tempted by the devil" (Matt. 4:1). As Jesus was ending a forty-day fast, the devil approached him and issued three successive challenges or temptations. In the first, the devil tempted Jesus to turn stones into bread so that he might satisfy the intense hunger he was undergoing at the time. But Jesus answered with the famous line, "Man does not live by bread alone, but by every word that proceeds from the mouth of God" (Matt. 4:4).

In the second temptation, Satan set Jesus on the pinnacle of the temple and challenged him to throw himself down, while reminding him that God had promised that no harm would come to his chosen Son. Jesus simply answered, "It is written, 'You shall not tempt the Lord your God'" (Matt. 4:7).

For his final challenge, Satan took Jesus up on a high mountain and showed him all the kingdoms of the world, promising to give them to him if he would but fall down and worship at Satan's feet. But Jesus, thoroughly disgusted with the suggestion (and with the whole incident by now), responded, "Away with you, Satan! For it is written, 'You shall worship the Lord your God, and him only you shall serve'" (Matt. 4:10).

In this manner, Jesus Christ began undoing the curse that had fallen upon mankind as a result of the disobedience of the first Adam. In successive attempts, Satan had sought to entice Jesus into doing several things: (1) doubt God's provision for him, (2) presume upon that provision (to "tempt" God), and (3) allow his own holy desire for ruling the nations to cause him to take a different path than the one God had chosen for him to trod—the Cross. And even though the conditions under which Satan offered his enticements were immensely less favorable for Christ than they had been for Adam, Jesus nevertheless succeeded where Adam had failed. Jesus resisted Satan's inducements to sin by responding to each with a terse, but poignant, quotation from Scripture.

What the New Testament doesn't reveal to us is the precise nature of the internal struggle (if any) that Jesus may have undergone prior to rejecting the individual temptations offered by Satan. But the text certainly suggests that Jesus rejected each of the inducements out of hand, without any hesitation or struggle whatsoever. Moreover, each of the three temptations was targeted not toward stirring up any inherent sinful desires within Jesus (since he possessed none) but toward causing him to use his powers to take an alternate path toward an otherwise perfectly good end (satisfying his hunger, demonstrating God's protection for him, and coming into his rightful inheritance as Ruler of the nations).

Although succumbing to any one of the three suggestions would have been sinful on Jesus' part, it was only because of the particulars of the individual temptations, and their source, that such is the case. There's nothing inherently sinful in turning stones into bread. But to do so on this occasion would have been to short-circuit his Father's will and to follow the leading of the evil one. Thus, Jesus dismissed the notion without so much as breaking a sweat, despite having not eaten for forty days.

By all indications, then, the temptation in the wilderness was purely external in nature. That is, it was likely a temptation consisting only in the suggestions of the devil, with no real struggle of soul ensuing in Jesus' person as a result. And it was a test, arranged by the Holy Spirit himself, that Jesus passed with flying colors. If Jesus did experience any internal struggle, it wasn't a struggle ensuing from any lack of desire to carry through with his Father's plan, much less any thought of rendering worship to Satan. Indeed, it's blasphemous for us to even consider that such could be the case. Rather, any struggle on Jesus' part would have consisted only of a momentary human desire to satisfy his physical hunger at the introduction of the tempting prospect of turning stones into bread.

The Temptation in the Garden

When we come to the second great temptation event in Jesus' life, however, we're faced with a very different situation. The gospel accounts are clear that Jesus underwent a great struggle of soul at the prospect of his impending death. On the eve of his crucifixion, Jesus went to the Garden of Gethsemane for prayer, where he told his disciples that his soul was "exceedingly sorrowful" (Matt. 26:38) and where his sweat became like "great drops of blood" (Luke 22:44). As the thought of his horribly cruel death weighed heavily on his mind, Jesus prayed, "Father, if it is Your will, take this cup away from Me; nevertheless not My will, but Yours, be done" (Luke 22:42).

A couple of things immediately strike us about the temptation that Jesus experienced in the Garden. First, at the risk of repeating ourselves, we must assert that it didn't (and couldn't) arise from any sinful desire on his part. The desire to avoid death—and particularly one as terrifying and grisly as the one he was about to undergo—is a perfectly natural inclination of the human soul, and there's no reason to expect Jesus to have reacted any differently in his humanity. Moreover, Jesus had to contend not just with the physical suffering that he was to undergo but with the very real spiritual separation from his Father that awaited him, as the sins of the world were placed on his shoulders. Is it any wonder, then, that his sweat became like great drops of blood?

Second, even in his great moment of despair, Jesus didn't stray one inch from the path that his Father in heaven had assigned to him. With regard to the possibility of an alternate course of action, he prayed only, "if it is Your will," and then he immediately added his own assent to the plan that had already been predetermined. Whatever temptation Jesus may have experienced that potentially would have saved him from the Cross, it was but a momentary one and arose quite naturally from a human will that shuddered at the thought of such a fate. On the other hand, his divine will, the controlling force of his person, was never for a moment out of unison with that of his Father in heaven (John 5:30).

In summary, the temptation experiences of Jesus were completely external in origin, emanating not from any desires within himself but from the barbs of the tempter. Because he had no sinful disposition or inclinations toward which Satan could direct his attacks, Jesus' temptations (or tests) consisted of the evil one suggesting that Jesus stray from the path of obedience to his Father. Whatever conflict of soul he experienced wasn't in consideration of doing anything that was inherently evil but was solely concerned with things that were otherwise good and proper in any other situation—and thus involved no moral defect on his part.

Jesus was never tempted to evil, for it was impossible that he should be (James 1:13). Rather, his temptation experiences were trials of virtue, arranged by God himself and designed to show forth his glory. By successfully resisting the seductions of the devil, Jesus "endured the full force of temptation's ferocity, until hell slunk away, defeated and exhausted."[3]

The Impeccability of Christ

Jesus' victory over Satan was no accident. It wasn't merely the fortuitous outcome of a chance encounter, for it was the Spirit who led Jesus into the wilderness to battle the tempter. Nor was the outcome ever in doubt, despite the reality of the trials that he had to endure. The first Adam had failed his test of obedience by falling prey to the devil's enticements. But the last Adam, Jesus Christ, quenched the fiery darts of the wicked one and won the victory over sin that Adam failed to secure for mankind. It was the very reason for which Christ had been sent to earth.

As a result, we may state with supreme confidence that if Satan's attacks upon the incarnate Lord had lasted, not just 33 years (the estimated length of Jesus' life), but 3300 years, the outcome would have been no different. As the only person who was both fully man and fully God, Jesus Christ couldn't possibly fall into sin. That Christ would win the victory over Satan wasn't merely a possibility, as it had been for Adam as well, but an absolute certainty, guaranteed by the immutable nature of his identity as the divine God-Man.

The doctrine or principle that the incarnate Lord wasn't able to sin is known as the impeccability of Christ. Though a few persons throughout church history have denied this truth, at the heart of its repudiation lies a faulty understanding of Christ's person. Those who seek to undermine the doctrine usually argue that unless Jesus was capable of sinning, both his humanity and the reality of his temptation experiences are compromised.

But that thinking is seriously flawed, for it reflects the logic found in the ancient heresy known as Nestorianism, whose followers were guilty of so radically separating the human and divine natures of Christ that the unity of his person was effectively denied. Those who argue that Christ must have been capable of sinning overemphasize the human side of his person and wind up doing the same thing as the Nestorians. A. W. Pink comments upon this tendency:

> Personality centered not in His humanity. Christ was a Divine person, who had been "made in the likeness of men" (Phil. 2:7). Utterly impossible was it, then, for the God-man to sin. To affirm to the contrary, is to be guilty of the most awful blasphemy. It is irreverent speculation to discuss what the human nature of Christ might have done if it had been alone. It never was alone; it never had a separate existence; from the first moment of its being it was united to a Divine person.[4]

To affirm that Christ was impeccable in his person in no way detracts from the reality of his humanity any more than the fact that he hungered and slept detracts from his divinity. Christ is fully God and fully man, two natures in one unique person. Thus, it's proper to say that Christ possesses a mutable human nature, since changeability in the creature isn't a result of the Fall but is an inherent characteristic of humanity. At the same time, however, we must affirm that it wasn't possible that Christ the person could have sinned, for to argue otherwise would be to say that God can sin, and the Scriptures won't allow for that. Thinking rightly of Christ requires us to cast out such unworthy (nay, blasphemous) thoughts.

As for the notion that affirming Christ's impeccability renders his temptations hollow, that they thereby become a mere fiction, we answer that such reasoning seems to be a conclusion in search of an argument. The certainty of the outcome in no way detracts from the reality of the struggle. Christ's victory over Satan cost him dearly. He became a Man of Sorrows, despised and rejected by men—stricken, smitten, and afflicted by God (Isa. 53:3–4). As W .G. T. Shedd writes in this context, "Because an army is victorious, it by no means follows that the victory was a cheap one."[5] It was hardly a cheap one in this case.

I can't help but believe that those who deny the impeccability of Christ have simply not thought through the implications of their argument here. Aside from the outright contradiction of Scripture that's involved in saying that it was possible for the God-Man to have sinned, a more practical question arises: How could God have promised salvation through Christ at the moment of Adam's transgression into sin? If Christ, like Adam, had fallen to the tempter's inducements to sin, the promise of Genesis 3:15 becomes a lie. Christ wouldn't have crushed the serpent's head, and the Old Testament saints who trusted in his work beforehand would have been sold a bill of goods by God himself. And they, like the rest of us, would be without hope.

Of course, such thoughts are ridiculous in the extreme. But they flow naturally from the argument that Christ wasn't impeccable. Instead, we should heed the words of Jesus himself, who told his disciples in the Garden of Gethsemane not to fight his arrest by the Jewish authorities since "it must happen thus" (Matt. 26:52–54). By use of a hypothetical, Jesus said that if he desired to, he could pray to his Father in heaven and have twelve legions of angels protect him from those who were seeking his destruction. But he didn't want to call on his Father for such deliverance, nor was it possible that he could have desired to do so on this occasion, for the Scriptures *must* be fulfilled.

As the omnipotent Son of God, Jesus lacked no power to prevent what was taking place. Rather, what he lacked was any desire to stray from his Father's will. The anguish of soul that he experienced in the Garden over his impending death, far from detracting from that reality, actually reinforced it in the most convincing ways. Jesus' human desire to avoid the Cross was simply no match for the controlling will of his divine personality, which wouldn't allow him to veer one inch from the path marked out for him. Thus, we confidently assert that even at that awful moment of struggle, Jesus' ultimate victory over temptation was never in doubt. His words stating that the Scriptures must be fulfilled were his own offer of proof to that effect.

Tempted in All Points

Given the unique nature of Christ's temptations, then, how is it that the New Testament can affirm that he "suffered, being tempted" (Heb. 2:18)? More importantly, if he didn't have the same sinful disposition as we, how can Scripture say that he "was in all points tempted as we are" (Heb. 4:15)? Doesn't his uniqueness in this regard contradict such a statement? We now turn our attention to a discussion of this issue.

First of all, Christ's entire life was one of suffering. The Westminster Larger Catechism (Q. 48) states that "Christ humbled himself in this life ... by conflicting with the indignities of the world, temptations of Satan, and infirmities in his flesh." The fact that the Son of God left his throne room in heaven to allow himself to be subjected to the "indignities of the world" means that the Incarnation was one constant act of suffering for Christ. It was bad enough that he had to receive in his flesh the most ferocious barbs that the tempter possessed. But the task of reconciling sinners to God required Christ to suffer something far worse—loss of communion with his Father in heaven. By choosing to carry on with the work assigned to him, Jesus was called upon to thwart the most holy affections and aspirations of which man is capable.[6]

Because Jesus possessed no sinful disposition or inclinations, the devil could only prey upon the natural infirmities that Jesus had assumed at his incarnation. As a man, Jesus needed food and sleep to survive, which explains Satan's attack in the wilderness. And as a man, Jesus would have had the natural inclination to preserve his own life, hence Satan's attack in the Garden. But those attacks consisted in calls to deviate from the way of the Cross, not in any appeal to the sins that so thoroughly characterize our lives.

We can say with the writer of Hebrews that Jesus was tempted in all points as we are, but we must not say that he was tempted in the same way or by the same things that we are, for that's an entirely different matter.

No doubt Christ was presented with the offers and opportunities to commit such sins as adultery, lust, and greed during his earthly life. He was, after all, the constant companion of sinners. But neither is there any doubt that he didn't experience, even for an instant, a desire to commit any of these sins. With regard to these sins of the heart, Jesus was tempted only in the sense that he had the offers to commit these sins placed before his mind by others. However, he did not undergo temptation in the sense that we usually define the term—that of experiencing an internal disposition toward, or of giving any serious consideration to, such sins.

Over the course of his life, Jesus was confronted with every type of temptation to which we are subject, for he was tempted "in all points as we are." He was tempted at the point of his intellect, his emotions, and his will. And he was tempted with every conceivable sin known to man. But in contrast to our own experience, such temptations consisted only in external presentations of the desirability of a certain sinful course of action. Unlike us, Jesus suffered merely by being the recipient of such despicable suggestions.

The Result of Christ's Temptations: His Sympathy with Sinners

Thankfully, there is good news in the fact of Christ's temptation experiences. The best news is that by successfully winning the war against sin and Satan, Christ has made reconciliation with God possible for lost sinners. That aspect of his work is largely the subject of the next chapter. But from his temptation experiences flows another blessing found in the verses from which we quoted in the previous section.

Hebrews 2:18 says of Christ, "For in that He Himself has suffered, being tempted, He is able to aid those who are tempted." Hebrews 4:15 adds that, for the same reason, Christ is able to "sympathize with our weaknesses." Together these two verses make up some of the most comforting words found in Scripture. They assure us that we aren't alone in our most trying times, and that we can find the strength of character to resist the temptations of life if we call on him who has been there before us. To know that Christ is able to sympathize with us in our weaknesses is comforting. But it's even more comforting to know that he is able to render aid to us in those times when we need him most.

A final question arises in this context: Does the fact that Jesus didn't partake of our sinful nature mean that he didn't fully experience humanity and thus is unable to sympathize with us in our trials? Richard Phillips responds to such a notion:

> The answer to this is that far from Jesus knowing less than we do about temptation because he never fell into sin, the opposite is the case. Jesus knows far more about temptation than we do because he endured far beyond the point where the strongest of us gives in to the trial. B. F. Westcott is surely right when he observes: "Sympathy with the sinner in his trial does not depend on the experience of sin but on the experience of the strength of the temptation to sin, which only the sinless can know in its full intensity. He who falls yields before the last strain."[7]

Rather than detracting from the reality of his sympathy for us, it is Jesus' sinlessness that gives it efficacy. Only One who is sinless could have resisted the devil's enticements and provide the victory that makes his sympathizing aid possible today. And only a sinless One could have endured temptation to the point where no mere mortal has ever been, giving him an insight into suffering that we ourselves will never possess.

In the end, every inducement to sin is merely one way among thousands by which the devil seeks to accomplish his single, ultimate purpose—to alienate us from the love of God. He tried his best with Jesus and failed. He'll try the same with us. But if you are Christ's, you have the sympathizing High Priest who is ready to provide you with all you need in order to withstand the devil's wiles. Jesus is willing and able to help you in your time of need. And because of his completed work on your behalf, your ultimate victory over Satan is already an accomplished fact.

8

He Was Perfected

(HEB. 5:9)

No Christian would argue with the statement that "Christ is perfect." Nor would they take issue with it worded solely in the past tense ("Christ *was* perfect") if the intent was to make specific reference to a fact that described his nature during the days of his earthly sojourn. But when the suffix *ed* is added to that otherwise innocuous statement of fact, it takes on an entirely different meaning, and becomes subject to potentially serious forms of misunderstanding. Nevertheless, that Christ was in fact "perfected" is a thoroughly biblical notion, one that receives quite an extended treatment from the writer of the book of Hebrews.

The purpose of this chapter is to explore the precise sense in which Christ may be said to have been perfected and to show how such perfection relates to the accomplishment of his earthly work on behalf of sinners. The fact that Christ has been perfect from eternity makes it natural that we would view with suspicion any statement that seems to imply that he needed anything to be added to his person. And it's true that we don't think rightly of Christ if we imagine for a moment that he needed improvement in anything related to his character or nature or that he lacked anything in the way of righteousness, power, grace, or any of the other divine attributes that he possessed from eternity.

Rather, the statement that "Christ was perfected" has reference to his role as Mediator of the new covenant—a role that he fulfilled by being and doing all that was required of him in order that he might heal the breach that had existed between God and us since Adam's fall in the Garden. Every aspect of Christ's incarnate life, from his birth in a stable to his death on a cross, was a part of the perfecting process that fitted him for his role as Mediator and Savior.

Made Like His Brethren

The first requirement for Jesus being made perfect relates to his being. The Mediator between God and men had to be both God and man himself. He needed to "have partaken of flesh and blood" (Heb. 2:14) and "to be made like His brethren" (Heb. 2:17) if he was to make atonement for the sins of his people. We have already discussed the necessity for the Incarnation in Chapter 3, so we'll not cover that ground again. But there's one aspect of that subject that figures prominently in the argument of the writer of Hebrews—Christ's priesthood. Because the Old Testament priests were God's appointed mediators between him and fallen men, it was necessary that they be able to represent those on whose behalf they were appointed to offer sacrifices to God. They could only do so if they too were made like their brethren. And this requirement applied with equal force to Jesus Christ, the great High Priest of his people.

Perfected through Suffering Obedience

Hebrews 5:8 says that Christ "learned obedience by the things which He suffered." This statement likewise tends to strike us as odd. It's just as strange to think of Christ learning obedience as it is to think of his being perfected. And yet his act of learning obedience was an integral part of that perfecting process that's our focus here.

So just what does the writer of Hebrews have in mind when he speaks of Jesus as having "learned obedience"? He means that Jesus, as the God-Man, entered into the human experience of what it was to obey, by denying himself and meticulously following the requirements laid down for him in God's law. A. W. Pink puts it this way: "As we learn the sweetness or bitterness of food by actually tasting it, so He learned what submission is by yielding to the Father's will."[1] And this obedience he rendered in "the days of His flesh" (Heb. 5:7).

Theologians generally speak of Christ's obedience as having taken two forms: active and passive. His active obedience refers to his faithfully fulfilling God's law in all of its particulars. He lived a perfectly sinless life, doing all that was required of him (in both letter and spirit) as well as refraining from all that was forbidden. Jesus submitted to the baptism of John and the rest of the Old Testament ceremonial law in order that he might "fulfill all righteousness" (Matt. 3:15). He told his disciples that he had come not to destroy the law or the prophets but to fulfill them (Matt. 5:17). He did everything that the law of God commanded of him, and he did it all perfectly. Moreover, his obedience wasn't given grudgingly. His nature was such that he loved righteousness and hated lawlessness (Heb. 1:9).

On the other hand, the passive obedience of Christ refers primary to his having willingly submitted himself to his role in God's plan of redemption—a role that called for him to be delivered up to evil men for a cruel and bloody death in order to make atonement for the sins of his people. Obviously, his submission to that plan could only be an active one from his perspective, requiring him to make a myriad of conscious choices to bring that plan to fruition. But because this aspect of his work consists primarily in accepting the cup from which God had given to him to drink, it is often referred to as his passive obedience. As Paul said, Christ "became obedient to the point of death" (Phil. 2:8).

The critical distinction in this is that Christ's passive obedience, or his atoning death on the cross, pays the penalty for sins that would otherwise be borne by his people. Christ's active obedience, or his perfect fulfillment of the law of God, is imputed to the believing sinner's account, allowing him to stand in front of a holy God and be pronounced righteous in his sight. Both are necessary if man is to be reconciled to God. Together, these two aspects of Christ's obedience constitute the sum of his atoning work on behalf of sinners. And it's in this sense that the distinction is most helpful.

Yet it should be obvious that it's nearly impossible to completely distinguish any particular aspect of Christ's atoning work as falling into one or the other category. Nor is it necessarily wise to do so, as J. Gresham Machen points out:

> How shall we distinguish Christ's active obedience from His passive obedience? Shall we say that He accomplished His active obedience by His life and accomplished His passive obedience by His death? No, that will not do at all. During every moment of His life upon earth Christ was engaged in His passive obedience. It was all for Him humiliation, was it not? It was all suffering. It was all part of His payment of the penalty of sin. On the other hand, we cannot say that His death was passive obedience and not active obedience. On the contrary, His death was the crown of His active obedience. It was the crown of that obedience to the law of God by which He merited eternal life for those whom He came to save.
>
> Do you not see, then, what the true state of the case is? Christ's active obedience and His passive obedience are not two divisions of His work, some of the events of His earthly life being His active obedience and other events of His life being His passive obedience; but every event of His life was both active obedience and passive obedience. Every

> event of His life was a part of His payment for the
> penalty of sin, and every event of His life was a part
> of that glorious keeping of the law of God by which
> He earned for His people the reward of eternal life.
> The two aspects of His work, in other words, are
> inextricably intertwined. Neither was performed
> apart from the other. Together they constitute the
> wonderful, full salvation which was wrought for us
> by Christ our Redeemer.
>
> We can put it briefly by saying that Christ took
> our place with respect to the law of God. He paid for
> us the law's penalty, and He obeyed for us the law's
> commands.[2]

Although Machen was hesitant to categorize any particular event in Jesus' life as belonging solely to either his active or passive obedience, he did most emphatically recognize the distinction between those two aspects of Christ's work. In the same sermon from which those words above are quoted, Machen utters praises for the fact that if Christ had come only to pay the penalty for our sins by dying on the cross, we would simply have found ourselves back in the probationary position in which Adam had originally been placed in the Garden. And yet we would have had none of the inherent advantages that he possessed, a fact that would render our situation hopeless in the face of God's demand for perfect obedience.[3] Indeed, it is a well-known anecdote that Dr. Machen's final words in a telegram to his dear friend John Murray, just before he died on January 1, 1937, were these: "I'm so thankful for the active obedience of Christ. No hope without it."

When the author of Hebrews writes that Christ was "perfected" through his suffering obedience (Heb. 5:8–9), he points to the fact that Christ's complete conformity to God's will was the means by which he was fitted or consecrated to the office of Mediator and High Priest. Only a mediator/priest could represent mankind and provide an acceptable sacrifice for sins that the law demanded. And no ordinary human priest would suffice for the work that Christ came to accomplish. Only one who had been perfected by a life of complete obedience to the will of God could offer the kind of sacrifice that would have infinite and permanent value for all of those who placed their trust in him. Christ's perfection made his sacrifice for sins acceptable, and it made his personal righteousness transferable to his people (Phil. 3:9).

Machen was right to give thanks for having a Mediator who has provided the perfect obedience we need in order to be reconciled to God. Our need is too great, and our abilities too inadequate. So God sent his Son to do the job for us. And the Son was perfected for the task by his obedience and suffering in our place. As a result of his perfection, his righteousness becomes our righteousness when we place our trust in him.

How wonderfully different is this biblical gospel from the one that is so popular today. Some who vainly imagine their own righteousness to be sufficient before God have attacked the doctrine of the imputation of Christ's righteousness to the believer's account. They would have men stand before God on the Day of Judgment clothed only in their own imperfect (nay, filthy—Isa. 64:6) "righteousness." To those who argue such sophistry and who seek to replace Christ's perfect righteousness with anything else, we simply, but firmly, respond with Machen that there is "no hope without it."

Our Great High Priest

Christ's perfection signifies his being brought into that completeness of condition for which his ministry was designed.[4] It was his glory to be made a High Priest on behalf of his people and then to achieve perfection through the conduct of his sinless life. This characterization of Christ's work is a central theme of the book of Hebrews, where the writer set forth Jesus as our great High Priest and Mediator of the new covenant.

From the opening words of his epistle, the writer of Hebrews sets out to demonstrate the superiority of Christ and his priesthood over all those who had come before him. He does this by appealing not only to the glory of Christ but also to the limitations of the Old Testament sacrificial system and the priests who were a part of it. The salient point for this part of our discussion is that neither the priests nor the system that they administered were able to provide the perfection that God required for sinners to be reconciled to him. If perfection could have come to sinful humans through the Levitical priesthood, it wouldn't have been necessary to repeat the sacrifices offered there on a daily basis.

More importantly, it wouldn't have been necessary to send Christ, a priest of an altogether different (permanent) order (7:11), to make a single, all-sufficient offering of himself on behalf of his people (7:27). But it *was* necessary, for the former system was "weak and unprofitable," being unable to make anything (or anyone) perfect (7:18). The work of the Old Testament priest was cut short by his own death, but Christ's work on behalf of sinners continues forever by virtue of his unchangeable priesthood (7:23–24). Thus, "He is able to save to the uttermost those who come to God through Him, since He always lives to make intercession for them" (7:25).

The implications of this teaching should be obvious to all. The ongoing efficacy of Christ's permanent priesthood, founded upon the perfect sacrifice of himself, means that the human office of priest is a thing of the past. It belongs to that system that was weak and unprofitable and which was a mere "shadow of the good things to come" (10:1). The New Testament knows of no such office surviving the death of Christ, and all those who presume to call themselves priests today denigrate the work of Christ and wickedly assume for themselves a prerogative that is his alone.[5]

The End of His Perfection: Author of Eternal Salvation

Our great High Priest didn't become obedient to the point of death for his own benefit. Rather, he did so that he might "bring many sons to glory" and thereby be able to call them his brothers (Heb. 2:10–11). The writer to the Hebrews tells us that it was by virtue of his perfection that Christ became the "author of eternal salvation" (5:9). That was the end for which he had come.

To say that it was by his perfection that Christ became the author of eternal salvation is to say that his work was the meritorious and efficient cause of our salvation.[6] Nothing we do, or do not do, can add a whit to that finished work of his. Neither the Old Testament sacrifices (10:1) nor our own works in the flesh (Gal. 3:3) could suffice. But in Christ, we're presented perfect to God (Col. 1:28).

When we come to the tenth chapter of Hebrews, the writer turns our attention from the perfection wrought in Christ to that which is ours by virtue of our union with him. In the first of several references to the perfection of believers, he writes that by Christ's one offering, he had perfected his people forever (10:14). Thus, the end of his perfection is ours. He is the author of *our* eternal salvation. And he is the "author and finisher" of the faith that unites us to him (12:2).

The Reward for His Perfection: Exaltation

In the midst of delivering one of his many warnings about the judgment that awaited the scribes and Pharisees, Jesus told his disciples that whoever humbles himself will be exalted (Matt. 23:12). Never was the truth of that statement more beautifully displayed than in his own case. As his humiliation was the greatest ever, so was his exaltation. After Jesus humbled himself to the point of an ignominious death on a cross, "God has highly exalted Him and given Him the name which is above every name" (Phil. 2:8-9). Christ is now seated at the right hand of the Father in heaven, crowned with glory and honor—a point that the author of Hebrews finds so important that he mentions it five times in the span of his letter (1:3, 13; 8:1; 10:12; 12:2).

It's certainly true that Christ was returning to the position of honor that he had before the world began—long before he was perfected by his spotless life (John 17:5). But the Bible also speaks of Christ gaining a measure of glory through the work he accomplished while on earth. Scripture affirms that there was an aspect of his personal glory to which he had not yet acceded prior to the completion of his incarnate work (John 7:39; Acts 3:13; Phil. 2:8–9; Heb. 1:3–4; 2:9–10; 5:5; 8:1; 1 Pet. 1:21; 4:11–13).

Nor is it inconsistent to say that despite the Son's exaltation he was no less glorious in his person prior to his incarnation. Infinite glory was his in eternity past. But it wasn't until he was perfected in his incarnate state that his human nature could be glorified. Philip Hughes captured the essence of this truth with the following observation:

> He left as the Son of God. He returned both as Son of God and also, by reason of the incarnation, as Son of man. He left as Lord. He returned both as Lord and also as Minister on our behalf in the presence of the Father. He left as King. He returned both as King and also as High Priest and Intercessor for those whom he is not ashamed to call his brethren (Heb. 2:11). He left as Sovereign. He returned also as Savior.[7]

From the moment of his ascension back into heaven, human nature has been forever glorified in the person of Jesus Christ. The human flesh and nature that the divine Son of God carried to heaven was perfected by his faithful obedience, and it's in this two-nature state that Christ the Lord received his exaltation and will thereby live forever. Moreover, the perfection that he accomplished will ultimately bring glorification and exaltation to all those who by faith are united to him. He has done all that is necessary to secure the blessings of salvation on their behalf.

Though Christ is ever at work on behalf of his people (see Chapter 17), he has ended his suffering labors and has taken his seat at the right hand of his Father in heaven. As our forerunner (Heb. 6:20), he has gone before us in obedience, suffering, and glory. He has shown us what real obedience looks like. It's now our solemn obligation and privilege to render unto him the same humble obedience that he offered to the Father. Such obedience on our part may likewise lead to suffering, and even death. But thanks to the work of Christ on their behalf, Christians who find themselves in such a situation may take comfort in the eternal perspective provided by the apostle Paul: "For I consider that the sufferings of this present time are not worthy to be compared with the glory which shall be revealed in us" (Rom. 8:18).

9

He Was Numbered with the Transgressors

(MARK 15:28)

Over the centuries, more than a few critics of Christianity have denounced it as a religion of blood. After all, a quick glance through any church hymnal will likely yield songs with titles such as "Jesus, Thy Blood and Righteousness," "Nothing but the Blood," "Are You Washed in the Blood?" and one of my personal favorites, "There Is a Fountain Filled with Blood." Add to that lineup the hundreds of others whose titles may not contain the word, but whose verses nevertheless sing the praises of Christ's blood, and you have a definitive testimony to the central place that blood plays in the Christian faith.

But these songs don't testify to any morose or bloodthirsty tendencies in Christianity. Nor do we sing about blood in any abstract manner. Rather, these songs call to mind the fact that after defeating Satan and being perfected through his complete obedience to God, Jesus Christ was delivered up for execution on a cross by the people of the very nation to which he had come to offer salvation. It's his blood about which we sing. The blood that we laud is holy blood; it's blood that was shed on behalf of sinners; and it's blood that is adequate to atone for the sins of all those who by faith embrace him as Savior.

Jesus' death on the cross of Calvary and his subsequent resurrection from the dead are the central events of redemptive history, and together these two actions of God form the nucleus around which all of the other tenets of the Christian faith coalesce. The Cross was God's answer to man's predicament. It was there that his justice and mercy met in the most visible of ways. The Son's death at the hands of sinful men constituted simultaneously the most despicable of human actions ever perpetrated and the most glorious of divine interventions ever undertaken.

Thus, when we sing of the blood of Christ being shed for sinners, we sing of his death on the cross. And when we sing of his cross (e.g., "When I Survey the Wondrous Cross," "The Old Rugged Cross," and "Lift High the Cross"), we sing of the shedding of his blood and the wonderful effects that flow from that divine act. So, while the concepts are intertwined, it's more meaningful and accurate to speak of Christianity as a religion of the Cross. All the hopes and aspirations of man are found at the foot of the cross of Calvary—not in the wooden beams that formed its structure but in the One who hung upon it and shed his blood that others might have life.

Isaiah 53: The Suffering Servant

The death of Christ is foretold in the Old Testament, many centuries before it took place. Some of the words of King David in Psalm 22 may have had an immediate application to his own life, but it's clear that the writers of the New Testament, as well as Jesus himself, understood the Psalm to describe the Messiah's suffering on the cross. Several other passages find their ultimate fulfillment in the details of the crucifixion account as well (Psa. 41:9; 69:21; Zech. 13:7).

However, it's Isaiah, the same Old Testament prophet who provides the clearest prophecy of Christ's virgin birth, who gives us not only a glimpse into the crucifixion event 750 years before it happened but more importantly provides a great deal of the theological interpretation of that event. It's Isaiah who first tells us that the Messiah would be "numbered with the transgressors," a fact that the evangelist Mark reiterates in his gospel account, after Christ had fulfilled the prophecy.

The fact that Isaiah's description of the Messiah and his sufferings identify Jesus and his crucifixion is explicitly confirmed in Acts 8:26–40, where Luke records the story of Philip's encounter with the Ethiopian eunuch in the desert of Judea. As Philip came upon the eunuch's chariot, he could hear the man reading from the Suffering Servant prophecy found in Isaiah 52:13–53:12. When the eunuch asked Philip whether Isaiah was speaking of himself or some other man, Philip proceeded to explain to him that Jesus Christ was the One to whom Isaiah had been referring. Christ's humiliation and death on the cross fulfilled Isaiah's prophecy of the Servant who would suffer for the sins of Israel and ultimately accomplish reconciliation between God and his people by virtue of his vicarious suffering on their behalf.

Because we'll make frequent reference to Isaiah's prophecy in the analysis that follows, the text is reprinted in its entirety:

Isaiah 52

[13] Behold, My Servant shall deal prudently;
He shall be exalted and extolled and be very high.
    [14] Just as many were astonished at you,
So His visage was marred more than any man,
    And His form more than the sons of men;
    [15] So shall He sprinkle many nations.
    Kings shall shut their mouths at Him;
For what had not been told them they shall see,
And what they had not heard they shall consider.

Isaiah 53

[1] Who has believed our report?
And to whom has the arm of the LORD been revealed?
[2] For He shall grow up before Him as a tender plant,
And as a root out of dry ground.
He has no form or comeliness;
And when we see Him,
There is no beauty that we should desire Him.
[3] He is despised and rejected by men,
A Man of sorrows and acquainted with grief.
And we hid, as it were, our faces from Him;
He was despised, and we did not esteem Him.
[4] Surely He has borne our griefs
And carried our sorrows;
Yet we esteemed Him stricken,
Smitten by God, and afflicted.
[5] But He was wounded for our transgressions,
He was bruised for our iniquities;
The chastisement for our peace was upon Him,
And by His stripes we are healed.
[6] All we like sheep have gone astray;
We have turned, every one, to his own way;
And the LORD has laid on Him the iniquity of us all.
[7] He was oppressed and He was afflicted,
Yet He opened not His mouth;
He was led as a lamb to the slaughter,
And as a sheep before its shearers is silent,
So He opened not His mouth.
[8] He was taken from prison and from judgment,
And who will declare His generation?
For He was cut off from the land of the living;
For the transgressions of My people He was stricken.
[9] And they made His grave with the wicked—
But with the rich at His death,

Because He had done no violence,
Nor was any deceit in His mouth.
¹⁰ Yet it pleased the LORD to bruise Him;
He has put Him to grief.
When You make His soul an offering for sin,
He shall see His seed, He shall prolong His days,
And the pleasure of the LORD shall prosper in His hand.
¹¹ He shall see the labor of His soul, and be satisfied.
By His knowledge My righteous Servant shall justify many,
For He shall bear their iniquities.
¹² Therefore I will divide Him a portion with the great,
And He shall divide the spoil with the strong,
Because He poured out His soul unto death,
And He was numbered with the transgressors,
And He bore the sin of many,
And made intercession for the transgressors.

Isaiah's prophecy makes it clear that the Servant's suffering and death was vicarious in nature; it was performed on behalf of others. The Servant (Christ) substituted his own life for those who were truly guilty and deserving of the death to which he voluntarily submitted himself. The reference to being "numbered with the transgressors" in verse 12 signifies Christ's complete identification with sinners in his death, which took two forms: the physical and the spiritual.

The Physical Numbering

As we have already learned, it was necessary for Christ to be "made like His brethren" if he was to be the great High Priest of his people. But he did more than simply take human nature unto himself in order to technically qualify as One who could offer a sacrifice on man's behalf. Rather, he specifically identified himself with sinners both in his life and in his death.

From the very outset, Christ's life was numbered with his fellow human beings. His birth in Bethlehem, in fulfillment of Scripture, came about only as a result of a census (numbering) called for by Caesar Augustus. His circumcision on the eighth day of life was undertaken in fulfillment of the terms of the Abrahamic Covenant and was intended for sinners, a class to which Christ himself didn't belong. The same may be said about his undergoing John's baptism in the Jordan, an act signifying repentance for sin and one to which he had no need (on that basis) to submit himself.

But it was at the cross where Jesus' physical numbering with transgressors found its most sobering application. It was there that the Son of God was treated as a mere criminal and subjected to the most grievous of insults and indignities to his person. He hung upon the cross as "despised and rejected by men," and yet we (Isaiah speaks as if including himself and everyone else here) didn't have the guts to look him in the face (v. 3). Moreover, we stupidly imagined that he was being stricken by God for something that he himself had done rather than for his work on our behalf (v. 4). He was "led as a lamb to the slaughter" (v. 7) and was "cut off from the land of the living" (v. 8), yet "He opened not His mouth" (v. 7) to utter a word of resistance.

The New Testament writers provide many more individual details of the humiliation that Christ endured in the final hours of his earthly life—the scourging by Pilate; the mocking, spitting, and slapping of the Jewish religious leaders, as well as the Roman guard; the platting of a crown of thorns on his head; and even the casting of lots for his garments. The end result of this physical abuse was that Jesus' "visage was marred more than any other man" (Isa. 52:14).

Charles Spurgeon comments upon this despicable scene with the following astute observation:

> Let us remember that our Lord's weakness was undertaken for our sakes: for us He became a lamb, for us He laid aside His glory, and therefore it is the more painful for us to see that this voluntary humiliation of Himself must be made the object of so much derision and scorn, though worthy of the utmost praise. He

stoops to save us, and we laugh at Him as He stoops;
He leaves the throne that He may lift us up to it, but
while He is graciously descending, the hoarse laughter
of an ungodly world is His only reward. Ah me! was
ever love treated so unlovely a sort? Surely the cruelty
it received was proportioned to the honor it deserved,
so perverse are the sons of men.[1]

In addition to the verbal and physical abuse that Jesus suffered at the
hands of sinful men, the very method of his execution was calculated
to add to the indignity of his sufferings. Death by crucifixion was
the most shameful form of execution in existence at the time and
was usually reserved for the lowest common criminals in Roman
society. This is why Paul could say that Christ had become obedient
to the point of death, "even the death of the cross" (Phil. 2:8; cf. Heb.
12:2). Such a death, says Paul, was "a stumbling block" to Jews, and
"foolishness" to Greeks (1 Cor. 1:23). But it was the form of death to
which Christ willingly submitted himself, and his death is the most
meaningful one in human history.

We live in an age when churches adorned with crosses are everywhere.
But, according to one scholar, this wasn't always the case:

> We have grown so used to the idea that the
> Crucifixion is the supreme symbol of Christianity,
> that it is a shock to realize how late in the history
> of Christian art its power was recognized. In the
> first art of Christianity it hardly appears; and the
> earliest example, on the doors of Santa Sabina in
> Rome, is stuck away in a corner, almost out of sight.
> The simple fact is that the Early Church needed
> converts, and from this point of view the Crucifixion
> was not an encouraging subject. So, early Christian
> art is concerned with miracles, healings, and with
> hopeful aspects of the faith like the Ascension and
> the Resurrection. The Santa Sabina Crucifixion is

not only obscure but unmoving. The few surviving Crucifixions of the early Church make no attempt to touch our emotions. It was the tenth century, that despised and rejected epoch of European history, that made the Crucifixion into a moving symbol of the Christian faith.[2]

However, one thing is clear from Scripture: regardless of when we date the emergence of the cross as a potent visual symbol of Christianity, its use in preaching was central to the apostolic message from the very outset. It was part of Peter's first recorded sermon at Pentecost (Acts 2:23), and Paul relished the fact that despite the obvious prejudicial view of Jews and Greeks toward the cross, he and his apostolic band were honored to "preach Christ crucified" to all (1 Cor. 1:23).

How sad it is today to see so many churches abandoning that message for a watered-down version of the gospel that focuses less on the objective reality of Christ's blood being shed for sinners and more on his ethical teachings. That form of preaching may indeed be more palatable to modern ears, but it's not more suited to the saving of souls. The fact of the crucifixion was never more problematic than it was for those in the first centuries after Christ's death, but the church preached it with gusto. And millions were saved in the process.

The Spiritual Numbering

If the fact of Christ's physical numbering with sinners provides the basis for his representing us before God, it's his spiritual numbering that provides the basis for our acquittal. Isaiah's testimony to this reality is truly overwhelming. In the first place, Christ has "borne our griefs and carried our sorrows" (v. 4); he was "wounded for our transgressions" and "bruised for our iniquities" (v. 5). Moreover, the chastisement that he received from God was for "our peace," and it's "by His stripes we are healed" (v. 5). Even though we like sheep have gone astray, "the Lord has laid on Him the iniquity of us all" (v. 6).

The end result of Christ's vicarious work on behalf of sinners is that God has made his soul "an offering for sin" (v. 10), and by that offering he "shall justify many, for He shall bear their iniquities" (v. 11). Thus, it's Christ who bears "the sin of many" (v. 12) and will thereby "sprinkle many nations" with his blood (52:15).

The theme of the substitutionary nature of Christ's death is just as prominent in the New Testament and provides the uniform theological interpretation of the event (1 Cor. 15:3; Heb. 2:17; 1 Pet. 2:24; 1 John 1:7). Paul tells us that God made Christ "to be sin for us, that we might become the righteousness of God in Him" (2 Cor. 5:21) and that "Christ has redeemed us from the curse of the law, having become a curse for us" (Gal. 3:13).

No one would deny that Christ's physical presence was a great blessing to those with whom he came into contact during the days of his flesh. But the blessing of his presence during those relatively few years was eclipsed by the magnitude of the blessing that his death on their behalf would provide some time later (cf. John 16:7).

Paul's language to the effect that Christ had become for us both "sin" and "a curse" speaks in no uncertain terms to the vicarious nature of his death. The death that he died was for the benefit of his people. He was numbered with them, the transgressors. And it was because of his identification with sinners that—for three hours on the cross when the sky turned dark in mid-afternoon—he had truly been forsaken by his Father in heaven. Not for anything that he had done but for crimes which we had committed and for which he had now taken upon himself the punishment. During that time, God had to look away from his beloved Son, as the innumerable sins of all those who would ever trust in Christ were laid upon him as their sin-bearer.

So intense was the agony of body and soul that Christ endured on the cross that the early church, in formulating the Apostles' Creed, would say that he had "descended into hell." Although the evidence suggests that many in that day wrongly understood the statement to be literally true, it nevertheless serves as an apt (if metaphorical) description of what Christ had to go through, since he suffered, both physically and spiritually, the cumulative punishment that was otherwise due for every single sinner (and every sin) for which he died. God's wrath against sin was poured out upon his Son at the cross of Calvary, and Christ thereby "poured out His soul unto death" (v. 12).

Christ Our Passover Sacrifice

The Gospels record that when Jesus became aware that "all things were now accomplished," he exclaimed, "It is finished," and yielded up his spirit to his Father in heaven (John 19:28–30; Luke 23:46). Only when he had completed the work that his Father had given him to do and which had been his very food while on earth (John 4:34), was he ready to succumb to the final act—his sacrificial death. He had already accomplished all that was prerequisite to yielding up his spirit. He had preached the gospel to the poor and proclaimed the acceptable year of the Lord to the people of Israel (Luke 4:18–19); he had seen to it that every last Scripture prophecy concerning his life had been fulfilled (John 19:28); and he had been perfected by his complete obedience to the will of God.

But even when we roll back the curtain on this final act, it's inappropriate to view Christ as merely a passive victim who endured divine judgment in our place. Though it's true that he was "led as a lamb to the slaughter" in his acquiescence to the Cross, he was actually performing a priestly work—he was "offering himself without spot to God" (Heb. 9:14). At Calvary, Jesus was more than just the spotless Lamb of God being presented to make atonement for the sins of the people. He was also God's High Priest officiating at the altar.[3] What he offered up to God was nothing other than himself. Thus, he was both the sacrifice and the sacrificer.

Paul writes in 1 Corinthians 5:7 that Christ was "our Passover" who was sacrificed for us. The statement recalls the event in Israel's history when God commanded his people to place the blood from an unblemished lamb over the doorposts of their homes in order to avoid his judgment against the firstborn sons of Egypt. By following these instructions, the Israelite sons would be spared when God would "pass over" their homes and direct his judgment only at Egyptians. In this way the Passover celebration was instituted and celebrated every year after that original occurrence.

Of course, it was no coincidence that Christ's death on the cross occurred on the occasion of the Passover celebration in Israel. His death was the antitype that fulfilled the type of the original Passover. He was the spotless Lamb who was offered to God to avert divine judgment. But because he was the fulfillment of the Passover event, there's no need for a daily, or even annual, repetition of his sacrifice. Christ has satisfied divine judgment once and for all. This is a point about which the writer of Hebrews is emphatic:

Hebrews 7

[26] For such a High Priest was fitting for us, who is holy, harmless, undefiled, separate from sinners, and has become higher than the heavens; [27] who does not need daily, as those high priests, to offer up sacrifices, first for His own sins and then for the people's, for this He did once for all when He offered up Himself. [28] For the law appoints as high priests men who have weakness, but the word of the oath, which came after the law, appoints the Son who has been perfected forever.

Hebrews 9

[23] Therefore it was necessary that the copies of the things in the heavens should be purified with these, but the heavenly things themselves with better sacrifices than these. [24] For Christ has not entered the holy places made with hands, which are copies of the true, but into heaven itself, now to appear in the presence of God for us; [25] not that He should offer Himself often, as the high priest enters the

Most Holy Place every year with blood of another—
[26] He then would have had to suffer often since the
foundation of the world; but now, once at the end
of the ages, He has appeared to put away sin by the
sacrifice of Himself. [27] And as it is appointed for men
to die once, but after this the judgment, [28] so Christ
was offered once to bear the sins of many. To those
who eagerly wait for Him He will appear a second
time, apart from sin, for salvation.

Now that Christ has appeared before the Father to put away sins
once and for all time, Christians are at peace with God. Though he
is God in the flesh and separate from sinners, Christ was numbered
with us for our benefit. The chastisement that we deserved has been
placed upon him, our Passover sacrifice. And the outcome of this
glorious transaction has been declared by the prophet: By his stripes
we have been healed.

His Numbering with Transgressors Was the Source of His Glory

We concluded the last chapter by noting that the reward for
Christ's perfection was his exaltation to the right hand of God in
heaven. A part of that obedient perfection that he achieved was
his active identification with sinners in the work of redemption
that he came to accomplish. Such identification was necessary if
we were to be saved from our sins. And according to Isaiah, that
identification with (and work on behalf of) sinners is the source of
Jesus' ultimate exaltation and glory. God the Father rewarded the
Son with exaltation and glory (Isa. 52:13; 53:12) on the basis of
his having done four things: (1) poured out his soul unto death, (2)
become numbered with the transgressors, (3) born the sin of many,
and (4) made intercession for those same transgressors (53:12).

In commenting upon this verse, Spurgeon points out that however
strange it may sound, "the extraordinary glories of Christ, as Savior,

have all been earned by His connection with human sin."[4] All of which is not to say (reiterating a point we made in the last chapter) that the Son didn't possess infinite glory even before his work on behalf of sinners. But it's on the basis of his saving work that he's now exalted to the right hand of the Father and rules the nations in glory. It was his glory to become "the Lamb who was slain" for the sins of mankind (Rev. 5:12). And as deep as his humiliation and degradation on behalf of sinners was, so shall be the heights of his exaltation.[5]

The Cross was no accident. Most Christians understand as much and will gladly affirm that statement without hesitation. After all, we have the prophecies of Isaiah and the Psalmist telling us beforehand that it would happen. And we have the uniform testimony of all four Gospel writers that Jesus had predicted his death, steadfastly setting his face to go to Jerusalem to make it happen (Luke 9:51) and calling it the hour for which he had come (John 12:27).

And yet there are some Christians whose basic theological system cuts against the grain of this fundamental understanding of redemptive history. Even if they would shrink from an outright denial of the statement above, they nevertheless talk about the event of the Cross as if it were God's plan gone awry and not his "determined purpose," as Luke tells us in Acts 2:23. They speak of it more as Plan B that was adopted by Christ only after coming to a realization that things weren't turning out for him the way he had anticipated.

But nothing could be further from the truth! Pouring out his soul unto death was the very reason for which he had come. And what a miserable estate we would all be in if it had turned out any other way (an impossible scenario, of course). Rather, Jesus endured the cross for the joy that was set before him (Heb. 12:2)—the joy of perfectly fulfilling the will of his heavenly Father and of being exalted as the Savior to his Father's right hand to rule for eternity. For this purpose he would gladly die the death that evil men had meted out for him to suffer.

It has also become popular in some circles today to assert that the cross of Christ demonstrates just how valuable humans are to God. The willingness of God to go to such lengths in order to redeem men unto himself is offered up as evidence of man's own inherent value. Perhaps it's not surprising that this type of thinking would find such a welcome audience in today's man-centered society. But it hardly does justice to the general tone of Scripture, which instead emphasizes the sheer grace of God in salvation, as he condescends to redeem those who are completely *unworthy*. In other words, the Cross demonstrates not so much the worth of man as it does the heinousness of sin. The reality is that our sin was such an affront to a holy God that only the extreme measures undertaken by him in the Incarnation and Cross of Jesus Christ could satisfy the demands of his justice.

To those who would urge us to abandon such "worm theology" in favor of a more "enlightened," modern approach, we answer simply, "Is sinful man worthy of more honor than Christ himself?" If it was necessary for the sinless One to undergo such torments of hell on our behalf, what does that have to say concerning those of us who are piled high with sins of every description and type? Just how many death sentences have we earned for ourselves over the length of our years so far?

The fact is that the value we assign to our own self-worth is inversely proportional to our view of the beauty of the Cross. It's only by understanding and appreciating the depths of our own depravity and need that we can truly appreciate the Cross of Christ for what it is—a gracious rescue from the pit of everlasting punishment. That's why Christians sing songs with titles such as, "There Is a Fountain Filled with Blood" and "Lift High the Cross." Because we understand the significance of Christ's blood that was shed for our sins, we cannot help but raise our voices in praise to him who saw fit to undertake such a merciful rescue mission.

To those who urge us to tone down our talk of the blood of Christ for the sake of modern sensibilities, we answer that they might as well ask a leopard to change his spots, for we are unable to remain silent about such a blessed thing. Like Paul, we've concluded that there's nothing else in which to boast except for the Cross of Christ and his blood shed for sinners (Gal. 6:14). As Spurgeon pointed out, even after we've joined him in glory, we'll forever sing praises to the Lamb that was slain, taking refuge in the fact that he suffered and bled on our behalf:

While the angels are singing "Hallelujah! Hallelujah! Hallelujah! Hallelujah!" we will bid them stop the song a moment, while we say, "He whom ye thus adore was once covered with bloody sweat." As we cast our crowns at his feet, we will say, "And he was once despised and rejected of men." Lifting up our eyes and saluting him as God over all, blessed for ever, we will remember the reed, the sponge, the vinegar, and the nails; and as we come to him and have fellowship with him, and he shall lead us beside the living fountains of water, we will remember the black brook of Kedron of which he drank, and the awful depths of the grave into which he descended. Amid all the splendours of heaven, we shall never forget the agony, and misery, and dishonor of earth; and even when they sing the loudest sonnets of God's love, and power, and grace, we will sing this after all, and before all, and above all, that Jesus the Son of God died for us, and this shall be our everlasting song—"He loved us and gave himself for us, and we have washed our robes, and made them white in the blood of the lamb."[6]

10

He Was Raised from the Dead

(JOHN 21:14)

The late D. James Kennedy used to say that Christianity lacked one thing that most other religions of the world possessed—a place to which its adherents could go and point with pride to the fact that the founder of their religion was buried there. Christians are unable to do so because the founder of our religion, though subjected to the reality of physical death, didn't remain in such a state but was seen by those who knew him only two days later, alive and well (nay—better than ever). Death's clutches were no match for his divine power. The grave could not hold him. It's to the empty tomb that Christians point with (biblical) pride and say, "Our Founder is not there, for he is risen!"

While "Jesus is Lord" is the most basic and primitive of Christian confessions, "he is risen" is the fact upon which it's based. The death of Jesus Christ on the cross together with his subsequent resurrection from the grave compose the central event of redemptive history. It's from these conjoined acts of God that all hope for human salvation depends. Without the resurrection, Christ's death on the cross would have been an empty gesture, devoid of any spiritual significance. It wouldn't have even been a noteworthy event on the landscape of first-century Judean society, much less the central event of world history.

But God didn't leave Christ in the grave to suffer decay. And in the act of raising him from the dead, the Father displayed to the whole world the significance of his Son's death on the cross, even if much of that world is unwilling to acknowledge that significance.

The Empty Tomb

The gospel accounts tell us that Jesus was crucified on Passover Friday between the hours of approximately 9 a.m. and 3 p.m. A sudden darkness over all the land marked the second half of this six-hour period (Matt. 27:45), undoubtedly signifying God's judgment upon both the sin that Christ was taking upon himself at that moment and the act of the crucifixion of his Son by sinful men.

After Jesus had yielded up his spirit on the cross, a rich man named Joseph of Arimathea asked the Roman governor, Pontius Pilate, if he could have the body of Jesus in order to bury it in a new tomb that he had cut out of a nearby rock. Pilate agreed, and Joseph gave the body of Jesus a proper, if hasty, burial. Joseph rolled a large stone against the door of the tomb, while Mary Magdalene and several other women disciples watched the proceedings from opposite the tomb (Matt. 27:57–61).

It was Friday evening, and the silence of the gospel accounts regarding the whereabouts of the apostles after Jesus died certainly leads to the impression that they had already fled the scene—just as they had done the night before after his arrest (Matt. 26:31, 56). In fact, there's no direct evidence that any of the apostles other than John was even present at the crucifixion (John 19:26). So it was left to those outside the apostolic band to see to it that Jesus' body received a proper burial.

The main reason that Jesus' body was given such a hasty burial was that the Sabbath began at sundown on Friday, and it wouldn't have been proper to leave his body on the cross during the time that

Jews were forbidden to work. The soldiers broke the legs of the other two men crucified next to Jesus in order to hasten their deaths. But Jesus had already died, so it was unnecessary to break his legs (John 19:33). Instead, one of the soldiers pierced Jesus' side with a spear to see if he was dead; blood and water flowed down, confirming that death had indeed already occurred (v. 34).

On Sunday morning, Mary Magdalene and several other female disciples (Luke 23:55–24:1) went to the tomb to anoint Jesus' body with spices that were traditionally used in Jewish burials. But when they arrived, they were met by a great earthquake and an angel of the Lord, who rolled back the stone and sat upon it. The angel told the women that Jesus wasn't there, for he was raised from the dead, and that they should go quickly and tell his disciples that he would meet them in Galilee (Matt. 28:2–8). As they prepared to do so, Jesus appeared to Mary and the other women and spoke to them, reiterating the words of the angel to go and tell his disciples of his resurrection (Matt. 28:9–10).

That same night, Jesus appeared to his disciples in Jerusalem. John tells us that Jesus showed the disciples his pierced hands and side, presumably because they couldn't otherwise believe what they were seeing. But one of the disciples, Thomas, was absent and expressed doubts about the reality of what the others had shared with him later. So the following Sunday, Jesus appeared again to the disciples. This time Thomas was present, and Jesus told the doubting disciple to place his fingers into his wounds, that he might believe what he was actually seeing with his own eyes. Thomas then did believe and exclaimed, "My Lord and My God" (John 20:19–28), the only appropriate response to such a wonderful discovery.

Over the forty days between Jesus' resurrection and his ascension into heaven, Jesus made several appearances to the disciples both in Jerusalem and Galilee. And he appeared not only to the Twelve but also on one occasion to over five hundred brethren at the same time (1 Cor. 15:6).

Perhaps it's emblematic of just how momentous the resurrection of Christ was that the apostles were caught off-guard by it. They shouldn't have been, however, for Jesus himself had told them on numerous occasions that he would have to suffer a cruel death but would be raised from the dead on the third day. Back in our introductory chapter, we looked at one such passage in which Peter's refusal to accept the inevitability of such a turn of events caused Jesus to rebuke him in the strongest of terms, "Get behind Me, Satan!" (Mark 8:33).

The apostles' initial reaction to the crucifixion and their failure to anticipate the fulfillment of Jesus' prophecy concerning his resurrection are even more surprising in light of the fact that Jesus' enemies seemed all too aware of his prophecy—and even took steps they hoped would prevent it from taking place. On the day following Jesus' crucifixion, the chief priests and Pharisees approached Pilate and requested that he post a guard at the tomb in order to prevent Jesus' disciples from removing his body secretly at night and then telling the people, "He is risen from the dead." Pilate agreed to their request and posted a guard detail at the tomb. But, of course, it was to no avail, for neither guards nor large stones are able to thwart the plan of God. And the angel's words to the women who arrived at the tomb that first Easter morning seem to be a mild rebuke for not having expected as much: "He is not here; for He is risen, as He said" (Matt. 28:6).

Over the centuries more than a few Christians have puzzled how Jesus could rise on the third day, when we know that he was in the tomb for less than forty-eight hours. Indeed, in all likelihood he was in the tomb for less than thirty-six hours or no more than a day and a half. This has led some to concoct alternative theories regarding the timing of events of the Passion Week. Some have argued that Jesus was crucified not on Friday, but Thursday. Some have even argued for a Wednesday crucifixion. But the gospel accounts are clear about the timing of the event: it was the day before the Sabbath (Mark 15:42–43; Luke 23:56), and for that reason the alternative explanations have never gained much traction with biblical scholars.

Rather, the problem that some have with the traditional dating of the biblical events reflects a failure to understand that first-century Jews didn't count time the same way that we do today. They spoke of time inclusively. In reckoning a period of time, they always included the day on which they spoke and any portion of a day that was involved in the period, as a full day. Jesus was in the tomb for a portion of two days (Friday and Sunday) and for the full day of Saturday. Thus, Sunday is the third day in first-century Jewish reckoning.

One might even conclude that Jesus was anticipating such confusion and attempting to provide guidance in this matter with a statement he made to the Pharisees recorded in Luke 13. When they warned Jesus to depart immediately because Herod was seeking to kill him, Jesus responded, "Go, tell that fox, 'Behold I cast out demons and perform cures today and tomorrow, and the third day I shall be perfected'" (v. 32). Clearly, we're justified in using this statement as a template for understanding Jesus' own prophecy that he would be raised on the third day. That translates into a Friday crucifixion and a Sunday resurrection, just as the church has always believed and taught.

The Post-Resurrection Preaching of the Apostles

Whatever fluctuation of spirit and resolve the apostles may have exhibited in the days leading up to the resurrection of Christ, they were new men after beholding him in his resurrected flesh. They went out and unabashedly proclaimed him as Savior of the world, and they did so in the face of severe persecution and rejection by their fellow Jews. Only ten days after Jesus' ascension into heaven, the apostolic band gathered for the traditional celebration of Pentecost, and Peter delivered a stirring sermon to the assembled crowd in Jerusalem in which he rebuked the Jews for their rejecting Christ. And the resurrection of Christ was the central component in Peter's teaching (see Acts 2:24–36), just as it would be in all of the sermons recorded for us in the book of Acts.

As far as the apostles were concerned, the resurrection is the clearest proof that Jesus is who he claimed to be and that God's raising him from the dead and exalting him on high was the final act in the redemptive drama that installed him forever as both Lord and Christ (Acts 2:32–36). Both Peter and Paul understood Psalm 16 ("For You will not leave my soul in Hades, nor will You allow Your Holy One to see corruption") as foretelling the resurrection of Christ, and both used it to great advantage in their preaching (Acts 2:25–31; 13:33–37).

What's so remarkable about the apostolic preaching in Acts isn't that they boldly proclaimed the resurrection of Christ—we should expect them to have done that—but that they did so in spite of the fact that it, more than any other aspect of their doctrine, was responsible for engendering the most vehement opposition and hatred from the enemies of the gospel. Of course, that merely underscores the fact that their enemies likewise understood the significance of the resurrection.

From Pentecost onward, the apostles fearlessly preached the resurrection of Christ to the people of Judea despite the opposition that it produced. The gospel accounts prove that they certainly would have faced stiff opposition and persecution even without the doctrine of the resurrection in hand, but the significance of that event ensured an even greater measure of resistance by those who wanted to put a stop to the preaching of the gospel.

By the time we get to the fourth chapter of Acts, we're able to see just how much trouble the preaching of the resurrection was causing the apostles. Acts 4:1–2 reads: "Now as they spoke to the people, the priests, the captain of the temple, and the Sadducees came upon them, being greatly disturbed that they taught the people and preached in Jesus the resurrection from the dead." In fact, on this occasion Peter and John were arrested for their preaching and placed in custody until the following day.

When Paul preached to the Athenians at the Areopagus (Mars Hill) in Acts 17, the assembled philosophers were eager to hear what he had to say (v. 20) and listened to his sermon with attentive ears. But when he mentioned the resurrection of the dead, some in the crowd mocked him (v. 32). Indeed, it's safe to say that Paul's later troubles with the religious and civil authorities were largely the result of this aspect of his preaching. When he defended himself before the

Sanhedrin (the Jewish ruling council in Jerusalem) after being arrested in the temple, he remarked that he was being judged "concerning the hope and resurrection of the dead" (23:6). Paul then reiterated this charge before the Roman governor Felix in Acts 24:21 and again in front of King Agrippa in Acts 26:6-8, where he called the resurrection "the hope of the promise made by God to our fathers."

God's Vindication of His Son

Of course, those who had opposed Jesus' ministry prior to his crucifixion understood (or at least should have understood) that his resurrection from the grave proved one thing in no uncertain terms: they had been wrong about him all along. It proved that he really was who he said he was—God's Son in the flesh and Israel's long-awaited Messiah. Christ's resurrection from the dead was a judgment upon his opponents' actions and the Father's vindication of his beloved Son and the work that he had accomplished.

Jesus' earthly work on behalf of sinners was accomplished when he cried out on the cross, "It is finished." But God's sending the angel to roll away the stone and bringing forth his son from the tomb prove to the world that Jesus' death is the atonement for sins that he promised. In the same way that the Old Testament priest, after he had offered the sacrifice on the altar, appeared before the people to prove that he hadn't been struck dead upon entering the Holy Place, Jesus' reappearance among the people proved that his sacrifice had been accepted by God.

According to Paul, it was by Christ's resurrection that he was "declared to be the Son of God with power" (Rom. 1:4), for it was through that act that God fulfilled the promise that he had made to the fathers of old (Acts 13:32). Paul even links Christ's resurrection to the prophecy of Psalm 2, where God the Father declared, "You are My Son, today I have begotten You" (Acts 13:33). Jesus didn't become the Son of God by his resurrection. But the resurrection declared to the whole world that he was now the Son of God *with power*. The resurrection was the final step in Christ's securing the nations for his eternal inheritance. All things have now been placed in subjection to him (Eph. 1:22; 1 Pet. 3:22), just as the Father had promised through David a thousand years earlier (Ps. 110:1).

The Power of Christ's Resurrection

The apostle Paul never tired of expounding the significance of Christ's resurrection. But he didn't write about it only from the perspective of what it says about Christ or meant for him. Rather, Paul was just as concerned to demonstrate what the resurrection of Christ means for us. Paul understood that God's raising his Son from the dead had tangible and glorious benefits for his people. He writes that Christ was "delivered up because of our offenses, and was raised because of our justification" (Rom. 4:25). It's the resurrection that makes it possible for Christ's righteousness to be imputed to all those who believe in him (vv. 22–24). And why is that the case? Geerhardus Vos articulates the essence of Paul's theology on this subject:

> Paul abhors and hates death because it is the wages—the penalty of sin. Whatever else it might be, to him it appeared first of all as a minister of condemnation, the personified, incarnate sentence of God against sin.... Now if this be [the] significance of death in general, it follows that the death of Christ in particular must be interpreted on the same principle. Christ was made sin on our behalf.... But if this be so, then the significance of the resurrection for the atoning work of Christ immediately springs into view. If the Savior's death was the embodiment of the curse which rests upon the world, then so long as he remained under the power of death there could be no assurance that satisfaction had been rendered, the condemnation of the divine wrath removed. On the other hand, as soon as at any point the process of death is suspended and life permitted

to emerge from death, this will be equivalent to a practical declaration on God's part that the curse has exhausted itself, the penalty been paid.... By raising Christ from death, God as the supreme Judge set His seal to the absolute perfection and completeness of his atoning work. The resurrection is a public announcement to the world that the penalty of death has been borne by Christ to its bitter end and that in consequence the dominion of guilt has been broken, the curse annihilated forevermore.... The very life of the exalted Christ is a witness to the blessed reality of the forgiveness of our sins.[1]

The resurrection of Christ wasn't merely some symbolic exclamation point that God placed upon the work that Christ accomplished by his death on the cross. Rather, it was part and parcel to the necessary complex of redemptive acts that God had ordained in eternity past for the salvation of sinners. This is why Paul could say that "if Christ is not risen ... you are still in your sins!" (1 Cor. 15:17). Even less does the resurrection represent an extraneous article of the faith that may be dispensed with by those who consider themselves too "enlightened" to believe such things in our modern age. Paul is very clear on this score: anyone who doesn't believe that God has raised Christ from the dead isn't a Christian, no matter what they may choose to call themselves (Rom. 10:9).

Our justification depends upon Christ's resurrection from the dead. Christians, who were once dead in their trespasses and sins, have been made alive together with Christ (Eph. 2:4–5), since it was impossible for us to be made alive without his having been so raised for our benefit.

In his letter to the church at Philippi, Paul writes that he desired to know Christ "and the power of His resurrection" (Phil. 3:10). Of course, the apostle was already redemptively united to Christ by faith and understood the power of his resurrection to bring that union into being. However, his emphasis here isn't on justification, but sanctification. Paul wanted to more fully experience the power to live a life wholly devoted to Christ. And he knew very well that Christ's resurrection is the source of such power, a point that he makes several times in his letter to the church at Rome (Rom. 6:4; 7:4; 8:11).

Christ's resurrection and ascension provided the basis for the Son dispatching the Holy Spirit to undertake the ongoing work of applying the benefits of his redemptive labors to those whom God has chosen for his own. It's the Spirit who brings people to faith (regeneration) and who gives them the power to live for Christ (sanctification). But neither work would be a reality if the One who called himself "the resurrection and the life" (John 11:25) didn't have the power to deliver on his promises.

Christ the Firstfruits

An unfortunate tendency in Christian circles today is to devalue the physical body, effectively adopting a view of humanity that's more akin to Greek philosophical dualism than the one espoused by Scripture. The ancient Greeks tended to view matter as inherently evil. And so it became popular to look upon the body as merely the prison house of the soul. Death thus became the gateway to true progress of the soul, which was freed up to exist without the encumbrances that characterize human nature.

This is hardly the view of Scripture, however. Man was created by God to be a physical being from the very beginning. Sin subsequently marred both body and soul, but God's redemptive acts are designed to bring both aspects of human beings back into their originally intended states. And Christ's resurrection from the dead is proof of such divine design. Paul writes that Christ is "the firstfruits" of all who have died or will die in the future, since he was raised from the dead and his soul reunited with his physical body forevermore (1 Cor. 15:20–23). In this way he has become the prototype for all believers, being the first to experience what will eventually transpire in their lives as well when in the twinkling of an eye the dead will be raised and every soul will be reunited to a then incorruptible and immortal body (1 Cor.

15:52–53). As in the case of Christ, that body will be the same one we inhabited in life, but it will now be glorified and no longer the "lowly body" we possessed from birth to death (Phil. 3:21). Scripture is vague as to precisely what that means for the physical abilities we'll possess in our immortal bodies. But it means that Christians will experience no more pain or suffering and no more sin.

On the other hand, for the unbeliever Christ is only the prototype in a general sense in that they, like he, will have body and soul reunited forever at Christ's Second Coming. But those who haven't trusted in Christ for their salvation will go not to the resurrection of life everlasting but to the resurrection of condemnation (John 5:28–29), where they'll suffer torment of both body and soul forever.

Christ is the first person to rise from the dead to newness of life in a glorified, spiritual body (Acts 26:23; 1 Cor. 15:44). But his rising is the guarantee that we'll follow in his footsteps one day. Christians who view death as a permanent separation of body and soul have a deficient understanding of both Christianity and Christ, for he's not our firstfruits if our bodies aren't also raised to newness of life with him.

The Effect of the Resurrection on the Apostles

From the very day of its occurrence, the enemies of Christianity have expended a great deal of time and effort trying to discredit the resurrection of Christ (Matt. 28:11–15). Every so often opponents put forth another ludicrous and fanciful theory in the hope of explaining away the event. And the fact that they have gone to such great lengths demonstrates that they understand the importance of the doctrine. But God has spoken in his Word and has left no doubt about the historicity and significance of the phenomenon. The New Testament church wouldn't exist without the resurrection of Christ from the grave.

Even the casual observer can't help but notice how the fact of the resurrection changed the demeanor of Christ's inner circle overnight. We noted above the prominence that the apostles gave to the resurrection in their preaching. But the fact that they even headed out to preach again after the crucifixion speaks to the transformation that occurred within the apostolic band after seeing the risen Christ. In a span of just seven short weeks, Peter went from being afraid of a little servant girl to standing up in front of thousands of hostile Jews in Jerusalem and proclaiming the name of Christ to them, while blaming them for crucifying him with their "lawless hands" (Acts 2:23).

John Calvin, the great Genevan reformer, believed that when Christ sent Mary Magdalene and the other women from the tomb to announce his resurrection to the disciples, he did so for the purpose of gently chastising those same disciples for their indifference.[2] Despite having told them on several occasions that he would be crucified and then rise from the grave, they appear to have seen the crucifixion event as the end of all their hopes and dreams. So Christ chose instead to make his initial post-resurrection appearance to these faithful women who had come to the tomb to anoint his body with spices and not to his inner circle of disciples who had been with him from the beginning of his public ministry. In first-century Judean society, women weren't even considered credible witnesses in a court of law.

But whether or not it was Jesus' design to shame his disciples in this way, the resurrection quickly turned those men into warriors for the faith. In no time at all they were staring down hostile mobs and civil authorities, preaching Christ crucified, being jailed, undergoing beatings, and even experiencing death for their efforts. Within a few years they would be accused of having turned the world upside down with their doctrine and preaching (Acts 17:6). And yet none of this would have occurred if Christ hadn't first been raised from the dead. Sunday would be just another day on the weekly calendar, and not the Lord's Day, a perpetual memorial of his entering into his own Sabbath rest after his earthly labors were complete.

When Jesus appeared to his disciples for the first time in his resurrected body, he showed them his hands, feet, and side (Luke 24:40; John 20:20). The apostle Thomas would later place his own fingers into those wounds in order to confirm Jesus' identity as the One who had truly suffered and died on the tree. His resurrected body had put on incorruptibility and immortality and appears to have had fewer limitations on movement than had been the case previously (John 20:26). But it still bore the scars from the wounds that soldiers had inflicted upon him at his crucifixion—wounds that he received as judgment for our sins. One day those wounds will be visible to us as well. They'll serve as an eternal reminder of the work that Jesus accomplished on our behalf. And we'll view them courtesy of the resurrection—his and ours.

11

He Was the King of the Jews

(MATT. 27:11)

Although there are several serious contenders for the award, there's perhaps no other truth statement about Christ that has spawned as much confusion and bad theology as the one under consideration here. That Jesus Christ was indeed the King of the Jews is a simple statement of fact, confirmed by him when the Roman governor Pontius Pilate interrogated him the night before his crucifixion (Matt. 27:11). But the meaning and significance of that statement has become obscured and mired in various misunderstandings, particularly in the last century or two, as new schools of theological thought have developed within the broader Christian church.

The goal of the present chapter is to examine what the statement meant in its original context, as well as what it means for us today. We'll look into a number of related issues, such as: (1) the nature of Jewish identity both before and after Jesus' earthly ministry; (2) the nature of the relationship between the saints of the Old Testament era and those of the New; (3) the identity of the people of God and what makes one a member of that community; and 4) the nature of the kingdom that Christ introduced with his arrival. All of these issues are in one way or another affected by the discussion here.

The Arrival of the King

Aside from the events that occurred in conjunction with Jesus' birth, there's no indication that anyone in the nation of Israel was aware of the presence of their long-awaited King for the next thirty years. Of course, it's likely that word of the birth of Israel's Messiah/King had spread throughout the land during those intervening years and was probably responsible for much of the messianic fervor prevalent in the first century AD. The people of Israel in AD 30 may have been expecting a different kind of King than Jesus turned out to be, and a different kind of deliverance than he offered them, but they were definitely waiting for a King to take his rightful place upon the throne of David, fulfilling a promise God had made to them a thousand years earlier.

Jesus, however, wasn't your everyday, run-of-the-mill Israelite king. Any other hereditary king of the nation could have rightly taken his place on the throne at a young age, as many had in previous centuries. But Jesus embodied within his person all three of the sacred offices that God had instituted for the nation of Israel—prophet, priest, and king. And it was only after being installed as the nation's great High Priest (at his baptism) that Jesus took upon himself the mantle of royalty. Immediately after receiving baptism, Jesus was led up by the Spirit to do battle with the devil in the wilderness, and upon his return from that encounter he began to preach repentance to the people for "the kingdom of heaven is at hand" (Matt. 4:17). Jesus went on to prove to the people that he had ushered in the kingdom of God by giving sight to the blind, healing the sick, preaching the gospel to poor sinners, and casting out demons by the Spirit of God (Matt. 11:2–6; 12:28).

As was fitting for such a King, his subjects (the Jews) weren't your run-of-the-mill people group, either. The Jews descended from Abraham, a man plucked out of obscurity and idol worship in a far-off country and sent by God to the land that would become the nation of

Israel. In doing so, God promised Abraham three significant things:
(1) he would have descendants as numerous as the stars in the sky;
(2) those descendants would one day possess the land to which God
was leading him; and (3) through him (and his descendants) all the
families of the earth would be blessed (Gen. 12:1–3; 15:5).

The descendants of Abraham thus enjoyed a special privilege; they
were a part of the nation that God would use to spread his gospel
message to the whole world. They would receive the covenants
and promises that God offered to a sinful human race in need of
redemption, and they would be the repository of his holy law given
at Mount Sinai. The descendants of Abraham were to be a light
shining in the darkness, serving as a testimony to God's goodness
and mercy to every other nation on earth. And they were the nation
through whom the Light of the World, Jesus Christ, would descend
to complete the work of redemption on God's behalf.

God's people, as embodied in the nation of Israel, didn't originally
have a king. God alone was to be their King and direct ruler. And
for nearly a thousand years after Abraham's journey from Ur to the
land of Canaan, that was the case. Although the Israelites were at
times ruled by military leaders, called judges, or by great figures such
as Moses and Joshua, it was a mark of their distinctiveness that they
had no king to rule over them, except for God himself.

All of that changed sometime in the eleventh century BC, however,
when God acquiesced to the Israelites' request for an earthly king.
Saul became the first king of Israel, but David was God's real choice
to rule the nation. So when David acceded to the throne, God
turned the unfaithfulness of the Israelites to their own advantage by
establishing an everlasting kingdom through David's descendants—
more precisely, through one particular descendant, from whom
God's mercy would never depart (2 Sam. 7:12–16). Of course, that
descendant is none other than Jesus Christ (Luke 1:32–33), the Son
of both David and Abraham (Matt. 1:1).

Whatever privileges and blessings attached to being a descendant of
Abraham, however, they had nothing to do with their recipients being
worthy to receive them. The Jews weren't chosen to be God's peculiar

possession because of any inherent qualities that marked them off for special blessing. On the contrary, being a Jew was strictly a matter of descent. More importantly, being Jewish didn't make one a believer, as the history of the nation so aptly demonstrates. God showered the same outward covenantal blessings upon believers and unbelievers alike. And there were even some from outside of the nation, known as Gentiles, who received God's grace to believe the gospel.

In this sense, then, we may say that the Jews were as run-of-the-mill as any other people group on earth. They were just as much in need of God's grace to turn from their sins as was any Gentile nation or person. It was God setting his love on Israel that made it a great nation, not the other way around. The Jews didn't merit God's blessing upon them; they received it as a matter of grace. And it's right here that so many in Jesus' day went off track in their thinking. Relying exclusively on their physical descent from Abraham, many of them began to take God's blessings for granted. They considered their racial origin to be proof of God's divine favor upon them individually. This was especially the case with the Pharisees, who took refuge in their descent from Abraham when Jesus confronted them for their harsh and unloving attitude toward others. With such a mindset holding sway among the religious leaders of Jerusalem in AD 30, the stage was set for a confrontation of epic proportions when Jesus arrived upon the scene, preaching the gospel of the kingdom.

Rejected by the Nation

The rejection that ultimately resulted from that confrontation didn't develop immediately, however. For the most part, the initial response of the people to Jesus' preaching was favorable. Great crowds gathered to hear him, and many became his disciples, following him wherever he traveled throughout the land of Palestine. To be sure, some came because they got their bellies filled or were healed from an infirmity. But others found hope in his message of God's grace toward sinners, a message that their leaders seem to have forgotten somewhere along the way.

This helps to explain why Jesus' relationship with the religious authorities in Jerusalem was rocky from the start. They didn't appreciate his message of grace, and they resented the influence he was beginning to exert over the populace. And so after Jesus had been among the people for about three-and-a-half years, the nation's religious leadership began to plot against him, hoping to have him killed and to put an end to his undermining their own authority and teachings.

Their plotting became that much easier as more and more of the people began to turn away from Jesus as well. Some were put off by his uncompromising gospel message (Matt. 19:22; John 6:66), while others were undoubtedly disappointed that he wasn't turning out to be the military rescuer for whom they had been waiting. When Jesus entered Jerusalem for the final time during the Passover Week, there were still enough committed followers awaiting his arrival that "a great multitude" went out to meet him, laying down palm branches before him and shouting, "Hosanna! 'Blessed is He who comes in the name of the Lord!' The King of Israel!" (John 12:12–13).

What a difference a few days would make, however. By Friday of the same week, the cry of the people would change from "Hosanna, King of Israel" to "Crucify Him." When given a choice by Pilate to have either Jesus or a notorious murderer named Barabbas released from custody, they chose Barabbas. Although Luke 23:23 intimates that Jesus still had his defenders among those assembled in Jerusalem for the Passover Feast, they were drowned out by the rest of the multitude and the influence of the chief priests. The nation had now formally rejected its Savior and King.

It's wrongly assumed by many that Jesus was executed because of his claim to be a king, which resulted in his being found guilty of treason to Rome. But this is a complete misunderstanding, one that has been propagated over the years by those who wish to portray Jesus as nothing more than a political revolutionary who ran afoul of the Romans for his royal claims. Although the Jewish authorities appealed to Jesus' claim to be the King when they brought him to Pilate (Luke 23:2), Matthew 26:63–66 demonstrates conclusively that that they sought to kill him for his claim to be divine. The charge against him was blasphemy, not treason. And Matthew 27 proves that Pilate didn't want to condemn Christ for making such a claim (vv. 11, 23). The governor seems to have understood all too well that the nature of the Jews' complaint against Jesus was religious, not political (v. 18).

Received by the Israel of God

In the prologue to his gospel account, the apostle John pens the following words concerning Jesus Christ: "He came to His own, and His own did not receive Him. But as many as received Him, to them He gave the right to become children of God, to those who believe in His name: who were born, not of blood, nor of the will of the flesh, nor of the will of man, but of God" (John 1:11–13). In this short passage, John makes three very important points: (1) Christ was rejected by his own people group (the Jews); (2) some individuals nevertheless did receive him and believed in his name; and (3) those who believed did so by the will of God.

When Christ came preaching the gospel of the kingdom, he did so primarily (though not exclusively) among the Jewish population of Palestine. This was natural, since he was himself a Jew and living in the land of Galilee. But it's also to be expected because it was God's design that the gospel would go to the Jew first and then the Gentile (Rom. 1:16). The covenants and promises were given to the Jews, and they were the ones to whom the Messiah was to be sent in fulfillment of those promises.

However, the great mass of Jesus' fellow countrymen rejected him. They chose instead to side with their religious leaders and lobby Pilate for his death. As John said, "His own did not receive Him."

Yet John's statement is susceptible to misunderstanding. There's even a sense in which the statement isn't true, but that sense isn't the one that John intends in this verse. Rather, it's obvious from the context that John is speaking of the Israelite nation (the Jewish people) when he refers to Jesus being rejected by "His own." From a racial and national perspective, the Jews were Jesus' own people. They were his blood kinsmen, descendants of Abraham.

John's statement is also intended to be a general statement of truth. Not all of the descendants of Abraham rejected him, as John goes on to tell us in the next sentence. But it was nevertheless true that as a people group and nation viewed collectively, the Jews had rejected their Messiah.

Still, we misunderstand John if we read his statement in a spiritual sense. Those who rejected Jesus weren't his spiritual kinsmen. They were not "His own" with respect to the mission for which he came: to save *his people* from their sins. Christ's people hear his voice, and they follow him (John 10:27). And because this is always the case, we may say that Christ has never been rejected by one who was spiritually "His own."

The importance of this truth lies in the fact that many Christians fail to make the proper connections and distinctions between the people of God in the Old and New Testaments and the terms that refer to them. A great deal of confusion and bad theology has resulted from a failure to recognize that the Bible uses the terms *Jew*, *Israel*, and even *Abraham's seed* in both a physical and a spiritual sense. Practically speaking, the ways in which this deficiency of thinking reveals itself is a tendency to see two different peoples of God with different paths to salvation, to be unaware of what makes one a part of the people of God today, and to be confused about how present-day (physical) Jews fit into that community.

But the Bible isn't really difficult to understand at this point. Rather, it's in our failure as Christians to adequately acquaint ourselves with all of Scripture that we have tended to adopt a theological view that results in confused answers to the questions above. Being familiar with only part of the biblical story of redemption will likely make one err at this crucial point of theology. On the other hand, having a firm grasp on how the Bible uses the terms that describe the people of God tends to bring clarity to the entire story of biblical redemption. In the most abbreviated manner possible, what follows is a summary of the Bible's teaching on this subject.

First, the terms *Jew*, *Israel*, and *Abraham's seed* typically refer to the visible people of God in the Old Testament period. That is, they primarily designate the descendants of Abraham, who made up a distinct people group and nation. The Israelite nation and race came into existence through the direct intervention and activity of God, who desired to establish a nation that would witness to his glory to the entire world. In this sense, then, they were the visible people of God. Every member of the nation of Israel was a part of the community of people that God had chosen to be his witnesses on earth.

But being an Israelite (or later, a Jew) didn't make one a part of God's people in the spiritual sense. That still required a separate work of the Spirit in the heart, and it was not guaranteed to anyone on the basis of his or her descent from Abraham. Indeed, there were times in the history of the nation when almost none were true believers. When the prophet Elijah despaired that there was no one left who was a true child of Israel except for himself, God assured him that he still had seven thousand true believers left in the nation (1 Kings 19:18). But at the time the population of the nation numbered in the millions!

When we come to the New Testament, however, the apostle Paul employs each of these three terms in a spiritual sense as well, as a designation for the true people of God, whether they're of Jewish or Gentile extraction. In Rom. 2:28–29, Paul says, "For he is not a Jew who is one outwardly…but he is a Jew who is one inwardly." In other words, true Jewishness consists not in one's racial origin but in possessing the proper spiritual condition of belief in Christ. The apostle John says essentially the same thing in Revelation 3:9.

Paul makes a similar argument in Romans 9:6, where he writes, "For they are not all Israel who are of Israel." Paul's statement here has two possible meanings. He could be speaking only of those who were of Jewish heritage. In that case, he would be distinguishing between elect Jews and all of those who are descendants of Abraham (those who are *of Israel*). On the other hand, he may be using the term *all Israel* to refer to the elect of God from all nations, in order to demonstrate that this designation for the people of God isn't limited to only those of Jewish extraction or to a particular nation or time.

Though it's possible that given the context, either interpretation of Romans 9:6 may be the correct one, Paul's epistle to the Galatians proves beyond a doubt that the appellation Israel is one that applies to those of any national or racial background, provided they have trusted in Christ. Paul wrote Galatians to counter the doctrine of the Judaizers, those of Jewish heritage who were teaching that believers in Christ must follow the Old Testament ceremonial law and be circumcised in order to be full members of the church. Paul wrote that, in Christ, "There is neither Jew nor Greek" (3:28) and that all those who believe in him constitute one people, "the Israel of God" (6:16; cf. Heb. 8:10). Moreover, those of whatever racial stripe who are Christ's "are Abraham's seed, and heirs according to the promise" (3:29).

The significance of all of this should be obvious. While the appellation *Christian* is the most appropriate one for those who trust in Christ (now that he has come and completed his work), it's merely the latest (and last) designation for the people of God that he has given to us in his Word. There is, however, an important distinction between this term and those that preceded it; it's a designation that's completely spiritual in its essence. It signifies all of those, and only those, who have truly placed their trust in Christ for salvation. It refers not to any visible collection of individuals, as was the case with the terms *Jew* and *Israel* but only to those who are a part of the invisible church, the true people of God.

Christians today, along with all believers who have come before them (including the Old Testament saints), make up the Israel of God and are Abraham's seed according to the promise of election. They are true Jews, those who are Jews inwardly, not merely in an outward (physical) sense. Those who are merely physical descendants of Abraham aren't a part of the people of God in either a visible or invisible sense. Jesus told a group of Pharisees who appealed to their descent from Abraham that they weren't Abraham's children, but children of the devil! (John 8:33–44).

Moreover, there's an important fact of biblical history that Christians frequently overlook today. In the book of Hebrews (7:1–11), the writer reminds his readers that long before the nation of Israel was established as a distinct people group, Jerusalem had a king named Melchizedek. Indeed, he wasn't only a king but a priest of the Most High God as well, which makes him a type of Christ himself, who is the only other person to ever hold both offices together. But the real significance of Melchizedek's identity is that the patriarch Abraham paid tribute to him and received a blessing from him. Since, as the writer points out, the lesser is always blessed by the greater, such an act on Abraham's part proved his recognition of Melchizedek's superiority.

But if Melchizedek, a Gentile, was superior to the patriarch of the Israelite nation, and if his priesthood and kingship predated those of Aaron and David, respectively, what does that have to say about the flow of biblical history, and the place of the Jews within it? When all is said and done, the significance of this reality can hardly be overstated: Abraham, the father of the Jews, paid homage and tribute to a Gentile king!

What the subsequent history of the nation shows us is that with the first advent of Christ, the national character of the church of God became a thing of the past. The nation of Israel was judged for its execution of the Savior in AD 70, when the Romans destroyed the temple and scattered abroad the inhabitants of Jerusalem for the final time. And all of this was according to the plan and purpose of God.

People in the Old Testament period were saved in the same way that we in the New Testament period are saved—by faith in Christ. The faith of the Old Testament saints may have been a prospective one, since they lived on the other side of Christ's earthly work, but it was faith in Christ nonetheless (Heb. 11). Was Abraham a Christian? Of course he was! Is a Christian today a spiritual Jew and descendant of Abraham? Of course he or she is. There's one people of God throughout all of human history, made up of all those who have placed their faith in Christ.

A Kingdom Not of This World

At this point, the perceptive reader may be asking what all of this has to do with the statement that Christ was the King of the Jews. Actually, there are at least three ways in which a grasp of the preceding discussion impacts our understanding of the statement. First, an awareness of the physical/spiritual distinction should keep us from being shocked by the Jews' rejection of their King. Although they're without excuse for having done so, it's merely evidence that the spiritual condition of the nation when Christ came wasn't much different than it had been in Elijah's day. The vast majority of those who were Abraham's physical descendants were simply not his spiritual descendants and thus not interested in the salvation that Christ offered. It's no surprise, then, that they rejected him. The same thing happens every day in the lives of those who have no use for Christ or his gospel.

Second, an understanding of the temporary and provisional nature of the national aspect of God's people gives us insight into the purposes of God in ordaining that Christ would be rejected. The rejection of Christ by the nation didn't result in God having to switch to a Plan B in order to accomplish the redemption of his people; rather, it was precisely the means that he had intended for doing so (Acts 2:23). And this was so, not simply because Christ needed to die for our sins (though that was certainly the case), but also because the nation's rejection of its King started the chain of events that God would use to send the gospel forth to all nations. The rejection of Christ in AD 30, the persecution of his disciples that followed, and the destruction of Jerusalem a few decades later all contributed to the spread of the gospel message, as God had intended all along.

The gospel was never meant to be the exclusive possession of any one nation. And by ordaining the end to the nation of Israel, God was advancing his redemptive plan to the next stage. No longer would he work only through a specific people group and nation. Instead, he was breaking down the "middle wall of separation" that had previously existed between Jew and Gentile and uniting them into his one church on an equal basis forevermore (Eph. 2:14–18).

Finally, the preceding discussion has hopefully clarified the issue of how we should apply the statement that "Christ was the King of the Jews" to our modern religious situation. It should be obvious by now that we err horribly if we take this statement to mean that Christ's kingship is limited in its sphere to a certain people group or nation. Jesus told Pilate that his kingdom was not of this world (John 18:36), which is to say that his kingdom is a spiritual one. This isn't to deny that as the Creator of the Universe, Christ is the owner of all and is rightly considered King over everything and everyone. But because his kingdom is first and foremost a spiritual one, those who don't recognize his reign are not his people in the spiritual sense, no matter what racial identity they may have. Christ's sheep hear his voice, and they come to him in submissive faith (John10:27).

Unfortunately, many Christians stumble badly at this point. Even some who are able to articulate the biblical gospel quite well seem to lose their way when confronted with the question of how modern Jews fit into this discussion. In some cases, the gospel message is completely compromised by a theology that seems to allow for two paths to eternal salvation—one by the blood of Christ and an alternative way by the bloodline of one's physical descent.

Moreover, some Christians mistakenly believe that the only thing that separates them from the modern religious Jew is the latter's lack of acceptance of Jesus as the Messiah. But such an assessment misses the mark entirely and only serves to demonstrate a lack of familiarity with both the Bible and modern Judaism. Scripture is clear on this point: The Judaism of today is not the religion of the Old Testament.

Even those in Jesus' own day who rejected him cannot be said to have been followers of the Old Testament religion, no matter how pious they may have otherwise appeared on the surface. Jesus told the Jews of his day that if they believed Moses, they would believe him (John 5:46). The simple fact is that the Old Testament saints were believers in Christ. Those who reject him thus bear no spiritual relationship whatsoever to Abraham, Moses, or any of the other faithful saints of that time period.

That's sufficient to prove the point, but many Christians also fail to recognize that modern Judaism doesn't merely reject Jesus' Messiahship but his divine identity as well. Whereas God reveals himself in the Bible to be a Triune being, Judaism has abandoned that belief in favor of a Unitarian view. When combined with the fact that the brand of Judaism that eventually won out in the course of Jewish history subsequent to the rejection of Christ was that of the Pharisees, the complete discontinuity of modern Judaism with the religion of the Old Testament should be obvious.

The sad irony is that in response to an otherwise laudable impulse to keep from offending, many Christians have effectively adopted a theological position that isn't only antithetical to the gospel message but hardly loving in its attitude toward modern Jews—they have determined that the gospel isn't to be offered to those of Jewish persuasion. Ultimately, however, such thinking runs directly contrary to the Bible's injunction to preach the gospel to every creature under heaven.

As Christians, we should stop being schizophrenic in our description and understanding of the people of God. There has never been more than one people of God at any time in human history, and there has never been more than one way to eternal life. Christians who suggest (even implicitly) that modern Jews might be able to rely upon their racial heritage to get them into heaven have mangled the gospel message in the worst possible manner. The New Testament couldn't be any more emphatic on this point than it is (Matt. 3:9; John 8:38; Rom. 9:8; Gal. 3:28).

To be sure, there was a physical aspect to the original title King of the Jews, for as long as the nation existed, it was Christ's prerogative to take his rightful place on David's throne and rule over the physical descendants of Abraham. But God's purpose for a separate nation to be his peculiar possession has run its course, and his redemptive plan doesn't move backward, but forward. Thus, we do well to stop trying to erect a new middle wall of separation between those whom God has united in one body.

That body includes all of those, and only those, who claim him as their King, regardless of their ancestry. The only pedigree that matters to God is faith in his Son. All such people are counted among those for whom he came to give his life as a ransom. They are counted as the true spiritual seed of Abraham. And the One for whom the spiritual seed was waiting, Christ, the King of the Jews, has now taken upon himself a new royal title—KING OF KINGS and LORD OF LORDS (Rev. 19:16).

12

He Was the End of the Law

(Rom. 10:4)

At the risk of repeating my introductory remarks from the last chapter, we deal here with another truth statement about Christ that has resulted in a great deal of confusion and bad theology over the centuries. Actually, these two chapters are closely related in that the modern confusion surrounding both statements tends to spring from the same theological source—an error known as dispensationalism.

We'll come back to discuss how dispensationalism plays into this controversy in more detail later. For now, the basic issue is how to understand Paul's statement in Romans 10:4 that "Christ is the end of the law for righteousness to everyone who believes." Does this mean, as some have suggested, that the law of God (however we may define that) is no longer binding upon the Christian? Was the law only for those who came prior to Christ's incarnation and work, or does it still apply to us today? Are Christians free to do as they please, or are they in some sense still bound by God's commands as revealed in Scripture? And if the latter, in what sense—and to which commands—are they bound? Moreover, how are we to reconcile this statement of Paul's with Christ's statement that "till heaven and earth pass away, one jot or one tittle will by no means pass from the law till all is fulfilled" (Matt. 5:18)? These are the questions we will seek to answer in the present chapter.

Biblical Law

It goes without saying that the meaning of Paul's statement can only be rightly discerned by first discovering what he means by the *law* and its modifying phrase "for righteousness." Once we have grasped this, Paul's meaning becomes abundantly clear. The only difficulty presented by this undertaking is to recognize that Scripture uses the term *law* in a variety of ways and with reference to different portions of God's revealed will.

In various places the Bible uses the term to refer to the law given to Adam in the covenant of works, the first five books of the Bible, the Mosaic Law in general, the ceremonial law, the national law of Israel, the Ten Commandments, or the entire Old Testament revelation. Although it's not always a simple matter to determine which meaning of *law* is intended, the particular context in which the word appears will usually lead the reader to the right interpretation. Of course, in a large number of the cases it's not altogether critical to know the particular sense in which the biblical writer uses the term. In other cases, like the one under consideration here, the issue isn't so much which sense of the law is being used but the purposes for which one seeks to keep the law. This latter point also helps explain why the law is sometimes spoken of in a decidedly negative sense, while in other passages it's given an altogether positive cast.

Although a comprehensive analysis of biblical law is beyond the scope or needs of our discussion here, it will nevertheless be helpful to begin where most such discussions do—with an explanation of the three categories of biblical law: the civil, the ceremonial, and the moral. All of the various commands found in the Bible fit into one or more of these categories.

The first category, that of the civil or judicial law, consists of laws given to the nation of Israel to guide the people in their daily lives as a body politic. Thus, they deal with matters such as making restitution for injuries to other persons or their property, the proper method for adjudicating disputes, and appropriate sanctions for violations of the criminal code.

The second category, the ceremonial law, concerns Israel's religious life. These laws set forth, often in precise detail, the regulations relating to the nation's worship of God. All of the stipulations concerning the priests, the temple, the various sacrifices, the Sabbath regulations, and the laws of purification fall into this category.

The third category, the moral law, consists primarily, though not exclusively, of the Ten Commandments given at Mount Sinai. Although any other commands or proscriptions falling into this category are essentially just applications of the Ten Commandments, to the extent that they offer more explicit guidance to us in what constitutes obedience to God, they too may be considered to be a part of the moral law. Jesus' commands to turn the other cheek and to love our enemies are examples of such moral strictures.

Christ as the Last Adam

Man has been subject to the law of God ever since the first man, Adam, was given life and placed in the Garden of Eden. The original covenant relationship between God and Adam consisted of a covenant of works, whereby the first man was bound to perfect obedience to God's revealed will, the fulfilling of which would result in eternal life for him and all of his posterity but with spiritual and physical death the threatened punishment for the breach of it. God gave to Adam and Eve the power and ability to keep the law, but they nevertheless failed their test of obedience by eating from the tree of the knowledge of good and evil in direct violation of God's express command to them.

From that point forward, Adam and Eve needed divine grace. They stood condemned by the law of God and were under its threatened curse. The rightful judgment of the Lord lay upon them and all their posterity. Only a Redeemer could reverse the effect of the fall and deliver Adam and Eve from their sin. And that's precisely what God immediately provided for them. He intervened directly by clothing them with animal skins, signifying that their sinfulness (as experienced in their awareness of their nakedness before him) was being covered and that the threatened penalty of death was being inflicted upon a substitute in their place. Moreover, he promised that a future Redeemer would come and crush the serpent's head once and for all (Gen. 3:15), providing the redemption of which Adam and his spiritual posterity were now in need.

In time, God would institute a system of sacrifices designed to point the way toward the salvation that this future Redeemer would provide through his own shed blood. Indeed, from all appearances the use of sacrifices began immediately upon God's clothing of Adam and Eve, since we see in the very next chapter the story of Cain and Abel bringing their offerings to the Lord (Gen. 4:3–5). Eventually, of course, God would provide the people of Israel with an elaborate and detailed ceremonial system to govern their worship of him and to point their attention forward to the work of Jesus Christ on the cross.

When Christ finally came, he who was made under the law (Gal. 4:4) fulfilled the requirements of the covenant of works that Adam had transgressed, just as he said he would do in the Sermon on the Mount (Matt. 5:17). He thereby redeemed his people and removed from them the curse of the law that had held them in bondage (Gal. 3:13), becoming, as Paul calls him, the "last Adam" (1 Cor. 15:45). Whereas the first Adam had plunged all humanity into sin and death, the last Adam's obedience to the covenant provided the means of escape for all those made righteous by his death (Rom. 5:19). For them, "there is therefore now no condemnation" (Rom. 8:1). By his work, Christ has "wiped out the handwriting of requirements that was against us…having nailed it to the cross" (Col. 2:14).

The End of the Law for Righteousness

This is the great theme of Paul's letter to the church at Rome: we're saved solely on the basis of Christ's work on our behalf and not by anything we have done or can do for ourselves. An individual sinner is declared righteous (i.e., justified) on the basis of that work through faith, which itself is the gift of God to the elect—and such faith is completely apart from the deeds of the law (Rom. 3:28). In short, we're incapable of being saved by any means other than by trusting in the finished work of Christ on our behalf; but when an individual does so, God imputes the righteousness of Christ to his account, and his sins are covered forever (Rom. 4:6–8). God still demands perfect righteousness on the part of all those who would enter his heaven, but he has provided it himself in the finished work of Christ, who fulfilled the law in all of its particulars.

This is why Paul says that Christ is the end of the law "for righteousness." The first Adam could have secured righteousness for himself and his posterity through perfect obedience to the law, but failed to do so. After that, no man had the ability to meet the demands of the law except Jesus Christ, who was born without the taint of original sin. But man was still liable to God to keep the whole law, even if he was now incapable of doing so. Thus, the law served to condemn man; it brought God's wrath with it (Rom. 4:15) and held everyone under its curse (Gal. 3:13). By fulfilling the law, Christ freed believers from its condemning aspects (Rom. 7:4, 6) and put an end to it as the way to righteousness, for his work needs no repetition. It's sufficient for all who embrace him by faith and who no longer trust in their own righteousness, but in his (Phil. 3:9).

On the other hand, the law retains its condemning character for those who persist in relying upon their own righteousness to gain standing with God (Gal. 3:10). Christ is only the end of the law for righteousness to "everyone who believes" and for no others. Only those who believe that God justifies the ungodly have their faith accounted for righteousness (Rom. 4:5).

That such was the intended meaning of Paul's statement is obvious from the context in which it appears. Paul is lamenting the fact that so few of his countrymen have embraced Christ, and he identifies the reason as none other than the fact that they were "seeking to establish their own righteousness" rather than submitting to the righteousness of God (10:3). But Paul has already made it abundantly clear that no one will be saved on the basis of his or her own works. And that isn't something that's true only prospectively, as if prior to Christ's completed work some persons had actually attained righteousness by way of the law. Rather, since the fall of Adam no human being has ever even had the opportunity to do so. Salvation has always been by grace alone and not by the works of the law. To prove the point, Paul earlier cites both Abraham and David as examples of those who were saved by their faith alone (4:1–12).

Unfortunately, more than a few Christians these days seem unaware of this most important of biblical facts. Under the influence of earlier dispensational theology, they imagine that the Old Testament saints were saved by their fidelity to the law. Thus, Christ was the end of the age (or dispensation) of law and the initiator of the dispensation of grace, wherein the terms of salvation have been altered. But Paul's treatise on justification in the letter to the Romans (as well as his other writings) leaves no room for doubt that this form of thinking is contrary to Scripture. The apostle reminds us that the Old Testament itself testifies to the fact that man is justified by faith alone (Rom. 1:17; 4:3-8; Gal. 3:6–14). And far from voiding the law, it's thereby that the law is established (Rom. 3:31).

Christ and the Moral Law

Returning to the questions with which we began our discussion, in what sense is the Christian still under the law of God? Does any portion of it still have binding authority as to us? If so, what portion(s)? Does affirming that Christ has fulfilled the law in its entirety mean that the Christian is free from its authority forever and may do as he or she pleases without regard for what it commands or prohibits?

Thus far we've looked at how Paul's statement that "Christ is the end of the law for righteousness" has a very narrow meaning, being limited to pronouncing the fulfillment of the covenant of works to which man was still subject until Christ completed his work. Although the covenant had promised righteousness to anyone who kept the law perfectly (Rom. 2:1–16), only Adam and Christ had the opportunity to fulfill the obligations contained therein—and the latter succeeded where the former had failed. No one can add a thing to what Christ has done, and to attempt to do so is to store up wrath for oneself. In this sense, then, the law that leads to righteousness (the covenant of works) is a thing of the past for those who believe.

The same thing may be said with respect to the ceremonial law. Because its main purpose was to point people to Christ by reminding them of their need for atonement from sin, it became obsolete when Christ finished his earthly work and presented himself to the Father in heaven (Heb. 8:13; 9:23–28). To return to the ceremonies of the Old Testament period after Christ has died and risen is to "serve the copy and shadows of the heavenly things" (Heb. 8:5) and to "trample the Son of God underfoot" (Heb. 10:29).

By the time Jesus came, the civil law in Israel was largely a thing of the past, since the Romans had occupied the nation for some time. Although traces of the civil law can still be seen in the gospel accounts (e.g., John 8:5), the Roman occupation of Palestine placed great restraints on the administration of the Israelite civil law. With the destruction of Jerusalem in AD 70, Israelite civil law was laid to rest once and for all. Christians are no longer subject to the civil law except as "the general equity thereof may require," as the Westminster Confession of Faith (19:4) puts it.

This brings us to the moral law of God. Is it too, like the civil and ceremonial law, a thing of the past now that Christ has come and ushered in the new covenant age? There are some who seem to think so. There is a general perception in some quarters that Jesus came as a "kinder, gentler Moses," who set about to replace the harsh demands of the old covenant law with an easier, more relationship-centered ethic summed up by the command to love our neighbor as ourselves. The case of the woman caught in adultery is frequently cited in support of this theory.

But those who argue in that manner seem to have missed altogether the significance of Jesus' statement, for he didn't proclaim the command to love our neighbor as a replacement for the second table of the Ten Commandments but as a summary of it (Matt. 22:39; cf. Rom. 13:9). Moreover, he called his disciples not merely to an outward obedience to the letter of the law but to a deeper, inward obedience that's vastly more difficult to live up to. For example, Jesus expanded the sixth commandment from a prohibition of murder into a prohibition of being angry at another without cause, which is committing murder in the heart (Matt. 5:21–22). Indeed, Jesus called Christians to a life of perfect obedience to the moral law of God (Matt. 5:48). And even though the Word of God is clear that none of us will ever attain to such a standard in this life, it remains our standard nonetheless, for we emulate our Savior in seeking to live such a life.

In Hebrews 2:2–3 (cf. 12:25), the writer employs a lesser-to-the-greater argument to make the point that if the law given by angels at Mount Sinai carried consequences for disobedience, how much more should we fear if we "neglect so great a salvation" that came by the hand of an even greater messenger—the Son of God. In commenting upon this verse, Richard Phillips writes:

> These words should dispel the common notion that the new covenant, or the New Testament, is an easier law than the old covenant.... If we think the New Testament represents God rejecting judgment and embracing an undiscriminating love for everyone, we can be corrected merely by remembering the woes Jesus pronounced on the Pharisees.... Jesus presents Old Testament laws in terms of their inner, higher, and spiritual demands.... On the night of His arrest, Jesus said, "A new commandment I give to you, that you love one another" (John 13:34). People

sometimes assume this means that God is willing to settle for less in the new covenant than in the old. Back in the Old Testament, they say, people wearied themselves obeying all kinds of rules and regulations. In the easier new covenant, all you have to do is love. That's it. Just love.... But of course, the command to love is vastly more difficult than the outward demands of the Old Testament law. It is easy to wash your hands. But washing your heart of anger, malice, and self-interest is another matter altogether. Therefore, the law's condemnation—always intended to drive sinners to God's grace in the gospel—is more intense in the light of Christ's coming.[1]

Paul wrote that the moral law is "holy and just and good" (Rom. 7:12) and that Christians were to walk so "that the righteous requirement of the law might be fulfilled in us" (Rom. 8:4). And even though the apostle writes about the internal struggle and difficulty that he faced in attempting to do that which the law demanded of him, he nevertheless said that he delighted in the law of God "according to the inward man" (Rom. 7:22). This, in fact, is one of the marks of a true Christian; he seeks to do the will of God out of gratitude for the salvation wrought in him by Christ (1 Pet. 4:1–2). The Christian recognizes that the law is but a reflection of God's holy character and that we show our love to him by keeping his commandments. For that reason, the commands of the Lord aren't burdensome to those who have been the objects of his redemptive love (1 John 5:3). Rather, along with the Psalmist, the Christian is able to declare that he loves the law of God, for by it (through Christ) he has been given life (Ps. 119:93, 163).

Throughout the centuries, Christians have spoken of three uses or functions of God's moral law. The first use is to promote civil righteousness—or negatively, to restrain sin within society. Although Christians may rightly lament the fact that the moral law of God seems to be losing more sway in the public arena each passing year, it's still hard to deny that, were it not for the general worldwide acceptance of the second table of the Ten Commandments, the planet would be a much more lawless place than it is at the present time. Millions of people around the world who wouldn't give a second thought to the first four commandments, which deal with our relationship to God, are nevertheless restrained in their behavior toward others by the general civil proscriptions that flow from the other six and which form a part of the law codes of most civilized nations today.

The second function of the moral law is to drive us to Christ. You may recall that this was the main function of the ceremonial law as well, but we may perhaps distinguish the way in which the two serve that function. While the ceremonial law served to remind the Israelites' of their unclean nature and need for an atoning sacrifice, the moral law serves more to remind us of our utter hopelessness to provide for ourselves what the law requires. By placing God's holy commands before us, the moral law of God shows us our sin and condemns us. Thus, in Paul's words, the law acts as a "tutor to bring us to Christ, that we might be justified by faith" (Gal. 3:24; cf. Rom. 3:20). Without the law, Paul wouldn't have even known he was a sinner (Rom. 7:7).

Finally, the third function of the law serves as a guide to kingdom living for the Christian. Christians are to be a holy people, even as our Lord is holy and perfect. A Christian is someone who has "died to sin" and no longer lives in its clutches (Rom. 6:2). Thus, he or she is guided in daily life by the holy precepts of God, whose very character is reflected in the commands that he has given us. Though the moral law no longer serves to condemn the Christian, to suppose that it's thereby annulled is simply incompatible with Christian thinking. B.M. Palmer states it this way:

> The attributes of justice, holiness, goodness and truth are stamped upon the law as a whole, and upon each individual part. They are impressed upon every precept and commandment, and just as distinctly upon the penalty which is their sanction. The law being

therefore the transcript of the Divine character, it is simply absurd to think or speak of it as cancelled.[2]

A New Covenant and a Better Hope

The writer of Hebrews does speak of a way in which the law has been annulled (7:18), but in this case he uses the term to refer to the old (Mosaic) covenant (i.e., the ceremonial law), which has been replaced by the new covenant in Christ. The new covenant is the "better hope, through which we draw near to God" (7:19), because the first system was "weak and unprofitable" and thus incapable of bringing in perfection. The author points out that if perfection had been available through the Levitical priesthood, then it wouldn't have been necessary to send Christ (7:11). But because Christ is a priest according to the order of Melchizedek, and not of Aaron, this change in the nature of the priesthood necessitated a change in the divine administration of the covenant (7:12).

The old order of things had now been set aside, not temporarily, but permanently. Christ's priesthood is unchangeable and eternal, and the sacrifice of himself that he offered for sinners is in no need of being repeated daily, as had been the case under the prior administration of the law (7:20–28). Because Christ fulfilled what the priesthood and the ceremonial law had anticipated, he rendered Old Testament Judaism obsolete. And this explains how the writer of Hebrews can refer to the prior administration as "weak and unprofitable," even though it too had come from the hand of God. It's not that there was anything wrong with the old covenant system or the law that accompanied it. But it was never intended to be a permanent arrangement. God used it to point the way to the work of Christ, and in that sense it served its purpose perfectly. A. W. Pink comments upon this matter:

> Absolutely considered no reflection can be made upon the Mosaic law, for it was the product of Divine wisdom, holiness and truth. But with respect unto the

people to whom it was given, and the *end* for which it was given, imperfection *did* attach to it. It was given to *sinners* who were defiled and guilty, and therefore was the law "weak through the flesh" (Rom. 8:3), its subject having no power to meet its high demands. Moreover, it was (in itself) incapable of meeting their deep needs; taking away their sins, bestowing life on them, conforming them to God's holiness. Why, then, was it given? It was "added because of transgression, till the Seed should come to whom the promise was made" (Gal. 3:19). It discovered the nature of sin, so that the conscience of man might be sensible thereof. It restrained sin by prohibitions and threatenings, so that it did not run out to an excess of riot. It represented, though obscurely, the ways and means by which sin could be expiated. Finally, it made known the imperative need for the coming of Christ to do for men what they could not do of and for themselves.[3]

It should also be pointed out that there was nothing sudden or unexpected about the change in covenant administration that took place at the coming of Christ. The prophet Jeremiah had foretold the new covenant more than six hundred years before it came into being. The fact that the people of first-century Palestine refused to accept the new reality at its appointed time of institution detracts not one iota from either the wisdom or effectual nature of God's redemptive plan. On the contrary, the events of that time and place happened in precisely the manner that God had ordained beforehand, as we have already discussed in an earlier chapter.

The failure to recognize this basic continuity of God's plan of salvation for the nations is at the heart of the theological error known as dispensationalism, which may be defined as both an interpretive approach to the Bible and as a movement that has been ascendant in American Christianity for the last hundred years. Dispensationalists tend to view the work of God in the Old and New Testament periods as quite distinct in character and design. They view the basic march of biblical history as having been interrupted by Israel's rejection of Christ and his subsequent crucifixion, which led to a fundamental change in God's redemptive focus—from the Jew to the Gentile. This state of affairs (or dispensation) is temporary, they say, for God will eventually return to his original plan of setting up an earthly kingdom with Jesus at the helm and with those of Jewish racial origin at the center.

Thus, dispensationalists argue for a basic discontinuity between the Old and New Testament periods and between the people of God in those two dispensations. As a result, this theological system is responsible for much of the wrong thinking about the subject of this chapter as well as the previous one. By drawing unwarranted contrasts between the two ages and people groups, dispensationalism leaves the impression that the heart of the old covenant consisted in keeping the law (thus, it's the "age of law") and was primarily concerned with temporal and earthly matters, most notably the land. On the other hand, the gospel dispensation (along with its people) is portrayed as the more spiritual of the two, being more concerned with the weightier matters of true religion and foregoing any interest in the temporal aspects of the covenant of grace.

Of course, there's a certain sense in which this latter statement is true, given the fact that the new covenant contains God's promise that he would write the law on the hearts of his people (Jer. 31:33). But the contrast drawn by dispensationalists is difficult to maintain in the face of the Bible's teaching that the promises and the people of God are fundamentally one and the same throughout the ages. Moreover, it makes it doubly hard to maintain the argument that the Christian is no longer under the moral law, when it's now written on his very heart in order that he might obey it!

However, it gets worse. It's one thing to contrast the ages of law and grace in such a way to leave the impression that the Christian is no longer under the moral law as a rule of life. But it's another thing altogether to suggest that the saints of the Old Testament era were saved by their fidelity to that law. And yet that is precisely what some dispensational theologians have done over the years. Some old-line dispensationalists, such as C. I. Scofield and Lewis Sperry Chafer, were quite forthright and explicit in teaching that the way to salvation during the days before Christ was by keeping the law, despite the clear and vehement declarations to the contrary by the writers of the New Testament.

To be fair, relatively few modern dispensationalists would agree with Scofield and Chafer that the Old Testament saints were saved by their works. Nor am I aware of a single dispensational teacher today who argues that we shouldn't seek to keep the moral law. But we must recognize that the language used by many a dispensational preacher has made them susceptible to both charges. The placing of the old and new covenants in complete opposition to one another, rather than seeing them as different administrations of the larger covenant of grace; the undue emphasis placed upon the law/grace distinction, which at times makes it sound as if there was no such thing as grace under the old covenant; and the dissemination of the so-called carnal-Christian myth (which we will address in a later chapter) have all contributed to the widespread notion that the moral law is an unnecessary (and undesirable) burden for the Christian.

Even some from within the dispensational ranks have begun to recognize the dangers inherent in their method of biblical interpretation. John MacArthur Jr. in *The Gospel According to Jesus*, which is a biblical refutation of the carnal-Christian myth, writes:

> There is a tendency, however, for dispensationalists to get carried away with compartmentalizing truth to the point that they make unbiblical differentiations. An almost obsessive desire to categorize and contrast related truths has carried various dispensationalist interpreters far beyond the legitimate distinction between Israel and the church. Many would also draw hard lines between salvation and discipleship, the church and the kingdom, Christ's preaching and

the apostolic message, faith and repentance, and the age of law and the age of grace.

The age-of-law/age-of-grace division in particular has wreaked havoc on dispensationalist theology and contributed to confusion about the doctrine of salvation.[4]

If there's one thing the church doesn't need, it's more confusion about the doctrine of salvation. But as MacArthur points out, dispensational theology has contributed much to this blight on the church in recent years. It's encouraging to see some men like him beginning to question the methods of these teachers and pointing out their errors. But it would be even better if they were to abandon the system altogether. The fact that so many modern dispensationalists have felt the need to retreat from the earlier form of the theological system espoused by men like Scofield and Chafer lends credence to the notion that the tree from which even the modern form springs is rotten. Unfortunately, dispensationalism continues to be the dominant eschatological and interpretive approach to the Bible in the broader evangelical church today. Is it any wonder, then, that confusion about the way of salvation is so prevalent in our age?

Paul's teaching, on the other hand, is crystal clear. Salvation is by grace alone, through faith alone, and not by the works of the law that we have done. And that has *always* been the case, from the moment of Adam's fall in the garden to the present time. Furthermore, that will continue to be the case until the day when Christ returns to claim his people. We're incapable of earning our way to salvation, but Christ has done the work for us by perfectly fulfilling the requirements of the law. Thus, he's the end of its condemning aspect for all those who place their trust in him—those who, by the work of the Holy Spirit, now have the law written on their hearts and are empowered to obey that law, even if imperfectly.

13

He Is the Destroyer of Death & Satan

(Heb. 2:14)

Twenty-first century Christians could learn a lot from Martin Luther's attitude toward the devil. The Reformer's own struggles and ravings against Satan are well known; one might even say they're the stuff of legend, since the most famous of tales, Luther's hurling of an inkwell at Satan while he was holed up in the Wartburg Castle, is most likely a later fabrication by others. But while Luther is often unfairly portrayed as having been obsessed with the devil, he actually can teach us a lot about striking the proper biblical balance between ignorance and obsession,[1] the two poles of thought that so frequently characterize our own meditations upon the subject.

Of course, many non-Christians dismiss the idea of the devil altogether. They think of him as the relic of a superstitious age, and portray him in caricature as a pitchfork-wielding red-suited impish rogue, someone upon whom they can facetiously foist their own personal indiscretions (what we would call sins) with a wink and a nod while muttering "The devil made me do it."

But Christians know better. We know that Satan is all too real, even if we struggle with exactly how to fit him into the present spiritual reality that is the New Testament age. At times we make the mistake of ignoring him altogether, perhaps in an otherwise laudable effort to focus on the reality of the statement under consideration here—that Christ has already destroyed him. But the New Testament makes it clear that despite the truthfulness of such a statement, Satan is still active in our affairs, even after Christ has defeated him and achieved the victory that has eternal ramifications.

An inordinate focus upon this latter truth can lead to the opposite tendency, however. There are a few within the church today who seem to be more concerned with the activity of Satan than with the finished work of Christ. Lacking a proper understanding of God's sovereignty, they often give Satan more credit for influencing and directing the daily affairs of men than he deserves.

And this is where we can take a cue from the great Reformer (as well as Scripture). Luther understood both of these truths and guarded each of them well, while managing at the same time to properly balance them against the teaching of the rest of Scripture. On the one hand, Luther took the devil very seriously. He was convinced that his own rediscovery of the gospel had roused Satan to a heightened level of activity, making him "more dangerous than ever before because he knows that he has only a short time left to rage."[2] Heiko Oberman's biography of Luther carries the subtitle *Man Between God and the Devil* for that's precisely the way in which the Reformer viewed himself in moving forward with the work of reformation to which he had been called.

At the same time, however, Luther could compare the devil to a "bad dog on a chain, which may bark, run here and there, and tear at the chain. But because it is tied and you avoid it, it cannot bite you."[3] He understood clearly that Satan exercises his power only within the strict confines that God allows. We're not to give him undue emphasis or attention, as if he were actually running the show here on earth.

Luther gave expression to this view of Satan in his hymn "A Mighty Fortress Is Our God." Of the devil it could be said that "on earth is not his equal"; nevertheless "his rage we can endure," for ultimately "one little word [from God] shall fell him." Thus, we aren't to fear Satan, "for God hath willed his truth to triumph through us."

I've no doubt that the writer of Hebrews would gladly join in singing Luther's hymn, for while he warns his readers against the ongoing work of the devil in seeking to turn the followers of Christ toward other pursuits, he also affirms that it was for the very purpose of destroying the devil (and his works) that Christ assumed human flesh and died on the cross. And the work of Christ in this regard is complete; the devil has been destroyed. Whatever tension may exist between the warning and the affirmation, both Luther and the writer of Hebrews understood that they don't amount to a contradiction. Demonstrating that to be the case is the goal of the present chapter.

The Ruler of This World

Although Satan is the most popular biblical designation for the devil, he is called by a number of other names as well, including Lucifer (Isa. 14:12–13), Beelzebub (Matt. 10:25), the evil one (Matt. 6:13), the adversary (1 Pet. 5:8), the serpent of old (Rev. 12:9), and the great dragon (Rev. 12:9). It's the more descriptive titles given to the devil that interest us here, however. Matthew calls him "the ruler of the demons" (Matt. 12:24), which is easy enough for us to understand and acknowledge. But more troubling are the titles that Paul and Jesus give him. Paul not only calls him "the prince of the power of the air" (Eph. 2:2) but also "the god of this age" (2 Cor. 4:4). And finally, on three separate occasions in the gospel of John, Jesus calls Satan "the ruler of this world" (12:31; 14:30; 16:11).

This latter designation for Satan is an important one for our understanding of both him and the contours of redemptive history. But it's also one that is susceptible to great misunderstanding. Both Jesus' and Paul's designations raise a number of thorny questions. If Satan is the ruler of this world, does that mean that God isn't ultimately controlling it? And if that's the case, doesn't such an affirmation contradict hundreds of biblical passages that seem to argue otherwise? Moreover, how can Satan be the god of this age, when he's no god at all? Isn't the God of the Bible the God of every age of human history? Indeed, is he not, as the Psalmist declares, the God who rules "from everlasting to everlasting" (Ps. 90:2; 145:13)? How, then, should we interpret and understand such titles given to one who opposes all that the God of Scripture seeks to accomplish in this world and in this age?

Frankly, the biblical evidence for God's control of the universe at all times and places is so overwhelming that it would be absurd to think that Jesus meant for the title to be understood in an absolute sense. Satan cannot be the "ruler of this world" in anything other than a restricted sense, for even he is a creature subject to the Creator of the universe. If God has chosen to give him and the demons that he commands a certain amount of freedom to conduct their activities on earth, it's nevertheless a freedom that our sovereign God is free to withdraw at any moment he chooses.

Rather, the designation "ruler of this world" is applicable to Satan by virtue of the fact that as a result of the Fall, he became the de facto spiritual head of all mankind, since from that time forward every human coming into the world by natural generation would be born in sin and subject to death. Their lot would be cast with Satan and his fate unless God chose to deliver them individually out of the abyss through a work of his particularized grace.

Thus, Satan could now lay claim to mankind as his legal possession. Sin had separated man from God and aligned him with the adversary. Death, as the wages of sin, now held sway over all of Adam's descendants, and Satan, the author of sin and death, had all of mankind in his evil clutches. The devil had a throne (Rev. 2:13) and a kingdom (Matt. 12:26), and the earth was the arena wherein he fought to protect and extend his influence and rule.

At the temptation in the wilderness, when Satan offered the kingdoms of the world to Jesus if he would worship him, our Lord didn't bother to correct him on that point because there was a sense in which the kingdoms of the world really did belong to the evil one.

Yet none of this takes place without God's permission and consent. We see that clearly in the story of Job, where Satan is unable to go any further in harming Job than God allows. Satan is a "bad dog on a chain," and isn't free to do whatever he pleases. He's subject to the ultimate control of God. Although this fact seems to bother some Christians, there's no reason why it should. God didn't create Satan as an evil spirit; to depart from righteousness was the devil's own free choice (Ezek. 28:11–19). Scripture says that he had been created perfect in all his ways, but that there came a time when iniquity was "found" in him by God (v. 15). However, as we shall see, God has chosen to bring good out of the evil that Satan committed, and thus he uses Satan to fulfill his own beneficent purposes on earth. As Luther was fond of saying, even the devil is *God's* devil.[4]

Christ the Conqueror of Satan

Nevertheless, an acknowledgment of that reality doesn't change the fact that Satan's works are themselves evil. God may bring good out of them, but Satan pursues them with evil intent and design. Thus, Christ was made manifest in the flesh for the very purpose of destroying the devil and his works (Heb. 2:14; 1 John 3:8). And, as if to point out the wonderful irony in God's redemptive plan, the writer of Hebrews tells us that it was "through death" that Jesus accomplished the destruction of both death and the one who wielded its awful power—the devil.

Here again we must be careful to not go too far in our thinking, however. Scripture is clear that it's God who has ultimate control over life and death. It's he who "kills and makes alive" (Deut 32:39; 1 Sam 2:6). But because the wages of sin is death, and Satan is the author of sin, it's with him that death is to be most closely identified and associated. Thus, the defeat of one is the defeat of the other as well.

When the time for battle arrived, Christ defeated Satan on the tempter's own battlefield. Though the devil pulled out all the stops in an effort to get rid of Jesus prior to the appointed time, it was only after Christ had fulfilled all the righteous requirements of the law that he submitted himself to the final act—death on the cross of Calvary. But if Satan thought that he had finally achieved his objective, it was only three days before he would discover to his horror that the cross signified his own defeat, not Christ's! The resurrection of Christ was God's message to the world that death and the devil had been defeated. What from a human perspective had looked like such a tragedy only days earlier was now revealed for what is really was—a glorious triumph for the Son of God, who had stripped the devil of his power and wrested from his hands the most awful weapon that he had in his possession.[5]

In his final address to the apostles on the night before his death, Jesus referred twice to Satan as "the ruler of this world." In the first instance, as he contemplated his impending death, he said that "the ruler of this world is coming" (John 14:30). But a little later on, when speaking of the work of judgment that the Holy Spirit would perform subsequent to his death, he said that "the ruler of this world is judged" (John 16:11). Clearly, then, the judgment of Satan has already taken place. He and his works have been destroyed by Christ's death and resurrection. Paul says that by his death on the cross Christ "disarmed" the evil spirits, having "made a public spectacle of them" and "triumphing over them in it" (Col. 2:15). The result is that Christians are freed from the fear of death, since they're no longer subject to its bondage (Heb. 2:15) and are assured of the same resurrection that Christ experienced.

The Present Conflict

But if Satan has already been destroyed and judged, how can he remain active today? Actually, the answer is hinted at in the last paragraph. In the same way that Christians have eternal life as a present possession but must still undergo death and bodily decay in the grave prior to experiencing the fullness of their redemption, so Satan's doom is already sealed and the futility of his rebellion against God on display to the whole universe, even if the final cessation of his evil activity won't take place until he is cast into the everlasting fire on judgment day (Matt. 25:41).

It's also important to point out that although Satan remains active to this day, his activity has been curtailed since the time of Christ's first coming. Jesus told his disciples that the arrival of the kingdom meant the division of Satan's spoils and that his (and their) ability to cast out demons was proof that Satan's kingdom was coming to an end (Luke 10:18; 11:20–22). Thus, it's no coincidence that with the coming of Christ, the gospel didn't continue to be the preserve of a single people group, since the one who had "deceived the nations" (Rev. 20:3) for so long was now on a shorter leash than he had been at any time previously.

Nevertheless, Satan continues to ply his diabolical trade, and even Christians must still reckon with him and his power to influence the world. And despite being curtailed at Christ's first coming, that influence is still considerable. The devil continues to oppose the spread of the gospel and is actively blinding men and women to its truth (Matt. 13:18–30; 2 Cor. 4:4). He hindered Paul in his missionary activities (1 Thess. 2:18) and is no doubt engaged in the same activity today. The apostle Peter even speaks of him as one who "walks about like a roaring lion, seeking whom he may devour" (1 Pet. 5:8). Satan is on the prowl at all times, looking for ways to tempt or ensnare both Christians and non-Christians (1 Cor. 7:5; 1 Tim. 3:7).

But even while he's plying his trade, Satan is being used by God to accomplish that which God has ordained for ultimate good. Erwin Lutzer lists four ways in which God uses the devil to bring about his divine ends: (1) to judge the unconverted (Mark 4:15; 2 Cor. 4:4), (2) to refine the obedient (Job), (3) to discipline the disobedient (Deut. 28:47–48; Ps. 78:49; 1 Cor. 5:5), and (4) to purify his chosen ones (2 Cor. 12:7).[6] This explains why Scripture may even speak of a particular event as emanating from the hand of both God and Satan (though separately), such as in the prophecy of the coming of the "lawless one" in 2 Thessalonians 2:8–12.

Does this mean that the devil is seeking to do God's will? Absolutely not! He's wholly inclined toward thwarting God's will and promoting evil wherever he may find a willing participant. But he does not, and cannot, operate independently of divine providence. Satan has no more freedom to do whatsoever he pleases, than do you or I. The entire universe and all creatures residing therein are ultimately subject to the will of God. And although Satan's actions may be used by God to bring about good, they don't change their evil intent or character when viewed from Satan's perspective. He alone is responsible for the evil in the world.

John Calvin, who called the devil "the author, leader, and architect of all malice and iniquity," offered this insightful observation about the origin of evil:

> Yet, since the devil was created by God, let us remember that this malice, which we attribute to his nature, came not from his creation but from his perversion. For, whatever he has that is to be condemned he has derived from his revolt and fall. For this reason, Scripture warns us lest, believing that he has come forth in his present condition from God, we should ascribe to God himself what is utterly alien to him.... Indeed, when Christ states that Satan "abode not in the truth," he hints that he was once in it, and when he makes him "the father of lies," he deprives him of imputing to God the fault which he brought upon himself.[7]

Then, commenting upon Satan's responsibility for evil, and God's use of it to achieve his own benevolent ends, Calvin adds:

> For inasmuch as the devil is by nature wicked, he is not at all inclined to obedience to the divine will, but utterly intent upon contumacy and rebellion. From himself and his own wickedness, therefore, arises his passionate and deliberate opposition to God. By this wickedness he is urged on to attempt courses of action which he believes

> to be most hostile to God. But because with the bridle
> of his power God holds him bound and restrained, he
> carries out only those things which have been divinely
> permitted to him; and so he obeys his Creator, whether
> he will or not, because he is compelled to yield him
> service wherever God impels him.[8]

Calvin's words remind us that whatever profit God may choose to bring out of Satan's evil machinations, the two are in no sense partners in carrying out the action (perish the thought!). God and Satan are immortal enemies, and the fact that God is able to use Satan's best efforts at thwarting the kingdom for its ultimate benefit only serves to demonstrate the utter foolishness of Satan's rebellion in the first place. The creature thought that he could be like his Creator but has found out to his horror that even in his rebellion he is forced to do the Creator's bidding.

Satan's opposition to the will of God also makes our duty clear: we are to resist him with all of our might (Jas. 4:7; 1 Pet. 5:9). We are to "put on the whole armor of God, that [we] may be able to stand against the wiles of the devil" (Eph. 6:11). God may indeed be using the devil to accomplish an end that is to our ultimate benefit, but our obligation remains the same. In fact, it's frequently in the very act of resisting Satan that God intends to bless us. It's one of his greatest tools for refining and maturing his saints.

Of course, that also means that resisting the devil may be one of the most painful things that we do. Very often it's the way of accommodation that leads to the most comfortable and trouble-free existence in this fallen world of ours. But if Christ had to suffer and die in order to defeat Satan, we should recognize that God's love for us doesn't exempt us from the same sort of fate.

Thankfully, the road of obedience to God's will seldom involves the path of martyrdom these days. For most of us, though, resisting the devil's invitations to sin or to compromise our faithful Christian witness will likely cost us something in the way of worldly comforts, even if resisting brings its own reward.

Knowing the Word of God and what he requires of us in every situation is the only surefire means of achieving victory over the temptations thrown at us by the evil one. That was precisely the method that Jesus used in his battle with Satan in the wilderness. Time and again he quoted Scripture to Satan with an unwavering confidence that God's truth was reliable and of sufficient force to withstand any form of testing.

This doesn't mean that we must all be professional theologians. But it means that if we want to resist the devil, we must be familiar with his methods and with God's instructions for defeating him, both of which we find in the written Word of God. Furthermore, we must never forget that Satan masquerades as an angel of light (2 Cor. 11:14). If more Christians had been mindful of this fact over the last two thousand years, it's certain that the history of the New Testament church would have been considerably different.

The Final Victory Assured

Paul tells us that Christ "has abolished death, and brought life and immortality to light through the gospel" (2 Tim. 1:10). Because he has delivered us from the sin for which death is the judgment, Christ now possesses the keys of death and hell (Rev. 1:18). As a result of his work, we'll one day put on incorruptibility and immortality. But even now the Christian is able to say, "O Death, where is your sting?" (1 Cor. 15:55), for he recognizes that death is now but his entrance into eternal glory.

As for the author of death, his days are numbered too. Christ has already destroyed him, the mortal wound having been inflicted at the Cross. But he limps along a little while yet, for God's redemptive plan is still in progress and Satan continues to have a role to play in it. Augustus Toplady, the author of the immortal hymn, "Rock of Ages," writes:

> Had evil never been permitted, how could the justice
> of God have been glorified in punishing it? How

could the wisdom of God have been displayed in over-ruling it? How could the goodness of God have been manifested in pardoning and forgiving it? And how could the power of God have been exerted in subduing it?[9]

Toplady's words point out a simple fact that's too often missed by those seeking to understand this issue more clearly: the presence of evil in the world serves to bring into high relief God's own holy attributes. To demonstrate this point further, we could add two questions to Toplady's list above: Would the holiness of God inspire the same level of awe within us if it didn't stand in such stark contrast to our own sorry state? And could we sing Toplady's hymn, or John Newton's "Amazing Grace," with the same emotion if we had never known the depths of human depravity from which we ourselves were delivered? When all is said and done, it's hard to imagine a more perfect scenario for revealing the righteous character of God and for bringing him the glory and honor that he deserves.

But make no mistake about it: evil is on its way out for good. The time will come when it will have served its purposes in full. Christ will have made his last enemy his footstool (Heb. 10:13), and the devil and his minions will be thrown into the lake of fire for all eternity. Sin will be banished from the presence of God and his saints once and for all. In the meantime, however, the saints of God are called upon to advance his kingdom. Every time the gospel is preached and another person turns to Christ, Satan's power is diminished accordingly.

At the end of his letter to the church in Rome, Paul commends the saints for their obedient faith and urges them to be "wise in what is good, and simple concerning evil." Then he adds this amazing proclamation: "And the God of peace will crush Satan under your feet shortly" (Rom. 16:20). What is so amazing about this statement? The words hearken back to the first announcement of the gospel in Genesis 3:15, where the eventual bruising of the head of Satan by the seed of the woman (Christ) is prophesied. But in this passage

Paul attributes the bruising of Satan's head to the church! Of course, there's no contradiction here. Rather, it testifies to the innate connection between Christ and his body, the church.

Has Christ left unfinished the work of destroying Satan? He most certainly has not. He has already struck the fatal blow. Satan's end is in sight, and he's gasping for his last breaths, even as he does his best to get in a few more bites before the appointed time for his expiration. But all the while that he lies prostrate and bleeding, the church continues to inflict additional wounds with each passing day as it carries the gospel to the nations. And the saints of God rejoice in the knowledge that Christ has given to his church the inestimable privilege of finishing Satan off! May we seek to do the job right—and to do it quickly.

14

He Is the Savior of the World

(JOHN 4:42)

Ask any professing Christian these days what it means to say that Christ is the Savior of the world, and you're likely to get one of several different answers. A relatively small percentage of those asked would probably say that Christ is the Savior of the world in the sense that his work on the cross secured salvation and forgiveness of sins for all those who have ever lived. Although this theological viewpoint, known as Universalism, is gaining considerable ground in the church today, it suffers from a debilitating defect—it's directly contradicted by Scripture. The Bible explicitly teaches the reality of the final judgment (Dan. 12:2; Matt. 5:22; 18:9; 23:33; 25:46; Rom. 9:21–23) and the imperative to trust in Christ in this life since there's no second chance for anyone to do so after death (Heb. 9:27). At the judgment, Christ will separate the sheep from the goats, and the latter will go into everlasting punishment (Matt. 25:31–46). The goats are also referred to as those whose names aren't written in the Book of Life; John tells us that they'll be cast into the lake of fire for all eternity (Rev. 20:11–

15). Thus, however attractive the belief in universal salvation may be to our human sensibilities, it's difficult to see how anyone who takes the teaching of the Bible seriously can hold to it.

Unfortunately, the answer likely to be given by the majority of professing Christians is no more biblical than the one outlined above, even if it's not as explicitly refuted by a quick recitation of relevant Scripture passages. Most Christians today seem to believe that Christ is the Savior of the world only in the sense that by his death on the cross, he made salvation a *possibility* for every person in the world by taking upon himself the penalty for their sins. At first blush, it's easy to see how this view has come to be so widely held. After all, it encompasses a valid recognition of the twin facts that Christ's death was a necessity if anyone was to be reconciled to God and that individual persons must still place their trust in him in order to experience that reconciliation. But it errs badly by ignoring the biblical evidence that Christ's work actually *accomplished* the salvation of those for whom it was intended. Rather, the popular view has the effect of diminishing the work of Christ by rendering it ultimately ineffectual and thereby making him only a *potential* Savior.

This chapter and the next form a single unit, focused on the atoning work of Christ in the salvation of sinners. Looking at the purposes for which Christ came, we'll seek to demonstrate how Christ is, at one and the same time, the Savior of the world, and the Redeemer of all those (but *only* those) whom the Father gave to him before time began. This chapter will focus upon answering the questions, "For whom did Christ die?" and "What did his death do for them?" The next chapter will delve more deeply into the nature of God's redemptive plan and how the work of Christ is applied to the salvation of sinners.

The Nature of Christ's Atonement

In an earlier chapter we discussed the necessity of the incarnation of Christ. When Adam plunged mankind into sin, the Incarnation became a necessity if anyone was to be reconciled to God, since God's righteousness and justice demanded a satisfaction for sin that only God himself could provide. We might wink at and find all manner of excuses for sin, but our holy and just God cannot and will not excuse the sinner with a wink and a nod. His justice must be satisfied. He had promised judgment for transgression of his command, and mankind freely brought such judgment upon itself through the sinful actions of Adam and Eve.

But God, who is also rich in mercy, determined to provide the means whereby sinners could be delivered from this predicament in a manner that also fully satisfied the demands of divine justice. Christ is the answer to man's predicament. Through his incarnation he was able to stand in our stead and pay the penalty demanded by God's law. His death on the cross was the atoning sacrifice that provides the means of escape for all those who would be reconciled to God. And it was the very reason for which he came (Mark 10:45; John 12:27; 18:37; Heb. 2:9–14).

The goal of the present section is to answer more precisely what that atonement was designed to accomplish. In other words, what was the ultimate meaning and purpose of Christ's death? Or to frame the question in a manner that's familiar to some and which effectively turns it into two interrelated questions, "What exactly was God doing on the cross?"

1. Christ's Death Was an Act of Substitution

In the first place, Christ's sacrificial death was vicarious in nature. He died in the place of others. He himself needed no atonement for sins because he had none for which to atone. The death that he suffered was undeserved with respect to himself. But as he bore the sins of others, he experienced the death that was rightly meant for sinners. This is the consistent testimony of Scripture, and the expressions of it take a number of different forms, reflecting the multifaceted nature of the transaction that took place on the cross. Thus, he died for our sins (1 Cor. 15:3; Gal. 1:4), he "gave Himself" for us (Eph. 5:2), he was sacrificed for us (1 Cor. 5:7), he laid down his life for his friends (John 10:11; 15:13; 1 John 3:16), he was made to "be sin" for us (2 Cor. 5:21), and he became a curse for us (Gal. 3:13).

2. Christ's Death Was an Act of Redemption

Christ's death on the cross was also an act of *redemption*. Although this term is often used as a synonym for salvation (and rightly so, as we shall see), for the moment we use it in the more commonly applicable sense of paying a price (or ransom) to secure the release of someone or something. In this case, the price paid was the accumulated penalty for our individual sins, and the payment was made in Christ's blood. Thus, as Scripture records, we were redeemed by the "precious blood of Christ" (1 Pet. 1:18–19, Rom. 3:24–25; Eph. 1:7; Rev. 5:9), we were "bought at a price" (1 Cor. 6:20), Christ "has redeemed us from the curse of the law" (Gal. 3:13), he has given his life as a "ransom for many" (Mark 10:45), and he thereby "became for us … redemption" (1 Cor. 1:30).

Note that a commonly held belief in the first millennium of the New Testament age was that this ransom price was paid to the devil in order to secure the release of individuals from his clutches. This idea, which is known as the Ransom Theory of the Atonement, was based upon the notion that subsequent to the fall of man in the Garden, Satan held a legal claim upon the souls of all persons born, and so God was now obligated to pay a ransom to deliver them from the devil's rightful ownership.

But this theory, which has now been widely discarded, ignores the fact that God owes nothing to Satan and could never be obligated to him in any way. It's true that fallen man is in bondage to Satan, but that's a very different matter from what's asserted in the Ransom Theory. Satan has no legal claim to anything or anyone whom God wants for himself. Whatever (or whomsoever) God wants is his by virtue of his sovereign claim over the entire universe. And he owes the devil nothing for taking (or redeeming) persons unto himself.

Rather, the ransom of Christ's blood was paid in order to satisfy the demands of divine justice. Sin required a sacrifice, and Christ became that sacrifice for us. He took the penalty for sin (death) upon himself, thereby redeeming us from the curse of the law.

3. Christ's Death Was an Act of Propitiation

A less familiar term that defines what Christ was doing on the cross is that of *propitiation*. Whereas the concept of redemption consists primarily in Christ's removing the penalty for sin, propitiation carries the transaction to the next level by asserting that his death actually appeased God's wrath against the individual sinner. In other words, Christ's death did not simply place the sinner back into a neutral position of non-indebtedness to the law of God. Rather, it actually restored him to favor with God. It didn't just satisfy God's divine justice; it turned God's temperament toward the sinner from one of wrath to one of favor.

There's probably no subject more unpopular in the modern church than the wrath of God (with the possible exception of the subject to be covered in the next chapter). But popular or not, the wrath of God against sin (Rom. 1:18) and consequently against the sinner himself (John 3:36; Eph. 5:6; Col. 3:6; Heb. 3:11) is explicitly taught in Scripture. Indeed, it necessarily issues forth from a Being who is holy and just and pure. God wouldn't be God if he weren't repulsed by human sin—and rightly at odds with the creatures who committed such transgressions. Psalm 7:11 says that, "God is a just judge, and God is angry with the wicked every day." But now that Christ has become the propitiation for our sins (Rom. 3:25; Heb. 2:17; 1 John 2:2; 4:10), believers may rest assured that God's wrath against him or her has been averted once and for all.

4. Christ's Death Was an Act of Reconciliation

The ultimate result of being redeemed from the penalty of sin and having God's wrath turned away from the sinner is reconciliation between the sinner and God. Christ's death on the cross doesn't only cancel the debt owed to God; it actually restores one to fellowship with him. Propitiation and reconciliation are related as cause and effect: Christ's death turns aside God's wrath, and the result is reconciliation between God and man.[1]

Paul writes that he and the other apostles had received the "ministry of reconciliation" and that God had entrusted to them the "word of reconciliation." And that word consists in this: "God was in Christ reconciling the world to Himself" (2 Cor. 5:18–19). Moreover, we were reconciled to God through the death of Christ while we were yet his enemies (Rom. 5:10–11). The glorious result is that God has actually "delivered us from the power of darkness and conveyed us into the kingdom of the Son of His love" (Col. 1:13; cf. 1 Pet. 3:18).

The Efficacy and Extent of Christ's Atonement

With this understanding of Christ's work as the backdrop, it should be obvious that his death was efficacious in bringing about that which it was designed to do. It didn't merely make salvation possible for all. Rather, it actually secured the salvation of individual sinners. And if by means of his vicarious death Christ intended to provide for the redemption, propitiation, and reconciliation of individual sinners, the objects toward which his death was directed must have been only those who are actually reconciled to God—the elect. To say otherwise is to argue that Christ's death failed in the most essential respect for which it was designed.

The Universalist rightly understands this concept of the efficacy of the atonement but wrongly argues that the intended recipients of its blessings were every person who ever lived, a concept known as universal (or unlimited) atonement. On the other hand, most of those who inhabit evangelical churches today have adopted the Universalist notion of the extent of the atonement but deny its efficacy. In their view, Christ's death didn't actually save anyone; it only made it possible for God to accept those who, of their own supposed "free will," eventually choose to avail themselves of its benefits. Thus, we may say that the Universalist at least gets one out of two concepts correct, while the modern evangelical gets neither the efficacy nor the extent of the atonement correct.

In contrast to both of those deficient positions, the Bible teaches that Christ's death secured the salvation of those for whom it was intended to benefit. Christ came into the world to save sinners (Matt. 1:21; 1 Tim. 1:15), and that's exactly what he accomplished by his death (Rom. 3:24–25; 5:10–11; Eph. 1:7; Tit. 2:14; 1 Pet. 1:18–19; Rev. 5:9). His blood wasn't shed for all men, but for the "many" who would be saved by his grace (Matt. 20:28; Mark 14:24; Heb. 9:28). Those for whom his blood was shed are variously referred to as the church (Eph. 5:25; Acts 20:28), the sheep (John 10:15, 27), his friends (John 15:13), and brothers (Rom. 14:15).

In short, the Bible doesn't teach a universal atonement but a particularized one. This is why the traditional doctrine is usually referred to as Particular Redemption, or Limited Atonement, since it is limited in its scope or extent to the elect of God. They, and they alone, are the ones for whom Christ died.

The Universal Passages

Despite the biblical evidence for particular redemption, however, there are some who point to a number of scriptural passages that, at a surface level, seem to imply that Christ's death was intended for all people. Indeed, those who argue against the traditional doctrine never tire of trotting out these passages, as if they were some magic elixir that could somehow overcome the thrust and weight of the numerous passages that speak directly to the very purpose for which Christ came. Nevertheless, these biblical texts must be addressed, and dealing with them only serves to further strengthen the case for particular redemption.

For starters, most of the so-called universal passages involve the use of the words *all* or *world* when commenting on some aspect of Christ's work. The title of this chapter takes its name from one such passage. But a closer examination of the relevant passages reveals a very different picture than is painted by the proponents of universal redemption. In every case, those who attempt to put a universal spin on such verses either reject the immediate context in which they appear, or they construct an interpretation of the verse that's at odds with the rest of the writer's argument. A few examples will suffice to prove the point.

A good example is 1 Timothy 2:6, where Paul seems to contradict the passages we cited above stating that Christ gave his life as a ransom for "many." Instead, Paul writes that Christ "gave Himself a ransom for all." Does this verse teach universal atonement? It certainly seems to. But when viewed in its context, we can see that Paul's use of the word *all* is designed to emphasize something quite different than the scope of the atonement. Paul is entreating Timothy to pray for all men, including "kings and those who are in authority" (v. 2), and Gentiles as well as Jews (v. 7). And why should Timothy do so? Because Christ is the one and only Mediator between God and *all* men (v. 5–6). No one, regardless of his or her social position or racial background, will be saved apart from Christ. But *all* who believe in him, from whatever class of men, will be saved. In this way, then, his death may be said to be a ransom for *all*.

Another example occurs in the epistle to the Hebrews. In 2:9 the writer states that Jesus assumed human flesh in order that he "might taste death for everyone." But that statement is immediately qualified in the next verse by linking the efficacy of his suffering to the "many sons" that he's bringing to glory as the captain of their salvation. Thus, the death that he tasted was for everyone who fits into the class of those he's bringing to glory—the elect of God.

Undoubtedly the most oft-cited passage in the whole debate is the familiar John 3:16, which says, "For God so loved the world that He gave His only begotten Son, that whoever believes in Him should not perish but have everlasting life." It's argued that this verse refutes the doctrine of particular redemption by demonstrating that it was God's love for every person on the planet that caused him to send his only Son. But one only arrives at that interpretation if one has already made up their mind that the atonement of Christ was universal. The text doesn't say that God loved every single person on the planet; it says that he loved the *world*. And that is a very different matter, as any study of the use of the word in Scripture will reveal.

The fact is that John and the other biblical writers use the term *world* in a variety of ways, and it is almost never used in the sense of referring to the entire human race! Indeed, there's at least one instance where John clearly uses the term to refer to believers only (John 6:33).

Perhaps the principle of judging the author's intent from his overall argument, as well as by a comparison with other Scripture passages, can be best illustrated by using the verse that is second only to John 3:16 in the frequency with which it arises in this debate. The verse is 1 John 2:2, where the apostle writes that Christ "is the propitiation for our sins, and not for ours only but also for the whole world." As one of only four propitiation passages in the New Testament, this would seem to be a clear statement supporting universal atonement. But John uses the term again only two chapters later in his epistle in a way that is restricted to believers only (4:9–10; the love of God was manifested toward those who "live through Him"; it is they who have been loved by God and have propitiation for their sins). The other two places where the term is used support the same interpretation, but especially Romans 3:25 where Paul says that redemption and propitiation come to us "through faith."

The Universal Aspect of Christ's Atonement

The bottom line is that many of the universal statements we find in Scripture are qualified or clarified in a more restrictive sense by other passages. What, then, are the biblical writers attempting to do by using such universal terms? In general we may say that the use of universal terms serves at least two important purposes. First, they help to emphasize the worldwide reach of the gospel by stressing that Christ's work is for every person in the world, regardless of race or class. This was particularly necessary during the decades when the

New Testament was being written, as many Jewish believers needed to be reminded that Christ was the Savior of Gentiles as well. When John told his readers that Christ was the propitiation not just for them, but also for the whole world, he was reminding them of this fact. The *whosoever* of John 3:16 testifies to the same truth.

This purpose is also clear from the reference to Christ as the Savior of the world in John 4:42. That title was ascribed to Jesus by the residents of Sychar, with whom he had just spent two days during which "many of the Samaritans of that city believed in Him" (v. 39). First-century Jews were repulsed by Samaritans and considered them to be hopeless heretics, a fact which John mentions in the narrative (v. 9). Indeed, Jesus told the woman at the well in this story that "salvation is of the Jews" (v. 22), which was a direct rebuke to her comments concerning the proper place of worship. But the fact that Jesus spent two days in their city, and preached the gospel personally to them, was proof that he wasn't just the Savior of believing Jews. If Christ could receive a despised and unclean Samaritan into his fold, then surely he was the Savior of the whole world.

The second purpose that universal terms serve is to emphasize the fact that Jesus' death looked backward as well as forward in time. That is, Christ wasn't just the Savior of those who believed subsequent to his death on the cross. On the contrary, all those who came before him, if they were redeemed by God, were also redeemed on the basis of Christ's work—a point that the New Testament writers make repeatedly (John 5:28–29; Rom. 5:18; 1 Cor. 15:18–23; Eph. 1:10; Heb. 9:15, 26; 11:40; 1 Pet. 1:10–12). Christ is the Savior of the world because he's the only Savior the world has ever known.

Finally, it should be recognized that in at least a few cases the biblical writers were simply using universal terms in a way that accords with our own common practice, not really intending for them to be understood as statements of literal truth. This interesting comment from Tom Wells demonstrates the reality of this tendency:

> To begin with, universal terms in every language with which I am familiar are almost always used with very

wide limitations. We do not often notice this, simply because we have taken it for granted since we were children. In fact, you may be surprised at this, but you will easily see that it is so. I'll take my examples from Scripture. Here are verses that illustrate it from John 3: "Behold, (Jesus) is baptizing, and all are coming to Him" (3:26). "(Jesus) bears witness; and no man receives His witness" (3:32). "He who has received His witness has set his seal to *this*, that God is true" (3:33).

Note the apparent contradiction in this account of Jesus' ministry. In verse 26, *all* receive His witness and come to Him. In verse 32, *no man* does so. But verse 33 assumes that some do in fact receive His witness. What's going on here?

Even if you have read this account many times you have probably never noticed this. The reason is simple: you are fully used to reading universal terms in a limited way, and you do it without giving it a second thought. You understand that verse 26 means only that a large number were coming to Christ, not literally *all*. In verse 32 you again grasp the idea: compared to the number of people who should have responded to Christ, *no man* means relatively few. And verse 33 confirms your understanding: some did, in fact, receive the witness of Christ. It never occurred to you to read *all* and *no man* as if they were true, universal assertions. You assumed the limitations on them and read on, without noticing what you were doing. You do that *all the time* (meaning *often!*).[2]

In summary, then, Christ's death on the cross has infinite value and is more than sufficient to have provided salvation for every person who ever lived—if that had been what it was designed to do. But it was designed to actually bring to God all those whose names were written in the Book of Life. It was of unlimited value but limited application, in line with God's intention for it. Christ gave his life as a ransom for many persons, and not a single one of them will be lost. His death didn't merely make the salvation of each of them possible—it actually secured it. Precisely *how* it did so is the subject of the next chapter.

The Importance of the Matter

At this point, however, I'm confident that more than a few thoughtful readers are asking themselves questions such as the following: Why is this issue such a big deal in modern theological circles? Isn't it sufficient for us to find agreement in the fact that no one will be saved except those who place their trust in Christ and just leave it at that? Do we really need to be concerned about whether the atonement was universal or particular in its scope and design? Don't such discussions represent the sort of theological hair-splitting that was characteristic of the church in earlier centuries? Finally, is there any practical value in resolving this dispute?

Those are good questions. And because this issue is just one part of the more comprehensive discussion of redemption that continues into the next chapter, we've reserved some of our response until then. But there are at least three significant ways in which our faith is impacted by our understanding of this issue.

First, how we view the work of Christ at this particular point cannot help but affect our view of him as Savior. Is Christ the Savior of the world because he made salvation a possibility for everyone on the planet or because he actually secured it for every person on the planet who would eventually come to God through faith? Did he really "bring us to God" by means of his death (1 Pet. 3:18), or did he merely place the initiative back into our hands to determine whether his work would be efficacious for us? Ask yourself which of these two positions paints Christ in the more glorious light, and you can see the implications that our view of the atonement has for our faith in him.

Second, our view of the extent of the atonement directly affects our view of the justice of God. Although I am convinced that few Christians have ever given thought to the implications of what universal atonement (not Universalism) teaches about the justice of God, it's a serious matter indeed, as Spurgeon pointed out long ago:

> To think that my Saviour died for all men who were or are in hell, seems a supposition too horrible for me to entertain. To imagine for a moment that He was the Substitute for all the sons of men, and that God, having first punished the Substitute, afterwards punished the sinners themselves, seems to conflict with all my ideas of Divine justice. That Christ should offer an atonement and satisfaction for the sins of all men, and that afterwards some of those very men should be punished for the sins for which Christ had already atoned, appears to me to be the most monstrous iniquity that could ever have been imputed to Saturn, to Janus, to the goddess of the Thugs, or to the most diabolical heathen deities. God forbid that we should ever think thus of Jehovah, the just and wise and good![3]

Finally, from a practical standpoint, it seems to me that the widespread preaching of universal atonement is at least partially responsible for the general lack of interest in the gospel that we see today. Though there's no way to prove the point, common sense would seem to dictate such a conclusion. When a man has been told over and over by those in the know that Christ died for his sins or that God loves him and has a wonderful plan for his life, it's difficult to see how such proclamations wouldn't lead the unconverted man to become comfortable in his present condition.[4] At the very least, it makes the self-introspection called for by the gospel a far less pressing matter.

The offer of the gospel is made to all people because from the human standpoint every person in the world is a potential believer.

God hasn't given a visible mark of identification to those for whom Christ gave his life. So we approach unsaved persons for what they are—those who just might be a part of that group. But in the process, we cannot let our preaching go beyond what Scripture will allow. We cannot make a pronouncement on God's behalf of something that he hasn't disclosed to us. Here is Spurgeon again:

> Another says, 'I want to know about the rest of the people. May I go out and tell them—Jesus Christ died for every one of you? May I say—there is life for every one of you?' No; you may not. You may say— there is life for every man that comes. But if you say there is life for one of those that do not believe, you utter a dangerous lie. If you tell them Jesus Christ was punished for their sins, and yet they will be lost, you tell a willful falsehood. To think that God could punish Christ and then punish them—I wonder at your daring to have the impudence to say so![5]

The world is full of those for whom Jesus Christ died, even if (perhaps) millions of them aren't yet aware of that fact. Some of them haven't even heard his name yet. But for every one of them, Jesus has made their ultimate salvation a certainty. He has already redeemed them to God through his work on the cross, even though for some that redemption has yet to be applied in time and space through the gift of faith. But rest assured that it will happen. Not one of them will be lost. Christ's work on their behalf won't fail in the slightest respect. He is their Savior, just as he is the Savior of all of those who ever have, or ever will, come to faith—from whatever corner of the world they hail. He's the one and only Savior of the world.

15

He Is the Redeemer of All Those Given to Him by the Father

(JOHN 6:39)

We hear a lot about church growth these days. The twenty-first-century church is teeming with experts and teams of consultants only too eager to share the latest sociological research detailing how you can pack your church with bodies on any given Sunday. The commonly accepted formula seems to revolve around one central idea: making church as comfortable as possible for the unbeliever. This usually involves creating an atmosphere that bears little resemblance to the traditional church of past generations. Thus, pews and sanctuaries are out; multi-purpose rooms with movable seating, as well as all of the latest audio and visual conveniences and contraptions, are in. Crosses are definitely out; they speak of blood and other primitive notions of justice and aren't acceptable to modern sensibilities. Entertainment and performance arts are in; after all, church shouldn't be dry and boring. And if you can offer a latte or cappuccino in the lobby for those who still get bored—well, all the better.

Ignoring the bigger issue of who should be the focus of our worship, one could perhaps defend this method of attracting unbelievers to church as a righteous form of the classic bait and switch if what these people got once inside the walls of the church was the unadulterated gospel truth. But the modern church growth movement has argued for change in this area of ministry as well. It calls us to focus on the felt needs of the audience and to avoid (or at least soft-pedal) biblical notions such as sin and judgment, the wrath of God, or even the blood of Christ shed for sinners. These things, we're told, only serve to further alienate the unconverted and attack their already low self-esteem. Thus, we should seek to present God in a more human light, and humans as more worthy of his loving attention and favor.

Robert Schuller, one of the earliest promoters and practitioners of this model, has castigated historic Christianity for being too 'God-centered,' when it should have been 'man-centered' instead. According to Schuller, the church should be proclaiming a message that exalts man by catering to his deepest need—his "spiritual hunger for glory."[1] This, of course, means that there's no place for talk of man's sin and helplessness before God. Even the gospel itself has got to go, since it "is not only faulty but potentially dangerous if it has to put a person down before it attempts to lift him up."[2] And what is Schuller's reply when someone points out that his teaching conflicts with the basic message of Scripture concerning these things? It's breathtakingly arrogant: "Just because it's in the Bible doesn't mean you should preach it."[3]

Jesus' Sermon in John 6

Thankfully, such self-appointed editors of the gospel are unable to bury the truth of God's grace toward sinners that we see displayed on every page of the Bible. Nor did Jesus seem to have much regard for the sermonic methods of modern church growth experts, as we can see from his discourse in John 6, which appears to violate all of the principles laid out above. It's for this reason that some have begun to refer to it as his Church Shrinkage Sermon.

Now our subject in this chapter isn't church growth but the redemption of sinners. But Jesus' sermon in John 6 teaches us a lot about both at the same time. And in the process it sheds a great deal of light on the state of the contemporary church, revealing serious shortcomings in both its theology and practice.

Jesus delivered the sermon in the synagogue at Capernaum on the day after he had miraculously fed the five thousand and had later walked on the water in the Sea of Galilee. John tells us that some of those who had been at the previous day's meal went to Capernaum to seek Jesus when they discovered that he had left their town on the eastern shore. When they ran into Jesus, he spoke of their felt needs all right but not exactly in the way espoused by many experts today: "Most assuredly, I say to you, you seek Me, not because you saw the signs, but because you ate of the loaves and were filled" (v. 26). Jesus knew that they weren't true believers, and he told them so (v. 36). But rather than toning down his message to suit the make-up of the crowd, he used the occasion to deliver one of the most memorable (and most blunt) sermons found in the New Testament.

The sermon consists of three main points dealing with the interplay between the Father, the Son, and individual sinners in the drama of redemption. The first point is this: Jesus is the bread of life sent from heaven by the Father to give everlasting life to all who believe in him. In contrast to the manna sent by God to the Israelites in Moses' day, the one who eats of this bread (Christ) won't die (vv. 27–35; 47–58). For this reason, the sermon in John 6 is often referred to as the Bread of Life discourse.

The second point expands upon the first. Christ's mission to give life to those who believe in him is the outworking of the Father's will, for the Father has given to him certain ones that Jesus will raise up on the last day (vv. 37–40).

If Jesus had hoped to get a reaction from the assembled crowd with these first two points, he succeeded nicely. Some of the Jews began to murmur among themselves concerning his statement that he had come down from heaven (vv. 41–43). But it's when we come to Jesus' third point that things get really interesting—and a bit too much for many of those present that day. In response to the Jews' murmuring, Jesus informs his hearers that "No one can come to Me unless the Father who sent Me draws him; ... It is written in the prophets, 'And they shall all be taught by God.' Therefore everyone who has heard and learned from the Father comes to Me" (vv. 44–45).

Although Jesus' words were sufficiently clear, they seem to have gotten lost in the uproar over his accompanying statement that only those who eat his flesh and drink his blood will be raised at the last day (vv. 50–54). When Jesus ended the sermon, he sensed his own disciples' unease over his comments and asked them, "Does this offend you? What then if you should see the Son of Man ascend where He was before?" (vv. 61–62). With these words, Jesus seemed to be turning up the rhetorical heat even higher, demanding some kind of response from his disciples. And then, as if to put the last giant log on the fire, he told them, "But there are some of you who do not believe ... Therefore I have said to you that no one can come to Me unless it has been granted to him by My Father" (vv. 64–65).

THUD! We can only imagine that for a split second or two it was possible to hear a pin drop onto the synagogue floor from twenty feet away—such was the reaction of the band of disciples gathered around Jesus at the time. And what was Jesus' great indiscretion? He had expressed the simple truth that salvation is by grace alone. Though he had made the same point a few verses earlier in the context of his sermon, his statement afterwards was even more direct than the first. The Father must not only draw someone unto Christ, he must actually grant that it will happen in each individual case—or else it won't happen! Those for whom it has been granted were given to Christ by the Father before time began.

This passage proves that salvation by grace alone has never been a popular teaching among the unconverted. And that should hardly come as a surprise to anyone, since it runs directly counter to the natural man's view of himself as the center of the universe and as one who is *worthy* of the redemption wrought by Christ. But that's also why it's so sad that the doctrine has become such a taboo subject, even in Christian circles. This teaching of Christ, which is definitely considered out-of-bounds within the modern church growth movement, is proclaimed in very few pulpits today. After all, it's hardly conducive to a seeker-sensitive approach to worship, since it tends to separate the wheat from the chaff. And yet, that appears to have been the very purpose for which Christ brought it up in the first place: "But there are some of you who do not believe ... *Therefore* I have said to you ...." So much for making the unconverted comfortable in their sin and unbelief.

The remainder of the chapter is dedicated to systematically presenting the Bible's witness to the gracious nature of salvation.

The Covenant of Redemption

The drama of human redemption begins in the divine councils of eternity past. Theologians refer to the covenant of redemption to designate that divine agreement between the Persons of the Trinity (or between the Father and Son), which was entered into before the creation of the world, wherein the Son agreed to become Redeemer of all those persons whom the Father chose to give to him out of fallen mankind. Although the precise term doesn't appear in the Bible, the concept of an eternal covenant of redemption represents the indisputable teaching of Scripture, with mounds of textual support behind it (see, e.g., Eph. 1:3–14; 3:10–11; John 3:16–17; 6:37–40, 65; 10:18, 29; 17:1–26; Rom. 8:28–30; 16:25; 2 Tim. 1:9; Tit. 1:1–2; Heb. 2:10–13; 9:12–15; 13:20; 1 Pet. 1:2, 20; Ps. 2:7–8).

The most basic expression of the covenant is found in Ephesians 1:3–14, a passage to which we'll refer numerous times throughout the rest of this chapter:

> [3] Blessed be the God and Father of our Lord Jesus Christ, who has blessed us with every spiritual blessing in the heavenly places in Christ, [4] just as He chose us in Him before the foundation of the world,

that we should be holy and without blame before Him in love, [5] having predestined us to adoption as sons by Jesus Christ to Himself, according to the good pleasure of His will, [6] to the praise of the glory of His grace, by which He made us accepted in the Beloved. [7] In Him we have redemption through His blood, the forgiveness of sins, according to the riches of His grace [8] which He made to abound toward us in all wisdom and prudence, [9] having made known to us the mystery of His will, according to His good pleasure which He purposed in Himself, [10] that in the dispensation of the fullness of the times He might gather together in one all things in Christ, both which are in heaven and which are on earth—in Him. [11] In Him also we have obtained an inheritance, being predestined according to the purpose of Him who works all things according to the counsel of His will, [12] that we who first trusted in Christ should be to the praise of His glory. [13] In Him you also trusted, after you heard the word of truth, the gospel of your salvation; in whom also, having believed, you were sealed with the Holy Spirit of promise, [14] who is the guarantee of our inheritance until the redemption of the purchased possession, to the praise of His glory.

This passage lays out a great deal of the basic framework of the covenant:

> 1. God the Father chose certain individuals ("us") to be in Christ (v. 4).
> 2. God did so "before the foundation of the world" (v. 4).
> 3. God's choice thus predestined us to adoption in Christ (v. 5).
> 4. God's choice was "according to the good pleasure of His will" (v. 5).

5. Our redemption and forgiveness were ultimately secured through Christ's blood (v. 7).

6. Through Christ's death we obtained an inheritance (v. 11).

7. Trusting in Christ and believing the gospel is the instrument that God uses to draw us unto himself (v. 13).

8. Having believed, we were sealed with the Holy Spirit (v. 13).

Under the terms of the covenant of redemption, the Father and the Son entered into an agreement whereby the Son promised to do all that was necessary to redeem human beings from the penalty and dominion of sin in a manner consistent with God's justice. This included taking on human flesh, perfectly fulfilling the law of God, and dying on the cross in our place. For his part, the Father promised to give to the Son an eternal kingdom with a people for his own special possession as a reward for the completion of that work. Thus, the Father sent the Son into the world (John 3:16) in order to do his work and will (John 4:34).

This, then, constitutes the eternal covenant (Heb. 13:20) that secures eternal redemption (Heb. 9:12; Eph. 3:11) and by which those who are called receive an eternal inheritance (Heb. 9:15).

The Helplessness of Man's Fallen Estate

Although the covenant of redemption was entered into before the foundation of the world, it plays out only within the context of time. There were no sinners in need of redemption until the fall of mankind in the Garden. God threatened death, both spiritual and physical, as the punishment for disobedience to his command (Gen. 2:16–17), and from the moment that Adam and Eve transgressed that law, mankind has been in need of a Savior.

The result of the death brought about by the fall was twofold. First, man was rendered a sinner by nature. He was corrupted in mind, will, and emotions. No part of his being (physical or spiritual) was left untouched by the stain of sin and the effects of the fall. Before long, the wickedness of man was so great that "every intent of the thoughts of his heart was only evil continually" (Gen. 6:5). Man now possessed a deceitful heart and was desperately wicked (Jer. 17:9). According to Paul, man's mind and conscience are defiled (Tit. 1:15), and his will is enslaved to sin (Rom. 6:15–22). The theological term for this condition of man is called total depravity, not that we're as bad as we can possibly be, but that we're corrupted in every aspect of our being.

The second result of death flows from the first. We're rendered incapable of doing anything to bring about our salvation. We're "dead in trespasses and sins" (Eph. 2:1) and completely dependent upon the grace of God in order to escape our present condition (Eph. 2:4–5, 8). We're not even able to respond to God's call to repent and believe without divine aid, since our understanding is darkened (Eph. 4:17–19) and our will is inclined toward evil. Paul writes that "the natural man does not receive the things of the Spirit of God, for they are foolishness to him; nor can he know them, because they are spiritually discerned" (1 Cor. 2:14). A similar statement occurs in Romans 8:7, where Paul says that "the carnal mind is enmity against God; for it is not subject to the law of God, nor indeed can be." Of course, these statements merely confirm Jesus' words that no one can come to him unless they are drawn by the Father (John 6:44).

It's for this reason that we can designate the doctrine of total depravity better as *total inability*. We're unable to save ourselves, or even to experience the desire to be saved, without the work of the Holy Spirit renovating our will into one that's no longer at enmity with God. That's why the renewing of the person by the Holy Spirit, in which the hostile sinner is enabled to embrace the gospel, is referred to as regeneration (Tit. 3:5). This is no slight tweaking of the affections; God's Word likens it to being born again (John 3:3), being made alive (Eph. 2:1, 5; Col. 2:13), becoming a new creation (Gal. 6:15; 2 Cor. 5:17–18), or of being given a new heart and new spirit (Deut. 30:6; Ezek. 36:26–27). Such is the estate into which mankind fell through the transgression of the first man, Adam.

The Father's Gift of Believers to the Son

God would have been perfectly just to leave all of mankind in that state. But he's also rich in mercy, and so before the world was founded, he chose some who would be born in the future to receive the grace of salvation—and he gave them to the Son as a special possession (John 10:29; 17:2, 6, 9, 12, 20; Heb. 2:13). Scripture refers to this choice of sinners by God as election and demonstrates that it's solely a work of his sovereign grace.

1. Election is Gracious

God's decision to save sinners was an act of pure grace. He was under no compulsion to save anyone. Nor was he in need of anything that sinful human beings had to offer. He was completely sufficient within himself, enjoying a loving relationship within the triune nature of his being. And sinners were completely undeserving of eternal fellowship with their holy Creator. But God graciously chose to exercise his mercy, and he pulled a great multitude of those otherwise destined for destruction out of their hopeless predicament. The scriptural testimony to God's grace and mercy in election is overwhelming. Here's just a sampling of passages that speak to the matter:

> Eph. 2:8—"By grace you have been saved through faith, and that not of yourselves; it is the gift of God."

> Rom. 3:24—Sinners are "justified freely by His grace through the redemption that is in Christ Jesus."

> Rom. 11:5—"Even so then, at this present time there is a remnant according to the election of grace."

> Eph. 1:7—"In Him we have redemption through His blood, the forgiveness of sins, according to the riches of His grace."

2 Thess. 2:16—God "has loved us and given us everlasting consolation and good hope by grace."

2 Tim. 1:9—God has "saved us and called us with a holy calling, not according to our works, but according to His own purpose and grace which was given to us in Christ Jesus before time began."

Titus 2:11—"For the grace of God that brings salvation has appeared to all men."

Rom. 5:17—Believers have received an "abundance of grace" and "the gift of righteousness."

Rom. 9:16—Salvation is "of God who shows mercy."

Rom. 9:23—Believers are "vessels of mercy ... prepared beforehand for glory."

Tit. 3:5—"Not by works of righteousness which we have done, but according to His mercy He saved us."

2. Election Is Unconditional

God's decision to save human sinners was an act of his mercy. But it's clear that although many are called to salvation through the gospel, only some have actually been chosen by God to repent and believe (Jesus refers to them as "few" in number—Matt. 22:14). The ones whom God chose are "the elect" (Mark 13:20), and it's they alone who obtain salvation (Rom. 11:7).

But this fact raises an important question: upon what basis did God choose certain individuals to future salvation? Scripture tells us that his choice of particular persons was made "according to the good pleasure of His will" (Eph. 1:5). That is, it wasn't dependent upon any good quality to be found within the recipients of his grace.

On the contrary, says Paul, if it had been on the basis of anything that we were to do, it would no longer be of grace (Rom. 11:6).

And Paul used the real life example of Jacob and Esau to prove the point. He says that God chose Jacob and rejected Esau before they were born—before either of them had done anything good or evil. And what does this prove? That "the purpose of God according to election [stands]," and that purpose is that salvation be "not of works, but of Him who calls" (Rom. 9:11). In other words, election to salvation is completely one-sided; we contribute nothing to the decision, nor do we do anything to provide the basis for God's decision. As Paul says, "So then it is not of him who wills, nor of him who runs, but of God who shows mercy" (Rom. 9:16).

Paul anticipated the obvious objection of self-centered mankind. But his answer in Romans 9:14–24 is a sharp rebuke to those who would raise such an objection:

> [14] What shall we say then? Is there unrighteousness with God? Certainly not! [15] For He says to Moses, "I will have mercy on whomever I will have mercy, and I will have compassion on whomever I will have compassion." [16] So then it is not of him who wills, nor of him who runs, but of God who shows mercy. [17] For the Scripture says to the Pharaoh, "For this very purpose I have raised you up, that I may show My power in you, and that My name may be declared in all the earth." [18] Therefore He has mercy on whom He wills, and whom He wills He hardens. [19] You will say to me then, "Why does He still find fault? For who has resisted His will?" [20] But indeed, O man, who are you to reply against God? Will the thing formed say to him who formed it, "Why have you made me like this?" [21] Does not the potter have power over the clay, from the same lump to make one vessel for honor and another for dishonor? [22] What if God, wanting to show His wrath and to make His

power known, endured with much longsuffering the
vessels of wrath prepared for destruction, [23] and that
He might make known the riches of His glory on the
vessels of mercy, which He had prepared beforehand
for glory, [24] even us whom He called, not of the Jews
only, but also of the Gentiles?

Paul appreciated the fact that God's sovereign choice to exercise
mercy toward some persons and not others would cause someone to
bring the charge of unrighteousness against God for not treating all
alike (v. 14). Paul also recognized that if we don't even possess the
ability to claim the mercy of God for ourselves, it might rightly be
said that no one has resisted God's will in the matter of salvation (v.
19). But Paul's rebuke is a stinging one. He points out that we have
no business complaining about such things, since God (the potter)
is free to make one vessel for honor and another for dishonor for the
sake of displaying the riches of his own glory (vv. 20–24).

Furthermore, it's implicit in Paul's statement that man is responsible
for his own predicament (1:18; 3:23). If he's unable to approach
God and claim eternal life on the basis of his own righteousness,
it's only because he rendered himself unable to do so at the Fall.
Since that time, divine mercy is the only basis upon which man
may be saved, and mercy is, by definition, an act of grace. Therefore,
God is perfectly righteous and fair to choose some and not others,
since all were deserving of eternal punishment. He'll have mercy
and compassion upon whomever he chooses (vv. 15, 18), and man is
without standing to complain about it.

It hardly needs to be pointed out that such a teaching doesn't sit well
with moderns, who tend to think of themselves, and not God, as the
center of the universe. But as Paul points out, there's nothing new with
that line of thinking. Indeed, it's more or less the essence of our sin
problem—thinking that we're somehow worthy of more than God is
obliged to give to us. As a result, some have attempted to evade the
force of Paul's words by positing the notion of a conditional election.
That is, they hypothesize that God's choice of individual sinners was

based upon their foreseen faith. In eternity past, God supposedly looked down the tunnel of time and saw who would eventually choose to believe in his Son and made his elective choice on that basis. Those who have developed this theory have tended to rely on Peter's salutation to the pilgrims of the dispersion, whom he called "elect according to the foreknowledge of God the Father" (1 Pet. 1:2).

But frankly, the problems with this view are so numerous that I'm surprised anyone can still make the argument with a straight face. Here are some of the ways in which the theory of conditional election fails to stand up to the test of Scripture:

> a) The foreknowledge of God is nowhere defined as his looking through the tunnel of time to see how people would respond to the gospel; in fact, 1 Peter 1:2 says nothing about faith at all. Rather, it's the pilgrims themselves who were foreknown by God. And this is nothing other than a reference to God's having fore-loved them, as the rest of Scripture makes clear. We're told that we love God only because he first loved us (1 John 4:10, 19), and that the elect are those who have been "beloved" by God (Col. 3:12; 1 Thess. 1:4). In Rom. 8:29–30, Paul says that the blessings of salvation are for those whom God foreknew. Also, "God has not cast away His people whom He foreknew" (Rom. 11:2). Indeed, Paul's great example of electing grace in Romans 9 is based upon the fact that God loved Jacob and hated Esau (Rom. 9:13). Furthermore, Peter uses the same root word only a few verses later in reference to Jesus, whom he said was "foreordained before the foundation of the world" (1 Pet. 1:20). Finally, Peter's sermon at Pentecost shows him using the term foreknowledge as a synonym for God's "determined purpose" to deliver Jesus up to death for our sakes (Acts 2:23). It seems clear, then, that foreknowledge isn't something for which God must rely upon his creatures to supply him.

b) The notion of foreseen faith as the basis for election runs contrary to Paul's description of grace as something that's completely unmerited. If God's choice of us is conditioned upon our work of faith, even if no other qualities are taken into account, then in what sense is it based upon mercy? As Paul says, "if by grace, then it is no longer of works; otherwise grace is no longer grace" (Rom. 11:6). Indeed, in the very next verse of Peter's epistle, after his reference to the foreknowledge of God, he chalks up his readers' salvation to God's "abundant mercy."

c) The notion of foreseen faith as the basis for God's election runs directly counter to the statement in Ephesians 1:5 that God "predestined us to adoption as sons by Jesus Christ to Himself, according to the good pleasure of His will" (cf. Rom. 8:28–30; 2 Tim. 1:9).

d) The theory of conditional election ignores the more basic fact that even faith is a gift from God, a subject that we'll take up in a moment.

e) Paul's hypothetical objections in Romans 9 make sense only if we understand election as being unconditional in nature. Why on earth would anyone raise the objection that God was unfair in not treating all alike, if he had actually based his choice on something he foresaw us doing—something that entailed obedience to his direct command to believe the gospel? And how could anyone argue that God shouldn't find fault because no one had resisted his will, if resistance to his will was the very basis upon which he made his electing choice?

Scripture tells us that "God has chosen the foolish things of the world to put to shame the wise" and "the weak things of the world to put to shame the things which are mighty." He has purposely chosen the "base" and "despised" things of the world to receive his grace. And for what reason? "That no flesh should glory in His presence" (1 Cor. 1:27–29). The doctrine of unconditional election is a blow to man's efforts to exalt himself; that's why Paul reminds us that we're but clay in the hands of the Potter and that he made us for his own glory.

3. God's Will Alone Is the Efficient Cause of Our Salvation

The gracious, unconditional nature of election is the reason why Scripture is explicit in attributing salvation to God alone. The constant biblical refrain is that God chose us, and that his will is the efficient cause of our believing to salvation:

> John 1:13—Believers were born, "not of blood, nor of the will of the flesh, nor of the will of man, but of God."

> Jas. 1:18—"Of His own will He brought us forth by the word of truth."

> 1 Thess. 5:9—"For God did not appoint us to wrath, but to obtain salvation through our Lord Jesus Christ."

> Ps. 65:4—"Blessed is the man You choose, and cause to approach You."

> Ps. 33:12—"Blessed is the nation whose God is the Lord, the people He has chosen as His own inheritance."

> Rom. 9:16—"So then it is not of him who wills, nor of him who runs, but of God who shows mercy."

> 2 Thess. 2:13—"But we are bound to give thanks to God always for you, brethren beloved by the Lord,

because God from the beginning chose you for salvation through sanctification by the Spirit and belief in the truth."

The Father's Gift of Faith to Believers

At this point, it seems almost superfluous to lay out our argument that faith in the gospel message is a gift from God to his elect. It should be clear by now that God's "purpose according to election" can only stand if he himself sees to it that each step in the process (including the elect believing unto salvation) comes to pass. And this is precisely what he assures us in his word. Romans 8:28–30, which is fondly referred to as The Golden Chain of Salvation, reads as follows:

> [28] And we know that all things work together for good to those who love God, to those who are the called according to His purpose. [29] For whom He foreknew, He also predestined to be conformed to the image of His Son, that He might be the firstborn among many brethren. [30] Moreover whom He predestined, these He also called; whom He called, these He also justified; and whom He justified, these He also glorified.

God (through Paul) tells us in this passage that all of those whom he set his love on (those he foreknew) he predestined to receive the grace of salvation. Thus, he preordains whatsoever comes to pass so that each individual elected to salvation will be called to faith by the gospel and ultimately justified and glorified. And because we're justified solely by faith in Christ, there's no chance that any of those called according to his purpose of election will fail to believe the gospel message. God's grace in election is irresistible. That is, it's efficacious; it never fails to bring about the change intended by God.

Of course, left to his own devices, no man would believe the gospel. His mind and understanding is darkened, and he's at enmity with God. But God graciously causes those whom he has chosen to repent and believe the gospel message. He does so through "the washing of regeneration and renewing of the Holy Spirit" (Tit. 3:5). He causes those whom he has chosen to be born again and to become new creations, breaking down their hearts of stone and giving them new hearts of flesh. At that moment, the righteousness of Christ is imputed to their account, and they're justified in the sight of God.

Although many people today love to deny that faith is a gift to the elect, the scriptural testimony to the truth of it is overwhelming:

> Phil 1:29—"For to you it has been granted on behalf of Christ, not only to believe in Him, but also to suffer for His sake."

> Eph. 2:8—"For by grace you have been saved through faith, and that not of yourselves; it is the gift of God."

> 2 Thess. 2:13–14—"God from the beginning chose you for salvation through sanctification by the Spirit and belief in the truth, to which He called you by our gospel."

> Jas. 2:5—"Listen, my beloved brethren: Has God not chosen the poor of this world to be rich in faith and heirs of the kingdom which He promised to those who love Him?"

> Matt. 16:15–17—"He said to them, 'But who do you say that I am?' Simon Peter answered and said, 'You are the Christ, the Son of the living God.' Jesus answered and said to him, 'Blessed are you, Simon Bar-Jonah, for flesh and blood has not revealed this to you, but My Father who is in heaven.'"

> 1 Cor. 4:7—"For who makes you differ from another? And what do you have that you did not receive? Now

if you did indeed receive it, why do you boast as if you had not received it?"

Rom. 12:3—"God has dealt to each one [believers] a measure of faith."

Acts 18:27—Paul "greatly helped those who had believed through grace."

Gal. 1:15–16—Paul says that God called him "through His grace, to reveal His Son in me."

Matt. 13:11—"He [Jesus] answered and said to them, 'Because it has been given to you to know the mysteries of the kingdom of heaven, but to them it has not been given.'"

1 Pet. 1:5—Peter says that believers "are kept by the power of God through faith."

John 6:65—"Therefore I have said to you that no one can come to Me unless it has been granted to him by My Father."

John 15:6—"You did not choose Me, but I chose you and appointed you."

Phil 2:12–13—"Therefore, my beloved, as you have always obeyed, not as in my presence only, but now much more in my absence, work out your own salvation with fear and trembling; for it is God who works in you both to will and to do for His good pleasure."

1 Cor. 12:3—"Therefore I make known to you that no one speaking by the Spirit of God calls Jesus

accursed, and no one can say that Jesus is Lord except by the Holy Spirit"

Eph. 1:17–18—Paul prayed that God would give to the Ephesians "the spirit of wisdom and revelation in the knowledge of Him, the eyes of your understanding being enlightened; that you may know what is the hope of His calling, what are the riches of the glory of His inheritance in the saints."

Acts 16:14—Luke writes with respect to a woman named Lydia, that "the Lord opened her heart to heed the things spoken by Paul."

Rom. 4:16—"Therefore it is of faith that it might be according to grace."

Acts 13:48—"Now when the Gentiles heard this, they were glad and glorified the word of the Lord. And as many as had been appointed to eternal life believed."

2 Tim. 2:24–26—"And a servant of the Lord must not quarrel but be gentle to all, able to teach, patient, in humility correcting those who are in opposition, if God perhaps will grant them repentance, so that they may know the truth, and that they may come to their senses and escape the snare of the devil, having been taken captive by him to do his will."

Heb. 12:2—Jesus Christ is "the author and finisher of our faith."

Faith in Christ is the instrument or channel through which the blessings of salvation come upon a son or daughter of Adam. The Holy

Spirit works repentance and faith in the heart of every single person for whom Christ died at the time appointed for such a work to take place. An individual Christian then turns from his prior ways and embraces the truth of God's Word in Christ. The faith that he exercises is truly his own; the Holy Spirit doesn't do the believing for him. But his belief is still a gift from God, for God sees to it that all those whom he foreknew are called and justified through the preaching of the Word. In this way, he's both "just and the justifier of the one who has faith in Jesus" (Rom. 3:26). And because of this, all human boasting is excluded (Rom. 3:27).

The Importance of the Matter

Martin Luther is reported to have said that the only thing that a man contributes to his own salvation is his sin. How true that is. The uniform testimony of Scripture is that "salvation is of the Lord" (Jonah 2:9). But that truth has fallen on hard times in our post-enlightenment society with its emphasis on the individual and his ability to be the captain of his soul. In a day when the "free-will" to choose any course of action without constraints is considered the ultimate path to authentic existence, the Bible's teaching that salvation is monergistic (a work of God alone) is about as popular as flies at a picnic.

But popularity has never been the determinant of what's true, as Luther himself learned in the sixteenth century. In his greatest work, *The Bondage of the Will*, Luther identified this as the essential issue between himself and those who sought to take the medieval church down the road that eventually became the modern Roman Catholic religion. Yes, the issue was justification by faith alone, but that's really just a shorthand expression for the more accurate "justification by grace alone, *through* faith alone, because of Christ alone." Luther and the other Reformers, in keeping with the historic position of the church since the days of Augustine, understood that man is incapable of doing anything to make himself worthy of salvation. His will is in bondage to sin, and he's spiritually dead in trespasses and sins. He needs God to rescue him from his predicament.

On the other hand, those who went on to found the Roman

Catholic religion at the Council of Trent (1545–1563) explicitly rejected the teaching of the Bible and adopted a synergistic model of salvation wherein God and man supposedly work together for a salvation that's never guaranteed and which man is required to merit through his own best (albeit grace-aided) efforts. And what's the essential difference that underlies these two opposing positions? It's whether the fall of Adam left mankind spiritually dead in trespasses and sins, as the Bible says, or merely sick and in need of only a general form of grace that's available to all people indiscriminately in order that they may believe unto salvation. It should be obvious that the latter belief makes the determining factor in salvation the will of man, not the will of God.

I don't believe that it's hyperbole to say that the supposed "free will" to choose for or against God to salvation is the holy grail of modern evangelicalism. The influence of men like Robert Schuller and earlier proponents of this myth, such as Charles Finney, have led to a near-total abandonment of the biblical teaching on this subject in mainline and broadly evangelical churches in America today. The doctrines of election and particular redemption simply won't fly in a day when the prevailing philosophy places man at the center of the universe. Teaching these doctrines won't pack churches with unbelievers, it's thought. Thus, they've got to go. And the expulsion has been devastating to the health of American (and worldwide) Christianity. If Jesus' sermon in John 6 teaches us anything, it's that where a person stands on this issue tells us a lot about their spiritual condition.

Perhaps the most tragic aspect of this state of affairs is that the doctrine that's so despised is one that's meant to provide Christians with their greatest source of comfort. What could be more comforting than the assurance that my union with Christ and the benefits which flow from that union are things that cannot be taken away, for God himself has predestined me to be conformed to the image of his Son—and his will cannot be thwarted by anyone or anything? How reassuring it is to know that my salvation doesn't ultimately depend upon my own strength but upon the will of God and the finished work of Christ. If it were the other way around, I would be in big trouble. Frankly, it's mystifying to me how anyone could find comfort in the "free will" of man to choose for or against God. That's a guaranteed death sentence.

To think wrongly about the work of salvation means thinking wrongly of the Savior who secured it for us through his life and death. The question for each of us is: Will I honor him by giving him the glory for my salvation? Or will I seek to hold back some glory for myself by asserting that he only made it *possible* for me to be saved, and that the determining factor was my personal choice to accept the gift that he offered to all?

Scripture says that Jesus made redemption for all those (and only those) that the Father had given to him before the foundation of the world. Out of his pure grace, and in accordance with his good pleasure, the Father chose a multitude of persons to be saved from the mass of fallen mankind. He then sent his Son into the world to undertake the work that was necessary to satisfy the demands of his justice and to provide the means for those whom he had chosen to be reconciled to him. Christ finished the work, and to this day the Holy Spirit continues the task of applying the redemptive benefits of that work to the recipients of God's grace through belief in the gospel message. Where is the place for human boasting in all of that? Of course, it's excluded. To God alone be the glory!

16

He Is Both Lord and Christ

(ACTS 2:36)

As long as the topic of church growth is fresh on our minds, the present chapter will look at biblical preaching having a very different effect from that which we just witnessed. If, as we saw in the last chapter, Jesus' sermon in John 6 demonstrates how faithful preaching of the truth will often repel unbelievers, Peter's sermon at Pentecost in Acts 2 demonstrates how it will also attract believers. In reality, Peter's sermon was even less seeker sensitive than Jesus' sermon, but the focus of Luke (the writer of Acts) is upon the positive effects that it produced. There's little doubt that it also drew the scorn of a great many hearers that day. Good biblical preaching will generally elicit both types of responses, at least when addressed to a mixed crowd of believers and unbelievers, as was the case at Pentecost.

But as with the last chapter, our focus here isn't so much on the art of preaching and the effects that it produces as with the content of the message—in particular, the message of Jesus Christ and his work in delivering sinners from the wrath and judgment of God. In this case, Peter's sermon adds yet another important detail to the picture of Christ that the New Testament paints for us, although it may not seem at first glance to offer anything new to what we have already produced.

Peter's Sermon at Pentecost

Peter's sermon on the Day of Pentecost is probably the most famous of all apostolic sermons. It's the first recorded sermon subsequent to Jesus' ascension into heaven and is truly remarkable for one reason: it shows the dramatic change that had occurred within the apostolic band (particularly Peter) as a result of their encounter with the risen Christ. No longer were they the scared rabbits that had abandoned him at his arrest and crucifixion. From this point forward, they would stare down hostile crowds, and even the Roman civil authorities, in their efforts to take the gospel to all nations.

Peter's sermon is the premier example of this newfound apostolic boldness. For one thing, he stood up at the temple in Jerusalem on that holy day and proclaimed that Jesus of Nazareth, who had been put to death only seven weeks earlier, had been raised from the dead by God, and that it was he who was heir to the throne of David. Perhaps even more shocking, however, is that Peter went so far as to place the blame for Christ's death squarely on the shoulders of his audience. And he did so twice in the space of a few sentences. In the first instance, speaking to the crowd, he said that "you have taken [Christ] by lawless hands, have crucified, and put [him] to death" (Acts 2:23).

Undoubtedly, there were some in the crowd that day who had been part of the multitude crying out, "Crucify him," only seven weeks earlier. But Peter was hardly proclaiming seeker-sensitive fare. Was it really necessary to blame all of those assembled in Jerusalem that day for the death of the Messiah? In a word, yes. Peter was speaking to Jews (2:5), and even those who hadn't participated in calling for the Messiah's death were a part of the nation that had collectively rejected him. Thus, Peter's second reference to their responsibility was even more explicit at this point: "Therefore let all the house of Israel know assuredly that God has made this Jesus, whom you crucified, both Lord and Christ" (2:36).

The words of verse 36 represent Peter's concluding statement to the crowd that day. The entire "house of Israel" bore the responsibility for rejecting the very One whom God had made both Lord and Christ. Luke tells us that the crowd (or at least a portion of it) was "cut to the heart" by Peter's words and asked what they should do. Peter responded, "Repent, and let every one of you be baptized in the name of Jesus Christ for the remission of sins" (vv. 37–38). The result was that about three thousand persons were added to the church that day (v. 41).

Luke doesn't tell us how many people were in Jerusalem that day. It's certainly possible that there were tens of thousands of Jews who either witnessed Peter's sermon firsthand or at least heard later reports of it. Nevertheless, for one sermon to produce three thousand converts is remarkable in any setting. In this case it was a vivid testimony to the fact that Peter (along with the other apostles) had now received the promise of being filled with the Holy Spirit (v. 4)—a promise that Jesus himself had given to them only a few days earlier (1:8).

The Son: Made Both Lord and Christ

What interests us here is Peter's statement that God has made Jesus both Lord and Christ. Of course, it should be obvious how this statement could be subject to misinterpretation. It is one thing for Peter to say that God had made Jesus the Christ. But what about Lord? How is it that Jesus, the incarnate Son of God, could be *made* Lord? Does this mean that there was a time when he wasn't Lord? Does this mean that he only became Lord upon the completion of his work? Or is something else going on here?

Clearly, something else is going on here, for in an earlier chapter we established the issue of Christ's eternal sonship. There was no moment, either before or after the foundation of the world, when the Son wasn't the divine Lord of the universe. That title belongs to him by virtue of his divine identity, just as it belongs to the Father and Spirit as well. But there's a sense in which the title applies more particularly to the Son as a result of his finished work and because of the agreement embedded within the covenant of redemption that we looked at in the last chapter. That covenant made the Son the recipient of a promised inheritance—a kingdom and a people of his own, all of which would be due to him at the completion of his earthly work. In this sense, God (the maker of the promise) has also made the Son Lord over all of creation.

Lord and Christ: How the Father Sees Him

Moreover, we mustn't lose sight of the fact that when the Son of God became incarnate, he entered into a new phase in his role as Savior of the world and Redeemer of his people. With his assumption of human flesh, the Son became the only Mediator between God and man, thereby making it possible for man to be reconciled to God. This was the work given to him by the Father in the eternal covenant of redemption. And it is what gives the title Lord added force in his case.

The distinction that we're driving at is nicely summarized by Berkhof:

> As the Second Person in the Holy Trinity, the eternal Son, Christ naturally shares the dominion of God over all His creatures. His throne is established in the heavens and His Kingdom ruleth over all, Ps. 103:19. This kingship differs from the mediatorial kingship of Christ, which is a conferred and economical kingship, exercised by Christ, not merely in His divine nature, but as Theanthropos (the God-man). The latter is not a kingship that was Christ's by original right, but one with which He is invested. It does not pertain to a new realm, one that was not already under His control as Son of God, for such a realm can nowhere be found. It is rather,

to speak in the words of [John] Dick, His original kingship, "invested with a new form, wearing a new aspect, administered for a new end"....

Christ was formally invested with this kingship over the universe when He was exalted at the right hand of God. It was a promised reward of His labors, Ps. 2:8,9; Matt. 28:28; Eph. 1:20–22; Phil. 2:9–11. This investiture was part of the exaltation of the God-man. It did not give Him any power or authority which He did not already possess as the Son of God; neither did it increase His territory. But the God-man, the Mediator, was now made possessor of this authority, and His human nature was made to share in the glory of this royal dominion. Moreover, the government of the world was now made subservient to the interests of the Church of Jesus Christ. And this kingship of Christ will last until the victory over the enemies is complete and even death has been abolished, I Cor. 15:24–28.[1]

Few of us fully appreciate that ever since the ascension and exaltation of Jesus Christ into the heavenly realms, a new state of affairs has existed in the government of the universe. It's not merely that human nature has now taken a permanent seat at God's right hand, as glorious as that fact may be. But the Father now sees the Son as the rightful ruler of that universe, as the One for whom "all things were created" and in whom "all things consist" (Col. 1:16–17). As a result of this, it's the Son who is to have the preeminence in all things (v. 18).

By virtue of the Son's completion of the work given to him by the Father in the covenant of redemption, he now has authority over the entire created order. He is Lord over all. And he is Lord in his capacity as the God-Man. His divine nature needed no augmentation, but human nature had never before shared in the government of the universe. Jesus (the name given to the God-Man) needed to be *made* both Lord and Christ.

Lord and Christ: How We See Him

The earliest and most primitive confession of the New Testament church was that "Jesus is Lord." Christians who lived in the decades following Jesus' death and resurrection boldly proclaimed his deity and sovereign rule in the face of stiff and deadly opposition. Peter's words at Pentecost testify to the confessional view of the post-ascension church: Jesus of Nazareth is both Christ (the Messiah) and Lord (the divine Son of God). And as both Christ and Lord, he alone is Savior.

Unfortunately, some in the church today deny this confessional formula in practice. They argue that people may take Jesus as their Savior and yet ignore his claims to be Lord over their life. To be clear, they don't argue that one can deny Christ's deity and still be a Christian; rather, they argue that one can be a true Christian and yet ignore the demands that Christ as divine Lord places upon them through his revealed Word. The refrain that's often heard by those who espouse such a view is that professing Christians who live an immoral life have accepted Jesus as Savior but haven't yet made him their Lord.

This theological notion, usually referred to as nonlordship salvation, is based upon a faulty reading of 1 Corinthians 3:1–4. In that passage, Paul chides the Corinthian Christians for acting carnally by creating divisions among themselves based upon whose ministry had been instrumental in leading them to the church. This single text has led to the development of the carnal-Christian myth, which posits the existence of two distinct classes of Christians—the carnal and the spiritual. Those who fall into the latter class have supposedly chosen to make Christ the Lord of their lives and to turn from their sinful ways. Some proponents of this view go even further by arguing that a second work of grace is necessary to lead one from the carnal to the spiritual stage.

But the biblical evidence against such a view is overwhelming. None of the New Testament writers ever separates Christians into two distinct classes. Rather, a person is either in a natural or fleshly (unsaved) state or in a spiritual (saved) state (cf. Rom. 8:1–9; Gal. 5:17–24). In fact, Paul uses this very distinction in the verses immediately preceding his rebuke of the Corinthian believers: "But the natural man does not receive the things of the Spirit of God, for they are foolishness to him; nor can he know them, because they are spiritually discerned. But he who is spiritual judges all things" (1 Cor. 2:14–15). Paul rebuked the Corinthians not for falling into a class of inferior Christians but for acting carnally in a particular area of their lives, a deficiency that Paul prays that they'll correct.

To be sure, individual Christians will be at different stages of the process of sanctification and will produce different levels of spiritual fruit. Some will still be clinging to the remnants of the old man more than others. Paul even describes himself as carnal in his saved state (Rom. 7:14), testifying that he continued to struggle against ongoing sin in his life. But all who are Christians have been given the Holy Spirit, and have become new creatures in Christ (2 Cor. 5:17). They are in the process of being transformed into the image of Christ (2 Cor. 3:18), and that process is assured for each and every one of them (Rom. 8:29). God is at work within the life of every believer, producing spiritual fruit, and making for himself a people who are zealous for good works (Phil. 2:13; Tit. 2:14). Anyone who lacks these qualities altogether, regardless of his or her self-confessed spiritual condition, isn't a carnal Christian but an unbeliever (James 2:14–26). Those who love Christ will confess him as Lord and delight in doing his will (Rom. 7:22; 1 John 2:3–5; 3:10; 5:1–3).

The dangers of the carnal-Christian myth and the whole nonlordship theological position are numerous. First, by setting up a false dichotomy within the church between those who are carnal and those who are spiritual, it opens the door to a great deal of judgmentalism and sectarianism. After all, someone will need to determine who falls into each category, since the two groups need very different calls to action. Those who are carnal need to embrace Christ as Lord and take the next step to the higher life, and those who are spiritual to reach even higher levels of spirituality. But who will do this? And what standard will they use?[2]

Second, the appeal to the so-called carnal Christian to become a spiritual Christian denigrates the conversion experience and exalts some imaginary second work of grace that supposedly leads to the deeper life.[3] But when this second work of grace isn't forthcoming after some period of time, the result is often multitudes of defeated and dejected Christians.

Finally, the perpetuation of the carnal-Christian myth, while tending to create despondency in some true Christians, also tends to give false assurance to those who haven't been truly regenerated by God's Spirit and brought into union with Christ. This is probably the most dangerous aspect of the nonlordship theological system; it tends to make unbelievers comfortable in their sin and unbelief by making them think that it's perfectly normal to have experienced no change in their desires or attitudes upon coming to faith. But if that's the case, what these folks need isn't a call to live the higher Christian life but a call to repent and believe the gospel in the first instance. Richard Phillips writes:

> Therefore, we see that the higher-life teachers err on both sides of the equation. There are no "carnal" Christians who have yet to pass through the veil into a personal relationship with God; such persons are not Christians at all. Likewise, there are no "spiritual" Christians for whom all struggle is gone in this life, who have entered into a stage of perfect sanctification. Indeed, the expectation of the latter stage is injurious to the Christian's spiritual life, for the struggle with sin and weakness is not a sign that we have not yet arrived as Christians. Rather, it is merely the reality of life this side of heaven, a life we are to live through faith as God's strength is made perfect in our weakness (2 Cor. 12:9). If anything, we are all carnal Christians, the word "carnal" meaning "fleshly." This is how Paul described himself, "The life I now live *in the flesh* I live by faith in the Son of God, who loved

me and gave himself for me" (Gal. 2:20). Instead of seeking some higher spiritual plateau, our calling is simply to grow in grace as we learn more and more to trust and to love the Lord our God.[4]

When a person comes to faith in Christ, they're a new creation. Though they struggle with sin until the day they die, their desires and attitudes have been fundamentally changed. They now embrace the One whom they had previously rejected and see that One as both Lord and Christ. In the end, it's absurd to say that Christ could be their Savior but not their Lord. If Christ isn't a person's Lord, then it's certain that he's not their Savior.

Lord and Christ: How We Speak of Him

There's a less conspicuous, though no less troubling, way in which some people effectively deny that Jesus is Lord and Christ. And in this case, I've no doubt that many of those who are guilty of this theological deficiency would vehemently protest that they don't in fact deny either Jesus' lordship or his Messiahship. At least some of them are probably not even aware of their own practice in this area. We refer here to the hesitancy of some to use these two titles in reference to Jesus when they speak of him, whether in the context of prayer, evangelism, or general conversation with others.

First, let me be clear that I'm *not* suggesting that it's never proper to refer to the Second Person of the Trinity as Jesus without any modifying title attached. On the contrary, I've already done so many times in this book. Rather, what I'm suggesting is that behind the hesitancy of some to use the titles of Christ and Lord lies a theological conviction that's, at best, a cowardly concession to the modern church growth movement, and at worst, a heretical attempt to strip Jesus Christ of his divine honors. For many today, the problem reflects a tendency to see Jesus Christ in an all-too-familiar light—as a spiritual buddy and accountability partner rather than as eternal Lord and Christ.

In his massive commentary on Hebrews, A. W. Pink makes the following observations regarding the way in which the New Testament writers refer to Jesus:

> 1. First, "Jesus" isn't a title but the name given to the Son in his human nature. The gospel narratives use the name Jesus in order to emphasize his humiliation.
>
> 2. Jesus' enemies referred to him as "Jesus of Nazareth" but not his disciples (see John 13:13). Only once in the four gospels do we find any of his disciples speaking of him with this identification, and that was when their faith had given way (Luke 24:19). Thus, says Pink, it was the language of unbelief.
>
> 3. When we come to the Acts and Epistles, which cover the period following his exaltation, Jesus is commonly referred to as either Christ or Lord, or in many cases both Christ and Lord in the same breath (as with our present passage). From this point forward, Christ is never referred to simply as "Jesus" except for the purpose of historical identification (e.g., Acts 1:11), to stress his humiliation, or when his enemies are speaking of him.[5]

A vivid example of this commitment may be seen in the opening words of Paul's first epistle to the Corinthians. In the span of only ten short verses, he refers to the Savior once as "Christ," once as "Jesus Christ," twice as "Christ Jesus," once as "the Lord Jesus Christ," twice as "Jesus Christ our Lord," and three times as "our Lord Jesus Christ." Thus, concludes Pink, "To address the Lord of glory in prayer simply as 'Jesus,' or to speak of Him to others thus, breathes an unholy familiarity, a vulgar cheapness, an irreverence which is highly reprehensible."[6]

No doubt some will object to Pink's words as too strong in their denunciation, but I believe that he was not only correct in diagnosing the problem but was also prescient in calling attention to it, as it has become an even more prevalent tendency in the years since he wrote. We live in an age when the siren call of humanism reigns supreme, and we in the church have been affected by it, whether or not we recognize that fact. We've become entirely too lax in the way we think and speak of the Lord Jesus Christ, and we've caved in to the cultural pressure to stress Jesus' humanity and tone down the talk of his divine identity. After all, the unbelieving world is only too happy to let us have our baby Jesus born in a stable. He's no threat to anyone. But if you want to speak of a Christ and Lord—well, that's an entirely different matter, isn't it?

And for anyone who may be thinking that this whole discussion falls in the realm of making a mountain out of a molehill, I simply urge you to consider the following: no enlisted man in our armed forces would dare address an officer without calling him "sir," nor would a person appear in any court in the land and address the presiding judge without the obligatory "your honor." Why, then, would we as Christians excuse or endorse the practice of addressing the Lord of glory by only his given human name?

The man Jesus is now the exalted and glorified Christ, and Lord of the universe. Is it not proper for us to address him in that way—at least as a general rule? Rather than succumbing to the prevailing pressure to bring Christ down to our level, we need to take our cue from Peter and the other apostles. Let us shout it from the rooftops: God has made Jesus both Lord and Christ.

17

He Is the Intercessor on Behalf of His People

(Heb. 7:25)

As we noted in Chapter 5, the Lord Jesus Christ holds an unchangeable priesthood that he now exercises at the right hand of the Father in heaven. Unlike the priests of old, whose ministries ceased upon their deaths (or earlier), Christ's priesthood "continues forever" for he's a priest after the order of Melchizedek, not of Aaron (Heb. 7:11–24).

Indeed, Christ's death was itself the most important aspect of his work, but it didn't end his work on behalf of sinners. His subsequent resurrection and ascension into heaven made possible the next (and present) phase of his priestly work—his ongoing intercession before the throne of God on behalf of his people. The writer of Hebrews sums up the implications of this fact with the following pronouncement: "Therefore He is also able to save to the uttermost those who come to God through Him, since He always lives to make intercession for them" (Heb. 7:25).

The intercession of Christ on behalf of his people isn't a terribly controversial or complex topic though it's subject to potential misunderstanding. There's no doubt, however, that it's one of the least appreciated aspects of the Savior's work. In all likelihood, few Christians today ever give much thought to the fact that Christ is interceding for them in heaven. But without that intercession, we would be lost forever. In recognition of that fact, this chapter will explore the nature and purpose of Christ's ongoing intercessory work and the role that it plays in the redemptive plan of God.

The Sinner's Advocate

When God's people returned to the Promised Land from the Babylonian exile and captivity in the sixth century BC, God gave them a very specific task: rebuild the temple. After an auspicious start, the work soon bogged down under a combination of Jewish indifference and Samaritan opposition to the rebuilding efforts. Around the year 520 BC God sent the prophet Zechariah to call the people back to the work. In his prophecy, Zechariah records a series of visions designed to assure the people of Israel that God's favor continued to rest upon them and to spur them on to the completion of their work.

In the first of his visions, Zechariah records the details of how the Angel of the Lord (the pre-incarnate Christ) interceded to the Lord of hosts on behalf of the people of Israel that their long exile and lack of rest in the land would finally come to an end. Zechariah 1:12–13 reads:

> Then the Angel of the Lord answered and said, "O LORD of hosts, how long will You not have mercy on Jerusalem and on the cities of Judah, against which you were angry these seventy years?" And the LORD answered the angel who talked to me, with good and comforting words.

The "good and comforting words" that God spoke to Israel included his promise that he would "return to Jerusalem with mercy" and would cause the cities of Judah to "spread out through prosperity" (vv. 14–17). Thus, his judgment upon the disobedience of the Israelites would end, and a new period of divine favor would be ushered in. Zechariah's vision shows the proximate cause of God's merciful change of disposition to be the intercession of the Angel of the Lord on behalf of sinful Israel.

In another vision recorded a couple of chapters later (3:1–10), Zechariah sees the high priest Joshua standing before this same Angel of the Lord in what may well be the throne room of heaven. However, this time another individual is present—Satan, who stands at Joshua's right hand ready to accuse him to God and to oppose God's extension of mercy to Israel, whom Joshua represents. But Satan's accusations fail for the Angel of the Lord steps forward to rebuke him instead. Moreover, in a remarkable picture that's symbolic of what Christ does for us in the transaction of justification, the Angel ordered those who stood before him to remove Joshua's filthy garments and to clothe him with the "rich robes" of righteousness (v. 4–5).

This latter vision poignantly captures the reality of the situation in which a sinner saved by grace finds himself. As a sinner, I stand guilty at the bar of heavenly justice. The Father, who sits as Judge in heaven, knows all my iniquities and my inability to plead my own case before him on the basis of personal merit. The adversary stands ready to make his case against me, holding in his hands a catalog of individual sins that I've committed, the sum of which is simply too numerous to count. But standing there beside me—ready to oppose the accusations of Satan and plead my cause before the Father—is Jesus Christ the righteous, who points out that I am one of his, at which point the verdict of not guilty is pronounced.

The very reason that Christ ascended into heaven was so that he could appear on our behalf in the presence of God (Heb. 9:24). For this reason the apostle John tells his readers that when they sin, they should remember that "we have an Advocate with the Father, Jesus Christ the righteous" (1 John 2:1).

The Nature of Christ's Ongoing Intercession

But it would be a mistake to think of Christ's intercession on behalf of his people as occurring only at the bar of judgment or as consisting only in legal claims put forth on their behalf. Rather, it's multifaceted and ultimately concerned with all that we ourselves are concerned to pray about—and much more.

No place is more instructive in this regard than Jesus' own prayer for his disciples in John 17. Delivered on the night before his crucifixion, it has come to be known as his High Priestly Prayer, and it gives us a glimpse into the kind of concerns that Jesus prayed about to the Father as he prepared to leave his disciples. It was delivered during his humiliation, but there's no reason to think that it's not indicative of the type of prayer that he continues to offer up to the Father in his glorified and exalted state today.

First, Jesus prayed that the Father would "keep" (protect) all those who had been given to him and that they might share the same kind of unity in all things that is enjoyed by Father and Son (v. 11). He also prayed that his disciples' joy be fulfilled (v. 13), that they be kept from the temptations and snares of the devil (v. 15), and that they be sanctified by the truth (v. 17–19).

In addition, Christ prayed for those who would believe in him later through the work of his disciples (v. 20); that they, too, would come to faith and be one in purpose and mind with those who came before them (vv. 21–23); that the world would thereby come to know that the Father had sent the Son and has loved the disciples of the Son as well (v. 23); that all those who are Christ's would eventually be glorified (v. 24); and finally, that they might exhibit the same kind of love for one another that the Father has for the Son (v. 26).

Jesus' High Priestly Prayer makes it clear that he exercises his intercessory work only on behalf of the elect of God. He told the Father, "I do not pray for the world but for those whom You have given Me, for they are Yours" (v. 9). In one of the Messianic psalms attributed to David, but which finds its ultimate fulfillment in Christ, he writes that his delight was in the saints on earth, but that with respect to those who hasten after other gods, he wouldn't even "take up their names on my lips" (Ps. 16:3–4).

Thus, it's critical to a proper understanding of the subject to note that Christ doesn't intercede for all men generally but only for those whom God has chosen for redemption before the foundation of the world. Nor are his intercessory prayers merely general in nature. As we can see from John 17, as well as from the prophecies of Zechariah, Christ's intercession is specifically directed toward the spiritual interests of his people. And in that sense it's also comprehensive in scope.

Christ prays to the Father that his people will receive every spiritual blessing that is available to them (Eph. 1:3). He prays that they might be brought to faith, united to others in faith, protected from the enemy, comforted in affliction, growing in the grace of sanctification, loving toward one another, seeking to know the truth of his holy Word, and empowered for service by the Holy Spirit.

The Necessity of Christ's Ongoing Intercession

The intercessory work of Christ in heaven isn't a mere adornment to the work that he performed on earth, as if it were somehow nice to have such work chalked up to one's account but not be essential in the final analysis. On the contrary, Christ's heavenly work on behalf of sinners is simply the continuation of the work that he began on earth, carrying it forward to its intended goal.

It's true that Christ's work on the cross secured the salvation of the elect once and for all and that nothing may be added to, or subtracted from, that accomplishment. But it's also certain that if Christ doesn't intercede on a person's behalf, that person won't see heaven. The testimony of the Son before the Father is absolutely essential to the salvation of the sinner.

Thankfully, no sinner for whom Christ died need worry about whether he'll be the object of Christ's intercessory work. It's not as if Christ dies for some and then fails to intercede on their behalf. Rather, his intercession is just one part of his comprehensive work that consists in our redemption from sin and judgment. Thus, just as is the case with our responsibility to believe the gospel, we may also say that we won't be saved without Christ's intercession on our behalf. But it *will* happen, for the grace of salvation cannot fail.

Someday, thanks to Christ having opened the way for them, the elect will stand in the throne room of God the Father and will be free from all guilt and vestiges of sin. But for now, we sin against him in thought, word, and deed every day. As a result, we need a Mediator through whom to approach the Father. Moreover, we need someone who's capable of making intercession according to the will of God, for we don't even know what it is that we ought to pray (Rom. 8:26–27). Only Christ is able to fill that bill on our behalf.

The Unity of Father and Son

Unfortunately, I fear that some Christians have a wholly inappropriate notion of what Christ's intercession in heaven looks like. They imagine that he's engaged in a great battle of wills with the Father, who stands like a guard at the gates of heaven seeking to keep sinners out. Even worse, they imagine that Christ must beg and plead with the Father to accept those for whom he died and that the Father gives his acquiescence to the Son's labors only in the most begrudging manner.[1]

What a pathetic and irreverent view of the heavenly reality! Those who would think such thoughts demonstrate their ignorance that it was the Father who sent the Son to redeem sinners in the first place. Eternal life is found in both the Father and the Son (1 John 2:23). We don't receive redemption from one only to have it denied by the other.

We should banish forever from our minds any thoughts of a war taking place in heaven. Father and Son are united in all that they do. Christ doesn't need to beg and plead with the Father to do something that he's otherwise not inclined to do. Rather, Christ is an authorized intercessor, one who presents legal claims on behalf of his people (John 17:24);[2] claims that the Father is only too eager to accept. The whole point of the author of Hebrews mentioning Christ's intercession is to assure us that we need not worry. His intercession on our behalf is proof that the Father has already accepted us.

Indeed, although we must allow for the possibility that Christ pleads our cause with audible words, it may be more appropriate to imagine otherwise. As Charles Wesley's great hymn reminds us, it's the Savior's bloody wounds that speak most loudly on our behalf:

> Arise, my soul, arise, shake off your guilty fears;
> The bleeding Sacrifice in my behalf appears:
> Before the throne my Surety stands,
> My name is written on his hands.
>
> He ever lives above, for me to intercede,
> His all redeeming love, his precious blood to plead;
> His blood atoned for every race,
> And sprinkles now the throne of grace.
>
> Five bleeding wounds he bears, received on Calvary;
> They pour effectual prayers, they strongly plead for
> me.
> "Forgive him, O forgive," they cry,
> "Nor let that ransomed sinner die!"
>
> My God is reconciled; his pardoning voice I hear;
> He owns me for his child, I can no longer fear;
> With confidence I now draw nigh,
> And "Father, Abba, Father," cry.[3]

Saved to the Uttermost

According to the writer of Hebrews, the significance of Christ's heavenly intercession lies in the fact that by it he's able to "save to the uttermost those who come to God through Him" (7:25). Paul echoes that sentiment in Romans 8 where he writes that no one is able to bring a charge against God's elect since Christ is at the right hand of God, making continual intercession for them (vv. 33–34).

We're secure in Christ because his intercession, like every other aspect of his saving work, is efficacious. It cannot fail to achieve its intended purpose. The Father hears the prayers of his Son and refuses him nothing (John 11:41–42). That fact alone demonstrates the absurdity of misguided attempts to invoke the intercession of dead saints or relatives. Christ is the only intercessor for his people; he's all they'll ever need.

What a tremendous comfort this truth ought to be for those of us who have placed our trust in him! When we understand Christ's work on our behalf as continuing even today, and not as existing only in the past, we're empowered to tap into the vast spiritual resources that are available to us through our union with him by faith.[4] And no sin that we commit could ever cause Christ to stop interceding on our behalf.

Are you suffering affliction or persecution? Pray to the Father through Christ, and he'll give you strength to endure whatever it is you're facing. Are you dealing with temptation and sin in a particular area of your life? Pray to the Father through Christ, and he'll give you the ability to resist the devil and flee from him. But above all, when you do sin, take comfort that you have an advocate with the Father in heaven—Jesus Christ the righteous.

18

He Is the Preserver
of His People

(JOHN 10:28)

One of the greatest lines in Christian hymnody also comes from one of the most beloved hymns of all time. The hymn is Augustus Toplady's "Rock of Ages," and the line reads, "Nothing in my hand I bring, simply to thy cross I cling." These words confess that a Christian has renounced all hope in himself or herself for salvation and is trusting solely and exclusively in the merits of Christ.

But Toplady also understood that even the act of "clinging" to Christ's cross is a gift from God to those whom he has called unto himself. The only reason any person clings to the cross of Christ is because God has given him or her spiritual life and, metaphorically speaking, wrapped his or her previously cold and lifeless hands firmly around his Son's cross—the only hope for a right standing before God. And this clinging isn't only a momentary act that otherwise suffices to transmit the benefits of Christ's work to the believer. Rather, it is a continuous, ongoing activity by which the Christian remains united to Christ through a wholehearted reliance upon his person and work.

But the question invariably arises: Is this act of continuous clinging something that will necessarily transpire in the life of every Christian? Is there any possibility that the hands of an individual Christian may permanently lose their grip upon Christ's cross? Is there any possibility that the believer may do something so heinous that God himself will pry that person's hands from the cross and return him to his prior state of lostness? In short, can the true Christian ever lose his or her salvation?

Thankfully, Scripture emphatically answers that question in the negative. Sadly, however, this immensely comforting doctrine, known as the preservation (or perseverance) of the saints, is unknown to—or worse yet, denied by—a great many Christians today, despite the mounds of biblical support undergirding it. We turn now to an examination of the evidence for this great doctrine of the faith.

The Comprehensive Nature of Grace

We've already seen that when God calls sinners out of the darkness of unbelief, he grants them repentance and faith that unite them to Christ. But that's not the end of God's work within the life of the newly regenerated believer; it's only the beginning. Every person who receives the grace to believe the gospel is thereby initiated into a life of faith, which has as its design the conformity of that individual to the image of his or her Savior (Rom. 8:29).

And although the extent of that conformity within the life of the believer will be different in each case (Matt. 13:23), Scripture is clear on this point: all of those who have been called to faith will undergo both sanctification (growth in conformity) in this life and ultimately glorification in heaven (1 Thess. 4:3; Rom. 8:30). In other words, God's grace to his people is comprehensive in scope. No one who receives the grace to believe will be allowed to later perish in unbelief, and anyone who says otherwise doesn't understand the nature of God's grace.

Psalm 97:10 states the matter clearly: "He preserves the souls of His saints." That is the consistent testimony of Scripture, and it is set forth in a number of ways, a few of which are laid out below.

1. Believers Experience Eternal Life as a Present Possession

Eternal life isn't something that we earn by faithful obedience to God. Rather, it's his gift to those whom he has chosen to be in Christ before the foundation of the world (Rom. 6:23; Eph. 1:4). Christ's work on behalf of his people has already secured eternal redemption for them (Heb. 5:9; 9:12), and when God applies it to the individual through the gift of faith, eternal life becomes his or hers to possess from that time forward. That's why Christ, and Scripture generally, speak of it as a present possession of the believer.

Time and again, Jesus said that whoever believed in him already has eternal life (John 3:36; 4:14; 5:24; 6:47, 54). Such people have already "passed from death into life" (John 5:24; cf. 1 John 3:14), and may rest assured that he'll raise them up on the last day (John 6:54). They cannot possibly perish or be snatched out of Christ's hand, because he has given them eternal life (John 10:28).

In an obvious reference to the new birth that occurs at the outset of the Christian life, the apostle Peter writes that once we've experienced this rebirth we have an inheritance that is "incorruptible" and "reserved in heaven" for us (1 Pet. 1:3–4). To argue, then, that this new life is eternal only in a provisional or potential sense is to do serious violence to the language and promises of Scripture.

God's choice of sinners is an act of his pure mercy, and that mercy "is everlasting" (Ps. 100:5). It isn't offered for a season and then withdrawn at a whim or dangled in front of the believer in some sort of spiritual cat-and-mouse game. To imagine that such things are true is to think of God in far too human terms. God promises eternal life to all those who believe in his Son, and that promise cannot fail or be thwarted by anyone or anything. It's precisely because eternal life is a present possession of the Christian that the apostle John may say to those he had addressed his first letter, "These things I have written to you who believe in the name of the Son of God, that you may *know* that you have eternal life, and that you may continue to believe in the name of the Son of God" (1 John 5:13).

2. Believers Are Sealed with the Holy Spirit

The apostle Paul also writes about the inheritance that believers have upon trusting in Christ. He notes that our inheritance is ultimately based in God's predestination of certain sinners to glory and that all those so chosen have been "sealed with the Holy Spirit of promise, who is the guarantee of our inheritance" (Eph. 1:11–14; cf. 4:30). Though the believer's subjective awareness of this sealing effect of the Holy Spirit may ebb and flow, the fact remains that all Christians possess the guarantee that the inheritance that awaits them is one that "neither moth nor rust destroys" nor one that thieves may "break in and steal" (Matt. 6:20).

3. Believers Are Preserved in Grace by the Power of God

Is it really true that the person who is trusting in Christ today may be assured that he or she will continue to do so until the end of life? Scripture says so. The most compelling textual argument for this doctrine comes from the promise of the new covenant given by the prophet Jeremiah:

> "Behold, the days are coming, says the LORD, when I will make a new covenant with the house of Israel and with the house of Judah—not according to the covenant that I made with their fathers in the day that I took them by the hand to lead them out of the land of Egypt, My covenant which they broke, though I was a husband to them, says the LORD. But this is the covenant that I will make with the house of Israel after those days, says the LORD: I will put My law in their minds, and write it on their hearts; and I will

be their God, and they shall be My people. No more shall every man teach his neighbor, and every man his brother, saying, 'Know the LORD,' for they all shall know Me, from the least of them to the greatest of them, says the LORD. For I will forgive their iniquity, and their sin I will remember no more… And I will make an everlasting covenant with them, that I will not turn away from doing them good; but I will put My fear in their hearts *so that they will not depart from Me*" (Jer. 31:31–34; 32:40; cf. Heb. 8:8–12).

But the truth finds expression in a great many other texts as well. Among the most notable is 1 Peter 1:5, which says that believers are "kept by the power of God through faith for salvation." Thus, believers will persevere in faith until the very end because God, who has chosen them for salvation, maintains them in that state. A true believer may stumble at times and may even go through an extended period of rebellion. But he won't fully or finally apostatize from the faith, for God will eventually renew his strength and bring him back into the fold.

Paul, who was confident that God would preserve him in faith (2 Tim. 1:12; 4:18), says that Christ would *confirm* his saints to the end (1 Cor. 7–8) and *preserve* them in their blamelessness at the coming of the Lord (1 Thess. 5:23). And how could he be so sure of this reality? Because, says Paul, "He who calls you is faithful, who also will do it" (1 Thess. 5:24).

4. God Finishes the Work He Has Begun

Similarly, Paul writes confidently "that He who has begun a good work in you will complete it until the day of Jesus Christ" (Phil. 1:6). The good work to which Paul refers is the work of grace within the heart of the believer, which begins at regeneration and concludes with glorification in heaven. God won't leave the work unfinished nor would he start it within the heart of a person if he didn't intend to bring it to fruition. All those whom he calls to himself will ultimately be glorified, for his gifts and calling are "irrevocable" (Rom. 8:30; 11:29).

5. Nothing Can Separate Us from the Love of God

Perhaps no other passage in Scripture is able to produce such sweet comfort as Paul's great statement in Romans 8:38–39: "For I am persuaded that neither death nor life, nor angels nor principalities nor powers, nor things present nor things to come, nor height nor depth, nor any other created thing, shall be able to separate us from the love of God which is in Christ Jesus our Lord."

Believers are united to Christ by the will of God, and not one of those whom the Father has given him will be lost (John 6:39; Matt. 18:14). The mountains and hills might crumble to nothing, but God will never remove his blessing from one for whom Christ died (Isa. 54:10). They are eternally secure in him, for his love abides forever; such is the comprehensive nature of God's grace.

Preservation and Perseverance

Is it more proper to speak of the preservation or the perseverance of the saints? Actually, either designation is appropriate, for they merely speak to the matter from different vantage points. Christ preserves his people in grace to the end, but he does so by causing them to persevere in the faith despite the attacks of the world, the flesh, and the devil. When Paul told the Philippian Christians to "work out your salvation with fear and trembling, for it is God who works in you both to will and to do for His good pleasure," he was acknowledging the bi-directional nature of this activity (Phil. 2:12–13).

Nevertheless, it should be obvious that even in the work of persevering to the end there's no room for Christians to boast of their accomplishment. They do so only because the Holy Spirit is at work within them. For this reason, it's probably preferable to use the term *preservation of the saints*, since it more appropriately directs our attention to the principal player in this drama—Christ, the preserver of his people.

The Warning and Apostasy Passages

The most common objection raised against the doctrine of preservation is that the Bible contains not only warnings to persevere and not fall away (e.g., Col. 1:23; Heb. 2:1) but also seems to record several actual cases of defections from the faith (e.g., 1 Tim. 1:18–19; 2 Tim. 2:17–18; 2 Pet. 2:1). The argument states that if perseverance in the faith is assured, it makes no sense for the Bible to warn us against falling away. Why warn against an actuality that's impossible in the first place?

But that line of argumentation ignores the way that God works out his redemptive plan in time and space. In the same way that the Word of God is the appointed means for bringing to faith those who have been chosen for salvation, so also it is with persevering in the faith. Like the original exhortation to repent and believe the gospel, God has ordained that his exhortation to persevere in the faith will have its desired effect as well. In other words, in both bringing to faith and keeping in faith, God has ordained the means as well as the ends. The warning passages in Scripture serve the function of calling the believer to stand firm against the temptations of the world and to strengthen himself with the armor of God's Word. But just as with the call to believe the gospel, there's no possibility that those for whom such exhortations are intended will ultimately fail to heed them. In the context of discussing his protection for those who were his, Jesus said, "My sheep hear My voice, and I know them, and they follow Me" (John 10:27).

What, then, should we make of the cases (known to us all) of someone who once had a credible Christian witness and later renounced the faith? Only two possibilities exist. Either that person is a true believer who has fallen away temporarily and will eventually be brought back into the fold through conviction by God's Word, or he or she was never a true believer (one who has been regenerated by the Holy Spirit) in the first place. And at least from our human perspective, this latter scenario most often seems to be the case.

In none of the several instances in Scripture where someone is mentioned as having turned away from the faith is that person said to have been a true believer. Indeed, in the most obvious case, that of Judas Iscariot, just the opposite is affirmed (John 17:12). Turning away from the faith, even after a period of what may look like faithful service to Christ, merely manifests one for what they truly are—an unbeliever. This is precisely what John affirms in his first epistle when he writes, "They went out from us, but they were not of us; for if they had been of us, they would have continued with us; but they went out that they might be made manifest, that none of them were of us" (1 John 2:19). The false believers of whom John speaks put on a good show for a time but were eventually revealed for what they were at heart. And how does he know this? Because, he says that if they had been true Christians, they would have continued (i.e., persevered) in the faith with the rest of us.

The point is that we humans aren't able to see the heart and know with absolute certainty whether someone is a Christian. There will be some who may fool us (and perhaps themselves) for a time. But their works will eventually reveal the reality. That's one reason why Paul urges Christians not to choose newer believers to be their overseers. Time in the faith is one of the best indicators of the genuineness of a person's profession. The Christian's faith will be tested over time, and only those who have truly received the grace of salvation will be left standing at the end.

Hebrews 6:4–6

No treatment of the subject would be complete without a separate consideration of the passage that some believe single-handedly disproves the doctrine of preservation. Hebrews 6:4–6 reads:

> ⁴ For it is impossible for those who were once enlightened, and have tasted the heavenly gift, and

have become partakers of the Holy Spirit, [5] and have tasted the good word of God and the powers of the age to come, [6] if they fall away, to renew them again to repentance, since they crucify again for themselves the Son of God, and put Him to an open shame.

1. Major Views of the Passage

Not surprisingly, there is serious disagreement within the church about the meaning of this passage. We turn now to a consideration of the two major views.

The first is represented by Arminianism, a popular theological system that denies the primacy of God's sovereignty in election and the nature of faith as his gift to believers. Because Arminianism ultimately places the human will at the center of the redemptive act, it should come as no surprise that those who hold to this system view this passage as speaking of true believers who have lost their salvation. Arminians contend that the descriptive phrases in verses 4–5 most naturally apply to someone who has been saved, having been "enlightened" and having "become partakers of the Holy Spirit" being two ways of saying that these people have received saving grace and knowledge of the truth. Given this assumption, then, the only conclusion to draw is that the reference in verse 6 to "falling away" is the loss of salvation.

On the other hand, the traditional Protestant position is quite different. This interpretation views the language of verses 4–5 as describing those who weren't true Christians but who had been more than casual participants in the sacramental life of the church. As a result of their association with God's people, they had enjoyed great privileges. Some of them may even have personally witnessed "the powers of the age to come" in their day, since great signs and wonders accompanied the preaching of the apostles, something the author of Hebrews had already mentioned in his letter (2:4). But their "falling away" simply revealed them for who they were at heart. The "repentance" that they had experienced wasn't true biblical repentance for sin but that of a temporary turning away from the old (now obsolete) rituals of Judaism. Now, after giving Christianity a try, their hearts would be hardened against ever returning.

According to this view, each of the descriptive phrases in verses 4–5 refers to a particular aspect of participation in the apostolic church. Although commentators over the centuries have differed somewhat in their specific identification of the individual phrases, there has been more-or-less general consensus around the following interpretations.

The phrase "once enlightened" refers either to having been baptized or to having received instruction in the Word of God. There's evidence that baptism began to be referred to as "enlightening" at a very early date in church history (although some deny that it arose this early). The second interpretation sees a parallel at Hebrews 10:26 where the writer refers to those who had received "knowledge of the truth" and yet weren't true Christians.[1]

Most commentators agree that to have "tasted the heavenly gift" means to have participated in the Lord's Supper while to have "become partakers of the Holy Spirit" is a reference to the laying on of hands that was common in the apostolic church. Alternatively, the latter could simply refer to having benefited from the Spirit's work, a description that certainly would have applied to anyone who had been involved in the early church for more than a brief period of time.

"Tasting the good word of God" most likely means to have sat under the preaching of the church, although A.W. Pink believed that it simply referred to experiencing that God had been faithful to his promise, in other words, it was having enjoyed the advantages of the new dispensation brought about by Christ.[2] The same could be said about the final phrase, "tasting the powers of the age to come," which is a probable reference to the signs and wonders that accompanied the original preaching of the gospel.

In recent years an alternative understanding of the phrases in this passage has been gaining ground—and for good reason. This new reading has the advantage of being particularly sensitive to the context of Hebrews, and has much to commend it. Under this view, the word pictures contained in verses 4–5 refer to the experience of God's people in the Exodus, an event that's on the writer's mind in the early chapters of the book.

Richard Phillips argues for this view with the following insightful comments:

> The Book of Hebrews contains five major exhortations, of which this is part of the third. Each of the other four makes explicit reference to an Old Testament situation. The lengthy exhortation in chapters 3 and 4 draws out the exodus as a basic counter-model for the Christian life, and it is extremely likely that this remains on the writer's mind in chapter 6.... [T]his epistle was written to show that the old covenant both pointed to and was fulfilled by the coming of Jesus Christ. That, along with the readers' familiarity with the Old Testament, is why the writer consistently draws from Old Testament texts and situations to make points about Christianity. This is his uniform method, and there is no reason to think he has departed from it in this passage which, like the others, derives its imagery from the life of Israel and looks back on the exodus as the general backdrop.[3]

Under this view, "once enlightened" is a reference to the pillar of light that guided the Israelites through the desert, the heavenly gift that they tasted refers to the manna they received from God, the good word refers to the word that came through Moses, and the latter two phrases remind readers of the astonishing works of power that God performed in bringing about Israel's deliverance from Egypt.[4]

The point of the writer, then, is to warn those in the first-century church against making the same mistake made by those who left Egypt centuries earlier. And he wants his readers to know that just as was the case in that earlier period, not all those who experience the blessings of participation in the church will prove to be true believers.[5]

2. Problems with the Arminian Reading

The problems with the Arminian reading of Hebrews 6:4–6 are almost too numerous to mention. We offer here only a few of the most serious objections to such a reading.

First and foremost, it directly contradicts the clear teaching of Scripture that we outlined above under the subject of God's grace. It's a generally accepted principle of biblical interpretation that less clear passages should be read in light of those that are more clear and explicit in their teaching. In this case, Scripture speaks loud and clear to the issue of preservation, and to read this single passage in any way that contradicts the great mass of passages testifying to that doctrine is to throw reason to the wind and commit grave error in the process.

Second, such a reading also contradicts several other direct statements made by the writer of Hebrews in his epistle. In 3:14 he writes that we have become partakers of Christ only "*if* we hold the beginning of our confidence steadfast to the end." Just a few verses later, he makes it clear that unbelief (not a fall from grace) is the root of apostasy (3:19). And if that's not enough, he has just finished telling us in the verse immediately prior to this passage (6:3) that *we will* go on to perfection *if God permits*. Whatever else the writer of Hebrews is trying to say, it's clear that he views the perseverance of the saints as something for which God is the determining factor.

Third, only a few verses later (6:9–10), the author distinguishes his readers from those mentioned in verses 4–6 by noting their faith and its fruits ("your work and labor of love"), remarking that they possessed those things "that accompany salvation." Conversely, there is no mention of grace or faith or any of its fruits in verses 4–6, the subjects of whom are spoken of as "those" and "they" in contrast to the "you" and "your" of verses 9–10. The implication is that the things listed in verses 4–5 aren't things that (necessarily) accompany salvation but may in fact represent merely temporary spiritual experiences.[6]

Fourth, it should be borne in mind that even the phrase that's most evocative of the blessings of salvation, "partakers of the Holy Spirit," is capable of being understood in a number of ways that don't render it as synonymous with "Christians." Although the writer of Hebrews has used the designations "partakers of the heavenly calling" and "partakers of Christ" back in Chapter 3 as synonyms for true believers, we can easily see how he may have used this phrase for the purpose of drawing an intentional distinction. As we have already pointed out, all those who were a part of the apostolic church could be said to have been partakers of the Holy Spirit's work to one degree or another. And when you take into account that the Greek word for *partakers* used here is different from the one used in 2 Peter 1:4 to refer to those who were "partakers of the divine nature," the case is even stronger. A. W. Pink points out that the word used here simply means "companions" and refers to what is external rather than internal. Thus, it means that they had shared in the benefit of the Spirit's supernatural operations and manifestations on behalf of the church.[7] But that's a very different thing from being "filled with the Holy Spirit" (Acts 4:31), "baptized with the Holy Spirit" (Acts 1:5), or "born of the Spirit" (John 3:6).

Finally, near the end of chapter 6, the writer of Hebrews issues a bold statement of assurance for those who have truly received Christ through the gospel. In verse 17 he refers to "the immutability of His [God's] counsel" toward "the heirs of the promise." Richard Phillips remarks, "These are hardly the words of someone who wants to convey a fundamental insecurity to those who have trusted in Christ."[8]

3. The Impossibility of Renewal

From a purely human standpoint, true repentance for sin is always impossible for those born of Adam. Only the regenerating power of God is able to bring one to the point of repentance and faith in Christ. Of course, from God's perspective such repentance and renewal is never impossible. What, then, did the writer of Hebrews mean by saying that it was impossible to renew again to repentance those who had fallen away from participation in the church?

The answer to that question seems to lie in the fact that the author still has the example of the ancient Israelites on his mind here. Beginning back at Chapter 3, he has been working to establish the inexcusable nature of Israel's sin during the days of the Exodus. They had seen God's mighty works for a full forty years (3:9), and yet they rebelled against him nonetheless. And why did they do so? The culprit was not a lack of evidence but sheer unbelief (3:19). What the Israelites had experienced wasn't a sudden departure from the fold but a gradual decline into disobedience and then complete apostasy. Their abandonment of the Old Testament church was nothing more than a public pronouncement of who they were at heart. But more than that, their hearts had now become hardened against ever returning, a point that the author makes twice in the span of only eight verses (3:8, 15) and once more a few verses later in the form of an explicit warning to his readers (4:7).

This is most likely the sense in which the author intends his statement to be understood. When a person's heart has been hardened by apostasy by having once been enlightened and then forsaking that knowledge of the truth, it renders them incapable of being brought back into the fold, since they thereby put Christ "to an open shame" and "crucify Him again." At that point they have become like those Jesus spoke of in Matthew 7:6—swine before whom our pearls should not be cast (see also Matt. 10:14).

John Owen, the great Puritan minister and biblical expositor, had this to say:

> When in things of duty God has neither expressly commanded them, nor appointed means for their performance, then we should think of them as being impossible. This is the impossibility that is meant here. It is a thing that God has neither commanded us attempt, nor appointed the means to achieve it, nor promised His assistance in it... [Thus], it is not for us either to look, or hope, or pray for, or endeavor the renewal of such people to repentance... What he [God] does we should gratefully accept; but our duty toward such people

is completely finished. And, indeed, they put themselves wholly out of our reach.[9]

Eternal Security

At one time, it was possible to speak of the "eternal security" of the believer and be fairly confident all would understand what you were trying to say. Traditionally, Protestant Christians have used the phrase to speak of the fact that believers are eternally secure in Christ since they're able to rely on God's promise to carry them through to the end of life in faith. Because Arminians uniformly denied this latter fact, they also denied the doctrine of eternal security, holding instead that true Christians may lose their salvation.

In recent years, however, a growing number of Arminians have begun to use the term, and defend a certain notion of "eternal security," albeit one that's very much at odds with the traditional understanding. This brand of Arminianism (drawn mostly from the dispensational, nonlordship community) still denies that believers will necessarily persevere in faith to the end. But unlike their predecessors, these modern proponents teach that the person who loses his faith will nevertheless retain the possession of eternal life. All that is necessary for one to inherit eternal life is to have experienced a momentary response of faith to the gospel; once that has been achieved, it matters not whether the person continues in the faith, at least as far as their eternal destiny is concerned.

Though many of those who teach this theological absurdity tend to stop short of discussing its obvious implications, some are at least honest enough to state the matter forthrightly. Here is what one of these adherents wrote, in what surely qualifies as one of the most biblically illiterate and inept statements of all time:

> It is possible, even probable, that when a believer out of fellowship falls for certain types of philosophy, if he is a logical thinker, he will become an "unbelieving believer." Yet believers who become agnostics are

still saved; they are still born again. You can even become an atheist; but if you once accept Christ as saviour, you cannot lose your salvation, even though you deny God.[10]

Atheists in heaven? "Unbelieving believers?" Such talk would be fodder for a good laugh if it weren't so dangerous and destructive. The rise of this brand of "eternal security" shows the depths to which dispensational theology in general, and nonlordship theology more particularly, has fallen. God won't be bringing unbelievers to heaven. There's another place designated for those who fall into that category. Rather, all those whom he has chosen to eternal life will retain the gift of faith while they live. They'll be made into "new creations" (2 Cor. 5:17). And God doesn't renege upon, or withdraw, his gifts and promises. Believers are secure in their faith because God has promised to finish the work he has begun in them.

Christian Assurance

Scripture is explicit in teaching that the Christian may attain to full assurance of eternal life (Heb. 3:14; 6:11; 10:22; 2 Pet. 1:10; 1 John 5:13), an assertion that would be nonsensical if it were possible to lose the basis upon which it's offered. True Christian assurance is grounded upon the objective nature of Christ's work and the absolute dependability of the promises of God. Although the believer may also derive a measure of assurance from the fact of the Spirit's sanctifying work in his or her life, such evidences of spiritual fruit are always secondary in importance to the concrete testimony of God to finish the work he has begun.

Nevertheless, Christians who rightly understand this truth will never allow themselves to become complacent concerning their spiritual walk and responsibility before God to continue steadfast in the faith. Protestant Christians have always appreciated the proper, biblical balance between God's sovereignty and man's responsibility in the matter of salvation. Scripture teaches both, and it's therefore no contradiction to hold to both. Too many Christians err by emphasizing one side to the exclusion of the other. But the fact is that although God is sovereign in bringing men to salvation (and keeping them there), he does so through the instrumentality of human means—the preaching of the gospel, including the ongoing exhortations to persevere in the faith. God doesn't simply bring persons to saving faith and then leave them to their own devices to see how things will turn out in the end. He ordains the means as well as the ends of bringing persons to faith and then keeping them in it.

True Christians will indeed persevere to the end. But they'll do so only by availing themselves of the means of grace that God has appointed for their benefit—something they're sure to do because God will be at work preserving them by those means. We need daily exhortations to remain steadfast in the faith, for we, like the Israelites who fell in the desert, aren't home yet. We won't enter the Promised Land until we've left this life. And it's the very threat of the fearful consequences of turning away from Christ to which the true Christian responds. God will never allow any of his chosen ones to be tempted beyond what they are able to bear; he himself will always provide the way of escape (1 Cor. 10:13).

Therefore, to argue that a Christian can be lost after experiencing true saving faith is to doubt the sufficiency and efficacy of the work that Christ undertook on our behalf. To imply, however innocently, that God's preserving grace is capable of failure is to impugn his faithfulness toward his people. Instead, we should adopt the attitude espoused by the late James Boice, who wrote that "the believer can be as certain that he or she will be in heaven as that Jesus himself will be there."[11]

The message of Scripture to the people of God is a clear one: cling to the cross of Jesus Christ. Indeed, do everything in your power to cling with all of your might. Heed the warnings of Scripture to continue steadfast in the faith, lest you end up like the Israelites of old. And then, when you have done all of that, rest assured that your hands will not slip, for he has promised to take you with him into glory. And no one is able to snatch you out of his preserving hands.

19

He Is the Way, the Truth, and the Life

(JOHN 14:6)

As we near the end of our study, the present chapter deals with a direct declaration of Christ that to some extent could be considered a summary statement of all that we have said thus far about his person and work. The full text of Jesus' assertion, found at John 14:6, is as follows: "I am the way, the truth, and the life. No one comes to the Father except through Me."

Jesus uttered this statement the night before his crucifixion. As he sat with his disciples at the Last Supper, he prepared them for his impending death and departure from their midst. First, he gave them a new commandment—that they love one another, even as he had loved them (13:34–35). Apostolic unity and example would surely serve the purposes of the gospel after Jesus had left the scene.

But there was more that Jesus would say to them. Not fully grasping the import of what Jesus had communicated, Peter asked him where he was intending to go (13:36). Jesus answered with some of the sweetest words in all of Scripture. He told them that he was on his way to his Father's house in which there were many mansions and that he was going there to prepare a place for each of them (14:2). Furthermore, he reminded them that they already knew the way there (14:4).

Despite the clarity of Jesus' words, at least Thomas still didn't fully understand. The disciples had been with Jesus long enough to know that when he spoke of going to the Father's house, he was referring to his return to heaven, the abode from which he had come (John 6:32–33). But Jesus' statement that they already knew the way there apparently caused enough confusion that Thomas was led (for our benefit) to press the matter further, as if to allow Jesus to place an exclamation point on the conversation.

It was to Thomas' statement and query, "Lord we do not know where You are going, and how can we know the way?" that Jesus gave the response that's our focus here. There could now be no mistaking what Jesus was saying to them. It was because they knew and loved him that he could say that they knew the way to the Father's house. Their union with him was the reason that there would be a place prepared in heaven for each of them.

The Way to the Father

Jesus' self-description in John 14:6 is as far-reaching in its implications as it is succinct in words. If we had no other information about Jesus Christ than what's contained here, we would still be alerted to the utter futility of placing our trust in anything or anyone else except for him alone. Christ is the one-and-only way to the Father by virtue of who he is and what he has done on behalf of sinners. That's the upshot of Jesus' threefold designation of himself as the Way, the Truth, and the Life. No one who seeks any other way to the Father will make it, because no one else possesses the credentials that Jesus does.

From the context of Jesus' statement, as well as his concluding remark about coming to the Father, it has generally been recognized that the latter two designations of *Truth* and *Life* occupy a supporting role in this passage.[1] That is, while both titles are immeasurably important in their own right, their primary function here is to help clarify how and why it is that Jesus is *the Way* to the Father. If no one is able to come to the Father except through Christ, there must be a good reason why that is so. In fact, there are two good reasons, for he is both the Truth and the Life.

In the first place, Christ is truth in the flesh. He's God's self-revelation in the person of the Son who came to earth for the very purpose of bearing witness to the truth (John 18:37). But he didn't only testify to the truth of God; he lived and embodied it. Every utterance from Jesus was a direct word from God (John 8:40), and his life and death were a revelation of both divine love and justice. Nothing could more fully demonstrate the truth of God's grace toward sinners than the death of the very One who was "full of grace and truth" (John 1:14). Only he who is in the bosom of the Father is able to declare him to mankind (John 1:18).

In much the same way, Christ has *life* in himself (John 1:4; 5:26). Not only does he have power over physical life and death, but he also has the prerogative to grant eternal life to whomsoever he wills (John 5:21). Indeed, it's only through faith in him that a person is reckoned to have life in any meaningful sense (John 10:10; 20:31). That's why Paul could say that Christ "is our life" (Col. 3:4), for it's only by being united to him that any of us will receive "the crown of life which the Lord has promised to those who love Him" (James 1:12).

Christ is the only way to the Father precisely because of his divine identity as both Truth and Life incarnate. No one else holds those credentials (nor could they), and no one else has provided the means of redemption (his atoning death) by which we may be reconciled to God. Those who do not avail themselves of the benefits of his redemptive work through personal faith in him are spiritually lost and will suffer everlasting punishment and separation from God. And this is true even if such persons never had a chance to hear the gospel message of salvation through Christ and personally reject it.

That's the traditional view of the Bible's witness to the doctrine of salvation. But despite the biblical evidence supporting that view, it is subject to increasingly intense attack in our modern secular society. And that attack comes not only from outside the church (which we would expect), but also, to some extent, from within.

Contemporary Attacks upon Christian Exclusivism

Although several factors are responsible for the growing tendency to reject the traditional view, the main culprit is the rise of humanistic thinking in the last century. Only rarely are the arguments offered against the traditional view exegetical in nature. Rather, it has simply become an unpalatable notion to many today that large numbers of the human race would be consigned to everlasting punishment without ever having had an opportunity to accept or reject the gospel. One scholar has stated the matter this way:

> It was relatively easy to think of those who had never heard of Christ as being lost, when such people could be thought of as primitive, savage, and engaged in bizarre religious practices. That they had committed sins worthy of endless punishment did not seem greatly incongruous, if they practiced head-hunting or cannibalism. With the shrinking of our globe, however, and increased contact with persons from other nations and other religions, we have come to see that many people are sincere and ethical. That they should be condemned to such an awful fate simply because they have not heard of Christ is unacceptable to many Christians.[2]

In June 2008, the Pew Forum on Religion and Public Life released the results of its "U.S. Religious Landscape Survey," in which 70% of Americans agreed with the statement, "Many religions can lead to eternal life." Although the number was slightly lower for those identifying themselves as members of evangelical churches, it still represented the majority opinion of that group as well (57%).[3]

Clearly, the religious landscape of America (and the world) has changed dramatically in the last hundred years or so. Numbers of the type reported by the Pew survey would have been unheard of in earlier centuries. America was a much less religiously diverse nation, and Christians especially understood and appreciated the uniqueness of Christ and the exclusivity of his claims. Nowadays, more and more Americans seem unwilling to accept the notion that their Muslim or Hindu neighbors, who are also quite sincere and devoted to their own religious practices, might not share in the salvation offered by Christ.

The result of this changing landscape has been the development of a number of theories proposed as alternatives to the traditional view. Although there are a variety of views contained within each of the three main alternatives, they may be summarized by the following broad definitions.

First, universalism posits that all human beings will be saved in the end. For some Universalists, the work of Christ is still the determinative factor in the salvation of man. But that work will be applied to all, regardless of whether they accepted or rejected him in this life.

Second, religious pluralism contends that Christ (and the Christian religion) isn't the only way of salvation but merely one of many ways to God. Some pluralists hold to a simple Universalist position, while others argue that only those who sincerely practice *some* religion will ultimately be saved. At the heart of the pluralistic system is the belief that all of the major world religions are merely different culturally based attempts to worship the same God. Thus, they're all equally valid and equally capable of producing salvation for the individual adherent.

But it's the third alternative, known as inclusivism, which is becomingly increasingly common in Christian circles these days. Unlike the pluralist, the "Christian" inclusivist holds to the uniqueness of Christ and of his being the only Savior available to man. But he argues that individuals may be saved apart from personal faith in Christ; indeed, it's possible for those who have never heard the name of Christ to receive the benefits of his redemptive work, usually by living a life in accordance with God's law.

Here is how one inclusivist described this system of thought:

> The unevangelized are saved or lost on the basis of their commitment, or lack thereof, to the God who saves through the work of Jesus. [Inclusivists] believe that appropriation of salvific grace is mediated through general revelation and God's providential workings in human history. Briefly, inclusivists affirm the particularity and finality of salvation only in Christ but deny that knowledge of His work is necessary for salvation.[4]

The inclusivist view was officially embraced by the Roman Catholic religion at the Vatican II conclave in the 1960s. Since that time, it has gradually gained adherents within the true church as well. And as the Pew survey shows, it (or worse) is effectively the majority view of those who make up the membership rolls of Christian churches today. As a result, it is becoming increasingly common to find Christians who assert that traditional evangelism and missionary efforts are no longer necessary and, in fact, may even be harmful to those targeted.[5]

The question for us is whether such emotional arguments can withstand the test of Scripture. Are any of the three alternative positions outlined above supported by an appeal to the final arbiter of all disputes—God's holy and infallible Word? Perhaps if John 14:6 were the only passage that speaks to the issue, the inclusivist could argue, with some justification, that the doctrine of Christ's exclusivity hung upon a thin reed of biblical support. But, as we noted earlier, Jesus' statement that he is the way to the Father is merely a summary of all that Scripture teaches upon the subject from cover to cover.

The Exclusivity of Christ

And that claim is no exaggeration. Scripture opens with God's promise to send a Redeemer to fallen mankind (Gen. 3:15) and ends with that Redeemer pronouncing himself to be "the Alpha and the Omega, the Beginning and the End, the First and the Last" (Rev. 22:13). Just as mankind is one in the fall, so also there is one Redeemer appointed to provide the way to reconciliation with God (Rom. 5:12–21). And every page of Scripture confirms the identity and uniqueness of that Redeemer—Jesus Christ, the "*one* Mediator between God and men" (1 Tim. 2:5).

Actually, none of the three universalistic alternatives is even able to survive the direct teachings of Jesus found in the New Testament. The pure Universalist is unable to account for the fact that Jesus left no doubt that there would be "many" who would suffer everlasting punishment for not having placed their trust in him (Matt. 7:13–14, 22–23; 8:12; 25:46; John 3:16–18). The pluralist is confronted by the fact that Jesus explicitly confined salvation to the church (as constituted in his day) in opposition to the syncretistic practices of the Samaritans, which weren't able to save (John 4:22). And the inclusivist must face the fact that Jesus made eternal life dependent upon one's personal commitment to him, a commitment that the apostle Paul said could only be secured through the preaching and hearing of the gospel (John 3:16–18; 6:47; Rom. 10:11–17).

Inclusivists are fond of arguing that general revelation (the knowledge of God that is available through nature and the created order) is adequate to lead into a saving relationship with God those who have never heard the gospel. But Paul makes it clear in Romans 1–2 that the effect of general revelation is to render everyone guilty before God. It places all people under divine judgment, a righteous judgment that can only be averted through repentance and faith in Christ (Rom. 3:21–28). Romans 2:12 reads, "For as many as have sinned without law will also perish without law, and as many as have sinned in the law will be judged by the law." Paul's point is that even those who have never received special revelation (those "without law") will perish in the end, not because they never heard the gospel but because of their guilt before God as sinners.[6]

Does this biblical truth have the effect of creating a narrow way to God? You bet it does. But that's precisely the reality to which Jesus himself testified: "Enter by the narrow gate; for wide is the gate and broad is the way that leads to destruction, and there are many who go in by it. Because narrow is the gate and difficult is the way which leads to life, and there are few who find it" (Matt. 7:13–14). Each of the seven "I AM" statements of Jesus in the gospel of John testifies further to the exclusivity of the salvation that he secured for his people.

Rather than causing us consternation, however, this truth should lead us into action. The gospel of Christ is the power of God unto salvation (Rom. 1:16). And except for those whom God has elected who are otherwise incapable of "being outwardly called by the ministry of the Word,"[7] all who would be saved need to hear that gospel message. That's why Jesus commissioned his disciples to go into the entire world and preach repentance and forgiveness of sins to every people group they could find. The goal wasn't so that those people might have an easier time of it here in this life, for very often just the opposite has been the case. Rather, the goal is that "they may have life, and that they may have it more abundantly" (John 10:10).

No Other Name

No matter how attractive a Christian may find the notion of an inclusivistic salvation to be, the Bible simply doesn't allow for it. Other religions, far from being equally valid ways to God, are an abomination in his sight (Deut. 18:9). Nor is it possible to speak of the so-called "anonymous Christian" who follows the dictates of his (sin-riddled) conscience and thereby qualifies himself as one for whom Christ died. Scripture is emphatic that none will be saved by the deeds of the law. The law condemns us; Christ, and he alone, delivers us from the curse of that law.

In the seventeenth century, the framers of the Westminster Confession of Faith wrote that to assert that any who didn't profess the Christian religion might be saved was "very pernicious, and to be detested" (10:4). These men had a keen awareness that such doctrines denigrated the person and work of Christ and were directly contrary to the clear teaching of Scripture. We might add, as Robert Reymond has pointed out, that any denomination or group claiming to be Christian and holding to such a notion has thereby "declared its own theological obsolescence and [rendered] itself a modern irrelevancy to most of the peoples of the world."[8]

Jesus Christ isn't merely the Way, the Truth, and the Life for some who want their salvation packaged in a particular culturally based form. Both Christ and the salvation that he offers transcend all cultures and people groups that have ever been or ever will be. All who would be saved must come to the Father through Christ, for he alone has accomplished the work of redemption by his life and death.

It's the work of the Holy Spirit alone to draw sinners into the kingdom. But it's to us that God has given the task of making known the truth of the gospel to all creatures under heaven. No matter how unpopular or foolish our message may be to those who are perishing (1 Cor. 1:18), we should be as bold as Peter was before the Sanhedrin (a hostile crowd if there ever was one), when he declared about Christ, "Nor is there salvation in any other, for there is no other name under heaven given among men by which we must be saved" (Acts 4:12).

20

He Is Coming Back

(2 Tim. 4:1)

"The blood of the martyrs is the seed of the church." That well-known axiom arose over the centuries in recognition of the fact that despite the best efforts of many a king and emperor, the Christian religion didn't merely survive in the face of official persecution, but actually thrived. Not only did Christianity gain a higher profile as a result of the numerous attempts to stamp it out, but also untold millions were attracted to the steadfast determination of individual Christians who went to their deaths rather than forsake the name of Jesus Christ as Lord and Savior.

Paradoxically, the greatest threats to the spiritual health and ministry of the church have always come from within her visible ranks rather than from the outside. The number of public officials who have sought to bring down the church through persecution pales in comparison to the tally of those who have sought to do so from within by spreading heresy and dissension amongst the faithful. That's why the New Testament church from its earliest days has sought to define, in increasingly explicit and careful ways, what constitutes valid Christian beliefs and entitles one to membership in the visible church.

The church did so through the development of creeds and confessions. One of the earliest attempts to define the faith is the so-called Apostles' Creed. Although not explicitly formulated by the apostles themselves, the creed represents a short summary of their teachings as deduced from the New Testament writings that they left behind. While later creeds, such as those developed at Nicea and Constantinople in the fourth century, deal with more narrowly defined issues concerning the nature of God and Christ, the Apostles' Creed was meant to be a concise summary of those beliefs that were most basic to confessing the Christian faith against all counterfeits.

One contemporary version of the Creed reads as follows:

> I believe in God the Father Almighty,
>> Maker of heaven and earth.

> I believe in Jesus Christ, his only Son, our Lord,
>> who was conceived by the Holy Spirit,
>> and born of the Virgin Mary.
>> He suffered under Pontius Pilate,
>> was crucified, died, and was buried;
>> he descended into hell.
>> The third day he arose again from the dead.
>> He ascended into heaven
>> and is seated at the right hand of God the
>> Father Almighty.
>> From there he will come to judge the living
>> and the dead.

> I believe in the Holy Spirit,
>> the holy catholic [i.e., universal] church,

    the communion of saints,
    the forgiveness of sins,
    the resurrection of the body,
    and the life everlasting. Amen.[1]

Our discussion so far has left unaddressed very little that appears in the Apostles' Creed. Thus it may seem odd that we find ourselves finishing off an in-depth study of the person and work of Christ with such a basic recitation of the facts concerning him. But we finish right where the Creed itself concludes its enumeration of the individual components of Christ's work—at that aspect that lies exclusively in the future. The final word on Christ from the Creed says, "From there [heaven] he will come to judge the living and the dead."

The Second Coming of Christ in History

The second coming of Christ has thus figured prominently in the expectations of Christians for almost two thousand years. Paul describes it as the Christian's "blessed hope" (Tit. 2:13), and the early church considered it an essential element of "the faith which was once for all delivered to the saints" (Jude 3). Those who denied it, or who denied any of the other events the New Testament says will accompany Christ's coming, were considered dangerous heretics and were to be shunned (1 Tim. 1:19–20; 2 Tim. 2:16–18).

And except perhaps for an occasional scoffer who appeared on the scene, that teaching of the faith had gone virtually unchallenged for almost nineteen hundred years after Christ's death. All of that began to change in 1878, however, with the publication of J. Stuart Russell's *The Parousia*. Russell argued that all of the New Testament prophecies relating to the second coming of Christ had been fulfilled in the events surrounding the destruction of Jerusalem by the Romans in AD 70. Thus, Christ's "coming" doesn't refer to a physical return to earth but to His act of sending down judgment upon the Israelite nation. Moreover, Russell argued that the general resurrection had also taken place in AD 70, as the dead in Christ were resurrected and taken to heaven and the saints then living were also transported there bodily as a part of that class who would never taste death in their earthly bodies.

Russell's thesis didn't gain many adherents in the decades following its initial publication, but it has gained a good many more recently. Those who subscribe to a modern heresy known as hyper-preterism have taken up Russell's ideas and gone even further astray by denying both the physical nature of the resurrection body and the future consummation of history. They have become the "scoffers" of whom the apostle Peter warns about in his second epistle. Peter writes that some will rise up and say to believers, "Where is the promise of His coming? For since the fathers fell asleep, all things continue as they were from the beginning of creation" (2 Pet. 3:3–4). But such scoffers forget "that with the Lord one day is as a thousand years, and a thousand years as one day" (3:8).

The Nature of Christ's Second Coming

Besides those who have adopted some form of Russell's thesis, there have been a few others along the way who have argued that Christ's forecast of his return was fulfilled at Pentecost, when Jesus poured out the Holy Spirit upon the disciples, which empowered them for the work of the kingdom. But Christ's promise to return to earth was distinct from his promise to send the Holy Spirit in the near future. They are two different events, separated by time and purpose. Indeed, this truth is evident by simply pointing to the many post-Pentecost references to his return as still future (e.g., Acts 3:20–21; 1 Cor. 1:7; Phil 3:20; Col. 3:4; 1 Thess. 1:10; 2:19; 3:13; 4:15; 5:23; 2 Thess. 2:1; Jas. 5:7-8; 2 Pet. 3:4).

The fact is that neither of these alternative theories, nor any others that have been offered as a substitute for that which is confessed in the Apostles' Creed, can square with the witness of Scripture. The New Testament is clear that the manner of Christ's return will be (1) personal, (2) bodily, and (3) visible.[2] It will be personal because Christ himself will actually return to earth. Although he has sent the Holy Spirit to be "another Helper" until he returns (John 14:16; 15:26), he'll come back in the flesh to set things right once and for all.

Christ's return will also be bodily and visible. The Second Coming cannot be equated with his ongoing spiritual presence in the church or within individual believers, nor can it be merely a metaphor for the judgment that befell Jerusalem. Scripture is clear that Christ will return in the flesh to earth in the future to be seen by all (Matt. 26:64; Acts 1:11; 3:20–21; 1 Thess. 1:10; Tit. 2:13; Heb. 9:28; Rev. 1:7). As Jesus was taken up visibly into heaven at his ascension, two angels assured his gazing apostles that "This same Jesus … will so come in like manner as you saw Him go" (Acts 1:11).

The Purpose of Christ's Second Coming

Although it's the same Jesus who will return to earth in the future, his return will be very different in nature from his first coming. Great signs and wonders accompanied his first arrival, but it appears to have been relatively unknown and unheralded outside the confines of Bethlehem. And his first sojourn ultimately resulted in the humiliation of rejection and death on a cross. But his Second Coming will be an event so glorious that every human being will be aware of it and affected by it, for Christ will appear with his heavenly angels in tow (2 Thess. 1:7) to set all things right once and for all.[3]

The New Testament speaks of Christ's return initiating four great interrelated end-time events: (1) the resurrection of the dead; (2) the judgment of the living and the dead; (3) the establishment of the kingdom of God in its fullest sense; and (4) the restoration and renewal of the created order.

1. The Resurrection of the Dead

In his first letter to the Corinthians, Paul writes that at the "last trumpet" the dead "will be raised incorruptible, and we shall be changed" (1 Cor. 15:52). And Paul makes it clear that this change isn't merely a nice benefit of Christ's work but an absolute necessity for "this corruptible *must* put on incorruption" (v. 53). It's a necessity for at least two reasons. First, man wasn't created as a disembodied spirit, and it's not his destiny to exist eternally in such form. Rather, being embodied goes to the very essence of what it means to be human.[4] The blessed uniqueness of human beings lies in the fact that they're created in God's image to be both spiritual and physical.

Second, humans must put on incorruptibility because Christ has done so, and his own resurrection was a representative act, one that secured for his people what he also personally experienced.[5] This is why Paul describes Jesus as the "firstfruits" of the resurrection (1 Cor. 15:23). If the curse of death hadn't been reversed through the power of Christ's resurrection, sin would still be the victor. But the Christian is able to sing, "O Death, where is your sting?" (1 Cor. 15:55) precisely because Christ has redeemed his people by triumphing over sin and death for all time.[6]

Even though Paul focuses his discourse in the fifteenth chapter of First Corinthians upon the resurrection of believers, Scripture is clear that both the saved and unsaved dead will experience bodily resurrection at the last day (Dan. 12:2; John 5:28–29; Acts 24:15; Rev. 20:13–15). Nevertheless, they're raised from the grave to quite different circumstances and effects. Berkhof explains:

> The resurrection of the wicked cannot be regarded as a blessing merited by the mediatorial work of Christ, though it is connected with this indirectly. It is a necessary result of postponing the execution of the sentence of death on man, which made the work of redemption possible. The postponement resulted in the comparative separation of temporal and eternal death, and in the existence of an intermediate state. Under these circumstances it becomes necessary to raise the wicked from the dead, in order that death in its widest extent and in all its weight might be imposed on them. Their resurrection is not an act of

redemption, but of sovereign justice, on the part of God. The resurrection of the just and the unjust have this in common, that in both bodies and souls are re-united. But in the case of the former this results in perfect life, while in the case of the latter it issues in the extreme penalty of death, John 5:28–29.[7]

Christians who experience death prior to Christ's second coming will also (at that latter event) experience the reunion of their soul and body. But they'll no longer "groan" under the weight of sin and the "futility" to which the creation has been subjected since the fall (Rom. 8:20–23). Rather, they'll enjoy perfect rest in a body which has been conformed to the glorious, resurrected body of Jesus Christ (Phil. 3:21).

2. The Judgment of the Living and the Dead

After the dead have been resurrected, they (along with those who are alive at Christ's coming) will appear before him at the great white throne in heaven to be judged. All those present will be judged on the basis of whether they placed their trust in Christ while they were alive on earth; those who had done so will find their names written in the Book of Life (Rev. 20:11–12). They'll enter into everlasting glory, but those whose names aren't there will be cast into the lake of fire, where they'll suffer everlasting torment (Rev. 20:15).

Of course, individual outcomes at the final judgment will confirm the judgment rendered at a person's death and for which they have already begun to experience either the blessings or sufferings due that status until Christ's return (John 5:24). But that hardly makes the final judgment an unnecessary or superfluous act. Rather, Christ's judgment of all humans at the consummation of history will serve to display the glory of God in a final, formal, and public act that will magnify his grace and mercy on the one hand and his holiness and righteousness on the other.[8]

Although it's proper to speak of the final judgment as an act of the triune God, Scripture ascribes the work to Christ in particular.[9] Jesus himself said that the Father, in recognition of the Son's mediatorial work on behalf of sinners, had committed all judgment to the Son (John 5:22, 27; Matt. 28:18). Thus, Christ "will judge the living and the dead at His appearing and His kingdom" (2 Tim. 4:1).

3. The Establishment of the Kingdom of God in Its Fullest Sense

This last statement of Paul's, in conjunction with 1 Corinthians 15:22–25, demonstrate that the establishment of Christ's kingdom rule climaxes with his appearing and with the resurrection and judgment that accompany that great event. Paul calls that time "the end" and describes it as the moment when Christ "delivers the kingdom to God the Father" (1 Cor. 15:24).

But we miss the significance of that event if we see it as merely the commencement of Christ's kingdom rule in the world, for there has never been a moment in time when he was not exercising his sovereign rule over all of creation, except perhaps (in a limited sense) during the days of his humiliation. We may distinguish between the divine rule that Christ, as the Son of God, has exercised over the created order since time began and the mediatorial rule with which he was invested at his exaltation to the right hand of the Father two thousand years ago. But it's only at the end of time that Christ ushers in the fullness of God's kingdom, after having put an end to all ungodly rule and placed all his enemies under his feet (1 Cor. 15:24–25). It's only then that righteousness will again reign supreme, every knee bow, and every tongue confess that Jesus Christ is Lord (Phil. 2:10–11).

4. The Restoration and Renewal of the Created Order

The final concomitant of Christ's second coming is what the apostle Peter calls "the restoration of all things" (Acts 3:21). This involves not only the inauguration of the eternal state but also the establishment of a new heaven and a new earth in which righteousness will dwell and sin and evil will be banished forever (2 Pet. 3:13; cf. Rom. 8:21; Rev. 21:1). Even the created order will be delivered from the corruption under which it has labored since God brought forth thorns and thistles in consequence of man's fall into sin. And the believer's salvation will be realized to the "uttermost," for Christ will appear this time "apart from sin," for the express purpose of "bringing many sons to glory" (Heb. 2:10; 7:25; 9:28).

The Timing of Christ's Second Coming

No one on earth knows the time of Christ's second coming. My guess is that very few of you who are reading these words will quibble with such an assertion. But even though that seemingly obvious statement of fact may not provoke a great deal of dissent in orthodox Christian circles, there have been a few vocal dissenters over the years who were unwilling to accept it as the truth.

Despite the fact that Jesus told his disciples that even he didn't know the hour of his return, it has become something of a sport in the last two centuries, and especially in recent decades, for some "seer" to claim that he has pinpointed the exact day and time of that great event. Indeed, whole religions have sprung up out of their founders' well-publicized prediction of Christ's return to earth, later proven to be faulty. But instead of slinking away in shame, which would have been the appropriate thing to do, the usual response of these "seers" has been to announce that they've since discovered some slight miscalculation in determining the date of their first prediction, whereupon they proceed to push the date further out.

Instead, Christians should stop giving ear to such nonsense and begin to live in *patient (but eager) expectation* of Christ's return. It's not necessary at this point to delve into the various millennial theories and their positions on what biblical prophecies, if any, are yet to be fulfilled before Christ can return in glory. Rather, the scriptural record calls Christians to strike a balance between our righteous longing for Christ to come and set things right and our responsibility to work at fulfilling the mandate to take the gospel to the nations in the meantime. As a result, we're to simultaneously live, work, and serve our King as if he could return at any moment, even if it be true that he just might tarry for another two thousand years. We're called to always "be ready" for his return (Matt. 24:44) but at the same time to go about the business of our daily lives, whatever that business may be. We should seek to avoid the extremes of being so entrenched in this life that we become "of the world" rather than merely "in it" for a time, and the opposite tendency often attributed to those who are described as being "so heavenly-minded that they're of no earthly good."

T. V. Moore, a nineteenth-century pastor and Bible teacher, spoke primarily to the latter tendency in this comment upon Acts 1:11:

> When longings for heaven unfit us for labours on earth, a voice from heaven should come, in gentle rebuke, "Why stand ye gazing up into heaven?" Instead of indolently longing for the rest of heaven, we should labour on earth to be fitted for that rest, and thus only shall we long aright. We may gaze upward toward the heavenly hills in faith and hope, and with such longings as Paul had when he was willing rather to depart and be with Christ, which was far better. But we are not to gaze with impatient discontent, and indolent desire to escape from the duties that God has assigned us here on earth. We must feel with Job, not when he exclaims in bitterness, "I loathe it; I would not live always," but rather when he says, "All the days of my appointed time will I wait, till my change come."[10]

Christ will come again to judge the living and the dead. That great day may be near in time or far off (as we measure such things), but it's getting closer with each passing hour. The faithful do well to ignore both those who prognosticate upon the precise date and the scoffers who deny the reality of his return altogether. The Lord has promised to come back for his people at the end of history, and the passage of time from the giving of that promise, rather than representing a slackness on his part, is an act of pure grace. Peter wrote that, "The Lord is not slack concerning His promise, as some count slackness, but is longsuffering toward us, not willing that any should perish but that all should come to repentance" (2 Pet. 3:9). Christ's forbearance in judgment will continue until the last of those whom he has chosen has come to him in faith—whenever that may be. Thus, we are to "consider that the longsuffering of our Lord is salvation" (v. 15).

Christians await the "glorious appearing of our great God and Savior Jesus Christ" (Tit. 2:13). One day he'll return to set all things in their proper order again. That day will be glorious indeed! Until that time, however, there's work to be done. The fields are plentiful and ripe, and we're to be about the business of reaping until Christ has gathered all of those who are his into one great harvest. We wait in patient expectation of that day. Yet at the same time, we join with the apostle John in singing, "Even so, come, Lord Jesus!" (Rev. 22:20).

Epilogue

"What Do You Think About the Christ?"

(MATT. 22:42)

No one could conduct a spiritual examination like the Lord Jesus Christ could. In his earthly ministry he repeatedly asked questions of people he met, questions often designed to direct his audience's attention toward a particular spiritual truth about himself and to test their understanding and acceptance of that truth. In our Prologue we saw Jesus employ such a technique by asking the question "Who do men say that I am?" to elicit his disciples' response to the more important question, "But who do you say that I am?"

The question with which we close our study is very similar to the follow-up one that Jesus asked his disciples that day. But this question ("What do you think about the Christ?") was directed to the Pharisees and only after they had "gathered together" against him (Matt. 22:34, 41) in the last days of his earthly life. This was Jesus' final confrontation with them. And when it was over, the unbelieving Pharisees moved to the home of the high priest to plot Jesus' murder (26:1–4).

Silencing the Pharisees

Although the question in its short form is an open-ended one, Jesus' subsequent words demonstrate that he intended to lead the Pharisees to a very specific place in their understanding of who he was. He didn't merely invite them to state their general opinions about the Christ but immediately followed it up with the query, "Whose Son is He?" With these added words, Jesus turned the question from an open-ended one to one that delved into the very heart of the Messiah's identity. The Pharisees knew their Scriptures, so they had no problem coming up with the answer: The Christ would be "The Son of David" (Matt. 22:42).

There was nothing particularly challenging or illuminating about Jesus' question as a matter of mere theological trivia. But it must have occurred to at least some of the assembled group that only two days earlier Jesus had accepted the title for himself from the throng of people who greeted him upon his triumphal entry into Jerusalem (Matt. 21:9). That was tantamount to declaring that he was, in fact, the long-awaited Messiah of Israel.

But even that wasn't Jesus' primary purpose for asking the question. His own unequivocal declaration to all that he was the Christ would come at his trial before the Sanhedrin two days later (Matt. 26:64). Rather, he used the occasion to indirectly issue a stunning pronouncement regarding the identity of the Messiah. The remainder of Matthew 22 reads as follows:

> ⁴³ He [Jesus] said to them, "How then does David in the Spirit call Him 'Lord,' saying:

> ⁴⁴ 'The LORD said to my Lord, "Sit at My right hand, Till I make Your enemies Your footstool"'?

⁴⁵ "If David then calls Him 'Lord,' how is He his Son?" ⁴⁶ And no one was able to answer Him a word, nor from that day on did anyone dare question Him anymore.

The Pharisees would have immediately recognized Jesus' words in verse 44 as a quotation from Psalm 110, where David states that the future Messiah would be One whom both the Father (LORD) and he would call "Lord." And what does such a statement represent, other than a declaration that the Messiah would be God incarnate? The Christ would indeed be David's Son according to the flesh. But he would also be David's Lord, the One about whom it may be said that he had no beginning or end. For both the Pharisees and us, the implications of such a truth are staggering.

The Question for the Ages

No philosophical question ever devised by man even comes close in significance to the one that Jesus posed to the Pharisees that day. What we think of Christ is the sole determining factor in the eternal destiny of every one of us. Some of those who have claimed to be his disciples have perished for the lack of a right understanding of who he truly is. While worshiping an idol of their own making, they have sought answers to the greatest question ever asked in places other than Holy Scripture. And the unbelieving world has been only too ready and willing to give the wrong answers.

Sadly, the very notion of *thinking rightly of Christ* is under attack today. To some, even the suggestion that there is a right form of thinking about Christ is a repugnant notion. Rather, to them, such notions represent an antiquated—and now highly objectionable— way of looking at the world. Truth, they argue, is determined personally by the individual as persons experience life through their own interpretive lens. And supposedly this is particularly the case in the realm of religious truth. Thus, it is commonplace in our day to hear someone pitting the mind against the heart and arguing that true worship is only possible when a person has set aside all notions of right thinking for the (supposed) bliss of uninhibited spiritual experiences. We might well describe the attitude of many in the church today as summed up by the statement, "You have your Christ; now let me have mine."

But Scripture tells a very different story. God's Word makes it clear that what we think of Jesus Christ is ultimately the *only thing* that matters! And far from being a relativistic enterprise, the true worship of Christ can flow only out of a right understanding of who he is and what he has done. Like it or not, the doctrinal position we take with respect to the person and work of Christ has eternal consequences. No one can love a Savior whom he doesn't know. We either worship the Christ of Scripture, or we don't. And if not, then no "Christ" whom we have invented in our imaginations will be able to satisfy our ultimate need—to be reconciled to a holy God.

In *Who Needs Theology?* Stanley Grenz and Roger Olson lament the lack of serious theological reflection among Christians today and write of their fear that if something isn't done to change this state of affairs, Christianity may soon be relegated to the status of mere folk religion, devoid of any public credibility whatsoever.[1] As Christians, we cannot allow that to happen. There's simply too much at stake. The world desperately needs a Savior, and it's our responsibility to proclaim the good news that the only One available to them has come in the person of Jesus Christ. Anything less than that is unloving.

Matthew 22:46 says that when Jesus had concluded his spiritual examination of the Pharisees, "no one was able to answer Him a word, nor from that day on did anyone dare question Him anymore." Of course, they dared not question him after that because the implications of his words were simply more than they could handle. The Pharisees, like so many who came before and after them, were comfortable in their misconceptions about Christ. They had created in their minds a "Christ" who was but a mere man, and nothing that Jesus or anyone else said about him was going to jar them from their delusional state.

Like some others over the centuries, however, the Pharisees weren't content to leave it at that. Rather than merely remaining firm in their own unbelief, they did their utmost to proselytize others to their position—even going so far as to concoct absurd stories in an effort to explain away Christ's miraculous works (Matt. 28:11–15).

Unfortunately, the spiritual descendants of the Pharisees are still with us. They come in several varieties, but they share a common purpose: make the world think wrongly of Jesus Christ. They're busy propagating their lies, continuing to spread absurd stories about missing gospels, apostolic hallucinations, mythological accretions, and the like. Wherever and whenever Christ is set forth as less glorious than he truly is, the Pharisaical spirit is at work.

Like the Pharisees (and Sadducees), those who spread such lies have gathered together in league against the Lord and his Christ (Ps. 2:2). But the Psalmist reports on the ultimate end of all their machinations: "He who sits in the heavens shall laugh; the Lord shall hold them in derision. Then He shall speak to them in His wrath, and distress them in His deep displeasure" (vv. 4–5). When the time is ripe, Christ "will dash them to pieces like a potter's vessel" (v. 9).

In the meantime, God will continue to gather his elect from the four corners of the earth. When they face the question of the ages, they'll join with Peter and the apostles in affirming that Jesus is "the Christ, the Son of the living God." They'll acknowledge him as God incarnate, the Word become flesh, and as the only way to the Father in heaven. They'll rejoice that God raised him from the dead for our justification and draw comfort in the knowledge that he gave his life as a ransom for theirs. With the rest of the faithful, they'll seek to do his will, while they eagerly await his future return in glory. And they'll look forward to the day when they cast their crowns before his feet and join with the saints in heaven in singing these words from Rev. 5:12:

> "Worthy is the Lamb who was slain
> To receive power and riches and wisdom,
> And strength and honor and glory and blessing!"

What Think Ye of Christ?

by John Newton

What think you of Christ? is the test
To try both your state and your scheme;
You cannot be right in the rest,
Unless you think rightly of him.
As Jesus appears in your view,
As he is beloved or not;
So God is disposed to you,
And mercy or wrath are your lot.

Some take him a creature to be,
A man, or an angel at most;
Sure these have not feelings like me,
Nor know themselves wretched and lost:
So guilty, so helpless, am I,
I durst not confide in his blood,
Nor on his protection rely,
Unless I were sure he is God.

Some call him a Savior, in word,
But mix their own works with his plan;
And hope he his help will afford,
When they have done all that they can:
If doings prove rather too light
(A little, they own, they may fail)
They purpose to make up full weight,
By casting his name in the scale.

Some style him the pearl of great price,
And say he's the fountain of joys;
Yet feed upon folly and vice,
And cleave to the world and its toys:
Like Judas, the Savior they kiss,
And, while they salute him, betray;
Ah! what will profession like this
Avail in his terrible day?

If asked what of Jesus I think?
Though still my best thoughts are but poor;
I say, he's my meat and my drink,
My life, and my strength, and my store,
My Shepherd, my Husband, my Friend,
My Savior from sin and from thrall;
My hope from beginning to end,
My Portion, my Lord, and my All.

Endnotes

Prologue: "Who do Men Say that I Am?"

1. Perry G. Downs, *Teaching for Spiritual Growth* (Grand Rapids: Zondervan, 1994), 105.

Chapter 2: He Is the Only Begotten Son

1. James R. White, *The Forgotten Trinity* (Bloomington, MN: Bethany House, 1998), 14.
2. Ibid., 158.
3. Ibid.
4. Louis Berkhof, *Systematic Theology* (Grand Rapids: Eerdmans, 1996), 93–94.
5. Arthur W. Pink, *An Exposition of Hebrews* (Grand Rapids: Baker, 2004), 239.
6. White, *The Forgotten Trinity*, 61.
7. To this point we have not offered any separate evidence for the divinity and distinct personality of the Holy Spirit, since he is not the focus of our study here. But the interested reader need only consult Acts 5:1–4 for explicit evidence of each.
8. White, *The Forgotten Trinity*, 26. I have modified White's spelling here for the sake of maintaining consistency.

Chapter 3: He Is the Word Become Flesh

1. White, *The Forgotten Trinity*, 109.
2. Ibid.
3. Berkhof, *Systematic Theology*, 333.
4. Stephen Charnock, *The Existence and Attributes of God* (Grand Rapids: Baker, 1996), 1:560–61.
5. Ron Rhodes, *Christ Before the Manger: The Life and Times of the Preincarnate Christ*, (Grand Rapids: Baker, 1992), 80–88.
6. Berkhof, *Systematic Theology*, 323.
7. Ibid., 322.
8. Rhodes, *Christ Before the Manger*, 195–97.
9. Donald Macleod, *The Person of Christ* (Downers Grove, IL: InterVarsity

Press, 1998), 168–69.

10. Benjamin B. Warfield, *Selected Shorter Writings*, ed. John E. Meeter, 2 vols. (Phillipsburg, NJ: P&R, 1970), 1:166.

Chapter 4: He Was Born of a Virgin

1. James Montgomery Boice, *The King Has Come* (Fearn, Scotland: Christian Focus Publications, 1995), 25.
2. Ibid., 100–02.
3. Ibid., 117.
4. Ibid., 157.
5. Ibid., 171–72.
6. Ibid., 43.
7. Charles Briggs, from his article "Criticism and Dogma," published in *The North American Review*, and cited without further details in Clarence E. Macartney, *Twelve Great Questions About Christ* (Grand Rapids: Kregel, 1993), 23–24. It should be noted that although Briggs' statement here is a valuable one, his views on a number of other issues were anything but orthodox.
8. Macartney, *Twelve Great Questions About Christ*, 25.
9. Macleod, *The Person of Christ*, 187.

Chapter 5: He Is the Same Yesterday, Today, and Forever

1. Pink, *An Exposition of Hebrews*, 1163.
2. Charnock, *The Existence and Attributes of God*, 339–40.
3. C. H. Spurgeon, "The Unchangeable Christ," a sermon preached at Metropolitan Tabernacle, 1888. Accessed: February 18, 2010. Online: http://www.spurgeon.org/sermons/2358.htm
4. Pink, *An Exposition of Hebrews*, 1161.

Chapter 6: He Was a Friend of Sinners

1. Jonathan Edwards, "Wicked Men Inconsistent with Themselves," a sermon preached in December 1738. Accessed: May 6, 2009. Online: http://www.biblebb.com/files/edwards/inconsistent.htm.
2. Arthur W. Pink, *Exposition of the Gospel of John* (Grand Rapids: Zondervan, 1975), 424.
3. Adoph Saphir (1873); quoted in Pink, *An Exposition of Hebrews*, 231–32, without further citation.
4. William Hendriksen, *New Testament Commentary: Matthew* (Grand

Rapids: Baker, 2002), 424.

5. B.M. Palmer, *Sermons* (Harrisonburg, VA: Sprinkle, 2002), 2:273.

6. Charles Haddon Spurgeon, *Spurgeon's Sermons,* 5 vols. (Grand Rapids: Baker, 1996), 8:206.

Chapter 7: He Was Tempted

1. J. I. Packer, "Temptation," in *New Bible Dictionary*, ed. J.D. Douglas et. al.; 2d ed. (Downers Grove, IL: InterVarsity Press, 1994), 1173.

2. Macleod, *The Person of Christ*, 226.

3. Ibid., 227.

4. Arthur W. Pink, from *Studies in the Scriptures* (Sept. 1932). Accessed June 4, 2009. Online: http:// home.att.net/~sovereigngrace/impeccability.html.

5. William G. T. Shedd, *Dogmatic Theology,* 3 vols. (Grand Rapids: Zondervan, n.d.), 2:345.

6. Macleod, *The Person of Christ*, 226.

7. Richard D. Phillips, *Reformed Expository Commentary: Hebrews* (Phillipsburg, NJ: P&R, 2006), 80–81.

Chapter 8: He Was Perfected

1. Pink, *An Exposition of Hebrews*, 254.

2. J. Gresham Machen, *God Transcendent,* ed. Ned Bernard Stonehouse (Edinburgh: Banner of Truth Trust, 1982), 190–91.

3. Ibid., 188.

4. Pink, *An Exposition of Hebrews*, 381.

5. Ibid., 411.

6. Ibid., 257.

7. Philip Edgcumbe Hughes, *A Commentary on the Epistle to the Hebrews* (Grand Rapids: Eerdmans, 1977), 283.

Chapter 9: He Was Numbered with the Transgressors

1. Charles Spurgeon, *Spurgeon's Sermons on the Cross of Christ* (Grand Rapids: Kregel, 1993), 11–12.

2. Kenneth Clark, *Civilisation* (London: B.B.C., 1961), 29; quoted in C. Fitzsimmons Allison, *The Cruelty of Heresy: An Affirmation of Christian Orthodoxy* (Harrisburg, PA: Morehouse, 1994), 29.

3. Pink, *An Exposition of Hebrews*, 230.

4. Spurgeon, *Spurgeon's Sermons on the Cross of Christ*, 133.

5. Edward J. Young, *The Book of Isaiah*, 3 vols. (Grand Rapids: Eerdmans, 1997), 3:337.

6. C.H. Spurgeon, *The Metropolitan Tabernacle Pulpit* (Pasadena, TX: Pilgrim Publications, 1969), 8:624.

Chapter 10: He Was Raised from the Dead

1. Geerhardus Vos, "The Meaning of Christ's Resurrection," *Modern Reformation* (May/June 2000), 8.

2. John Calvin, *Calvin's Commentaries*, trans. William Pringle, 22 vols. (Grand Rapids: Baker, 1998), 17:338–39.

Chapter 12: He Was the End of the Law

1. Phillips, *Hebrews*, 52–53.

2. Palmer, *Sermons*, 2:125–26.

3. Pink, *An Exposition of Hebrews*, 397–98.

4. John F. MacArthur, Jr., *The Gospel According to Jesus*, rev. ed. (Grand Rapids: Zondervan, 1994), 31.

Chapter 13: He Is the Destroyer of Death and Satan

1. Don Matzat, "How Martin Luther Dealt with the Devil," *Issues, Etc.,* (Dec. 1996). Accessed August 19, 2009. Online: http://www.issuesetcarchive.org/issues_site/resource/journals/luther.htm.

2. Heiko A. Oberman, *Luther: Man Between God and the Devil*, trans. Eileen Walliser-Schwarzbart (New York: Doubleday, 1992), 154.

3. Martin Luther, *What Luther Says: An Anthology*, comp. Ewald M. Plass, 2 vols. (St. Louis: Concordia, 1959), 1:402.

4. Erwin W. Lutzer, *The Serpent of Paradise: The Incredible Story of How Satan's Rebellion Serves God's Purposes* (Chicago: Moody, 1996), 16.

5. Pink, *An Exposition of Hebrews*, 134.

6. Lutzer, *The Serpent of Paradise*, 103–13.

7. John Calvin, *Institutes of the Christian Religion*, ed. John T. McNeill, trans. Ford Lewis Battles, 2 vols. (Philadelphia: Westminster, 1960), 1:174–75.

8. Ibid., 1:176.

9. Augustus Toplady, *The Complete Works of Augustus Toplady* (Harrisonburg, VA: Sprinkle, 1987), 387.

Chapter 14: He Is the Savior of the World

1. Tom Wells, *A Price for a People: The Meaning of Christ's Death* (Edinburgh: Banner of Truth, 1992), 42.
2. Tom Wells, "For Whom Did Christ Die?," *Reformation & Revival Journal* (Vol. 5, No. 1, Winter 1996), 60–61.
3. Charles Spurgeon, *A Defense of Calvinism* (Pensacola, FL: Chapel Library, n.d.), 18.
4. Thomas R. Thompson, "John 3:16 (Limited Atonement)," with further citation to J. Hufstetler, The Doctrines of Grace, Limited Atonement tape TE-BL-009. Accessed September 21, 2009. Online: http://members. truevine.net/ shadrach/john3_16.htm
5. C.H. Spurgeon, *The New Park Street Pulpit* (London: Banner of Truth Trust, 1963), 1:400.

Chapter 15: He Is the Redeemer of All Those Given to Him by the Father

1. John F. MacArthur, Jr., *The Vanishing Conscience* (Dallas: Word, 1994), 85; quotation from Robert Schuller, *Self-Esteem: The New Reformation* (Waco: Word, 1982), 31.
2. Ibid., quoting from *Self Esteem*, 127.
3. Ibid.

Chapter 16: He Is Both Lord and Christ

1. Berkhof, *Systematic Theology*, 406, 411.
2. Ernest Reisinger, *What Should We Think of the Carnal Christian?* (Edinburgh: Banner of Truth, 1992), 3.
3. Ibid.
4. Phillips, *Hebrews*, 295.
5. Pink, *An Exposition of Hebrews*, 103.
6. Ibid.

Chapter 17: He Is the Intercessor on Behalf of His People

1. Pink, *An Exposition of Hebrews*, 249.
2. Berkhof, *Systematic Theology*, 405.
3. Charles Wesley, "Arise, My Soul, Arise," *Trinity Hymnal*, Rev. ed. (Suwanee, GA: Great Commission, 1990), 305.

4. Phillips, *Hebrews*, 239.

Chapter 18: He Is the Preserver of His People

1. Pink, *An Exposition of Hebrews*, 290.
2. Ibid., 292.
3. Phillips, *Hebrews*, 189.
4. Ibid., 190.
5. Ibid.
6. John Owen, *Hebrews* (Wheaton, IL: Crossway, 1998), 147. See also Pink, *An Exposition of Hebrews*, 323–30.
7. Pink, *An Exposition of Hebrews*, 291.
8. Phillips, *Hebrews*, 188.
9. Owen, *Hebrews*, 151.
10. R.B. Thieme, *Apes and Peacocks or the Pursuit of Happiness* (Houston: Thieme, 1973), 23; quoted in MacArthur, *The Gospel According to Jesus*, 105.
11. James Montgomery Boice, *Psalms*, 3 vols. (Grand Rapids: Baker, 1998), 3:902.

Chapter 19: He Is the Way, the Truth, and the Life

1. See, e.g., D. A. Carson, *Pillar New Testament Commentary: The Gospel According to John* (Grand Rapids: Eerdmans, 1991), 491.
2. Millard J. Erickson, "The State of the Question," in *Through No Fault of Their Own?: The Fate of Those Who Have Never Heard*, William V. Crockett and James G. Sigountos, eds. (Grand Rapids: Baker, 1991), 24–25.
3. The full survey report is available at http://religions.pewforum.org/reports#.
4. John Sanders, *No Other Name: An Investigation into the Destiny of the Unevangelized* (Grand Rapids: Eerdmans, 1992), 215; quoted in W. Gary Crampton, "Christian Exclusivism," *Trinity Review* (May 2002), 3.
5. William V. Crockett and James G. Sigountos, "Foreword," in *Through No Fault of Their Own?*, 9.
6. Robert L. Reymond, "The 'Very Pernicious and Detestable' Doctrine of Inclusivism: Part 2," *Trinity Review* (June 2003), 2.
7. Westminster Confession of Faith 10:3.
8. Robert L. Reymond, "The 'Very Pernicious and Detestable' Doctrine of Inclusivism: Part 1," *Trinity Review* (May 2003), 4.

Chapter 20: He Is Coming Back

1. *Trinity Hymnal*, 845.

2. Berkhof, *Systematic Theology*, 704–06.
3. Ibid., 706.
4. Paul Helm, *The Last Things: Death, Judgment, Heaven, Hell* (Edinburgh: Banner of Truth Trust, 1989), 53.
5. Ibid., 50–51.
6. Ibid., 51–52.
7. Berkhof, *Systematic Theology*, 723–24.
8. Ibid., 731.
9. Ibid.
10. T.V. Moore, *The Last Days of Jesus* (Edinburgh: Banner of Truth, 1981), 204.

Epilogue: "What Do You Think About the Christ?"

1. Stanley J. Grenz and Roger E. Olson, *Who Needs Theology?: An Invitation to the Study of God* (Downers Grove, IL: InterVarsity Press, 1996), 10.

General Index